ONE WEEK LOAN

Rich Britain: The rise and rise of the new super-wealthy

Other books by Stewart Lansley

Poverty and Progress in Britain (with G. C. Fiegehen and A. D. Smith; Cambridge: Cambridge University Press, 1977)

Housing and Public Policy (London: Croom Helm, 1979)

Poor Britain (with Joanna Mack; London: Allen and Unwin, 1985)

Beyond Our Ken: A Guide to the Battle for London (with Andy Forrester and Robin Pauley; London: Fourth Estate, 1985)

Councils in Conflict: The Rise and Fall of the Municipal Left (with Sue Goss and Christian Wolmar; Basingstoke: Macmillan, 1989)

After the Gold Rush: The Trouble with Affluence – 'Consumer Capitalism' and the Way Forward (London: Century, 1994)

Top Man: How Philip Green Built His High Street Empire (with Andy Forrester; London: Aurum Press, 2005)

Rich Britain:

The rise and rise of the new super-wealthy

Stewart Lansley

POLITICO'S

First published in Great Britain 2006 by
Politico's Publishing Ltd, an imprint of
Methuen Publishing Ltd
11–12 Buckingham Gate
London
SW1E 6LB

10 9 8 7 6 5 4 3 2 1

A CIP catalogue record for this book is available from the British Library.

ISBN 1 84275 147 6

Typeset by SX Composing DTP, Rayleigh, Essex
Printed and bound in Great Britain by The Cromwell Press, Trowbridge, Wiltshire

Contents

Preface and acknowledgments

The super-rich have rarely strayed far from the public's consciousness or from political controversy. In the nineteenth century, their immense power may have provoked political outrage in some quarters and spawned great social movements but their wealth stayed largely intact. The twentieth century brought the first serious challenges to their political and economic dominance. For a generation and more, a period straddling the Second World War, the rich found both their wealth and influence at least partially eclipsed.

It seems to have been a temporary phenomenon. In the last two decades the rich have bounced back in dramatic style, regaining their former status and their fortune-making prowess. In the process, they have recaptured some of the share of the national cake that they had relinquished to middle England for a while. It was as if it was merely on short-term loan. Moreover, although the wider implications of the growing concentration of wealth at the top that has occurred in the last two decades are profound, the transformation has occurred with barely a political whimper.

Rich Britain sets out to explore the return of the super-rich. What has been driving the remarkable turnaround in their fortunes? Is the trend towards an ever-rising gap in wealth between the top and the bottom to be welcomed or deplored? What of the future – should the super-wealthy be allowed a free hand to continue up the path of further personal enrichment, or is it time to ask some serious questions about the impact and implications of the continuing wealth explosion amongst the ultra-rich?

It might at first sight be thought that this book starts from an anti-rich stance. It does not. It will argue that many of those at the top of today's rich lists are inspirational, successful and deserving of their rewards. It will also argue that others are much less so. The book attempts to provide a way of distinguishing between the deserving rich, those who, for example, are enjoying the benefits of wealth they have personally created and built and who also put something back, and the less deserving, those who have done little more than exploit today's more favourable political climate to seize for themselves a larger chunk of the nation's existing wealth, irrespective of the nature and consequences of their methods.

The issues surrounding the growth in the number and size of super-fortunes in recent years might be of less concern if the rising personal wealth had been largely justly earned, the result of exceptional and superior skill, effort and risk-taking that contributed to increasing the size of the national cake. But the evidence presented in the book is that today's deserving rich are likely to be outnumbered by those whom society will mostly judge as somewhat less than deserving.

Many people have been generous enough to help with this book, sharing ideas, stories and information. Andy Forrester, Chris Garsten, Paul Ormerod, Linda Palmer, Steve Schifferes, Janet Williamson and Christian Wolmar all read and made helpful and perceptive comments on draft chapters. Not all of them will agree with its findings. Jonathan Shaw and Andrew Shephard at the Institute for Fiscal Studies guided me through some of the statistics and provided the data used as a basis for Figure 2.2. John Clemens at Tulip Financial Research and analysts from Datamonitor's Global Wealth Reports provided helpful information from their own work on trends in the numbers of rich and in the concentration of wealth in recent years. The press office at HM Revenue and Customs was very patient and helpful in dealing with my repeated requests for information and interpretation. I am also grateful for the support provided throughout by my agent, Pat Lomax of Bell Lomax, and by Alan Gordon Walker and Jonathan Wadman at Politico's.

Stewart Lansley
December 2005

Introduction

An economic megashift

'Britain's super-rich have seen their wealth soar into the stratosphere.'
(Sunday Times Rich List, 2005)

In May 2004, hundreds of people gathered in the heart of London's West End. The men wore formal dress, for the women only top designer jewellery was on display. It was no ordinary party. The guest-list was a roll-call of Britain's rich – royal, landed, business and celebrity wealth mingling side by side. The party had been thrown by Asprey, jewellers to the royal family, to celebrate the opening of their Bond Street store in a refit that cost a staggering £50 million. For the lavish and much-publicised event, the whole street had been closed off and carpeted in purple. Bellboys in purple pillbox hats lined the route to the 44,000 square foot store. Guests included the Duchess of York, Sir Elton John, the actress Keira Knightley, Zara Phillips, the Duke of Marlborough and retail billionaire Philip Green, new and old society mixing together in the giant new shop. It was a party that culminated in dinner for 250 at Annabel's, the private members' Mayfair nightclub frequented by celebrities and minor aristocrats. It was certainly a sign of the times.

In the last two decades, a remarkable revolution has been occurring in Britain – a great surge in both the numbers of the very rich and in the level of their wealth. Whether we take the company boardroom, the football pitch, the presenter's couch or the modern deal-making entrepreneur, the story is the same – rewards have been escalating at unprecedented rates. The number of those with incomes of over £1 million rose eightfold in the ten years to 2005.[1] In the five years to 2002, the number of Britons with more than £5 million in 'liquid assets' rose at the rate of 13 per cent a year, despite the carnage of the 2000 stock market crash. Between 2002 and 2004, the number rose again by 50 per cent.[2] The number of billionaires in Britain – a mix of aristocrats, entrepreneurs, businessmen and tax exiles – has more than tripled since 1990 while the number worth over £100 million has risen more than fivefold over the same period.[3]

This is tearaway growth by historical standards. Existing fortunes have leapt forward. New entrants have climbed aboard. The *Sunday Times* – in its annual charting of the nation's richest 1,000 – described the 2004 personal wealth increase at the very top as 'an explosion'. A year later, in 2005, as the assets of the top 1,000 soared yet again, they called it 'stratospheric'. A wealth boom on such a scale has not been seen in Britain in recent or even distant memory, in fact not for over a century. It has been driven by a combination of a benevolent political climate, a new pro-rich culture and benign economic conditions. When the assets of the rich soared to new heights at the end of the nineteenth century they were viewed with a mixture of awe and disdain by the public. By contrast, the members of today's super-rich club are lionised by leading politicians and much of the public alike.

Increasingly the limits of what the rich can buy are being raised. Richard Branson and the Barclay brothers both own their own island. Indeed, privately owned islands have become sufficiently big business that a company has been formed – Vladi Private Islands – specialising in selling them to the mega-rich. Recent islands on their books have included Therese Island in the Seychelles for £3 million or Musha Cay in the Bahamas for £31 million. Premiership football clubs are being used, in effect, as toys of the global super-rich. International motor shows unveil ever more exclusive and luxury models by Porsche, Bugatti and Rolls-Royce at previously unheard-of prices. A Bugatti Veyron, introduced at the 2005 Frankfurt Motor Show, for example, is the fastest, most powerful and most expensive production car in history. It would set you back £810,000. For a swimsuit for that special occasion, you'd need £15 million in spare cash to buy one 'dripping in diamonds' designed by Gideon Oberson. And if you're after an exclusive 'Ghengis Khan' Westminster watch, designed by Swiss craftsmen, which comes with tiny, moveable hand-carved figures on a black onyx dial and chimes the sounds of Big Ben on the hour and half-hour, it would set you back £320,000. A modern tycoon lifestyle certainly doesn't come cheap.[4]

The emergence of the multi-millionaire class has spawned new industries including a rapidly expanding professional and very well-paid 'servant class' that looks after the mega-rich. They research and provide expensive and exclusive holidays; they buy, deliver and construct the personal cellars to store the world's finest wines; they conduct the bidding to acquire the world's most expensive Impressionists, Post-impressionists, Picassos and Modiglianis; they organise the purchase of the yacht, the mansion and the private jet. And for those who can't yet afford one of their own, they will hire one – at a cost of up to £400,000 a day – from firms such as NetJets and Bookajet.

Britain has never been short of the very rich and the trappings that go with them. But what has been witnessed in the last decade and a half is altogether of a different order. Today's mega-rich may not compare in power and fortune with the Victorian aristocracy and the Edwardian industrialists and financiers, but they greatly outclass their predecessors in the era before and after the Second World War. Today's rich are wealthier, less embarrassed by their wealth and much happier to flaunt and trumpet it. The 'stealth wealth' culture and 'conspicuous abstention' that characterised the post-war decades has been replaced by a voracious consumerism, especially by the younger breed of the enriched. Although the wealthiest classes have long indulged in some sleight of hand in their dealings with the revenue, today's super-rich are even more adept at hiding it away from the taxman through what one critic has dubbed 'the seedy backstreets of global finance'.

The last two decades have not just seen a remarkable swelling of the ranks and a sharp rise in the value of the wealth of those at the top. Top fortunes that would once have taken a lifetime to accumulate can now be built, and sometimes lost, in just a few years. Joanne Rowling, the author of the Harry Potter novels, has become a half-billionaire in just eight years, and moved in the process from downtown Edinburgh to 'millionaire's row' in Morningside. James Dyson, the inventor of the bagless vacuum cleaner, has built a business empire worth a billion pounds in twelve years. John Caudwell's £1.28 billion mobile phone business took sixteen years to build. Philip Green, the high street retailer, has gone from nowhere to close to £5 billion in little more than a decade. This is breakneck speed, bringing him billionaire status faster than anyone else in British history.

You also don't have to be a landowner, property tycoon or entrepreneur to make it to the rich lists. Top company executives, once generously rather than lavishly paid, have, in the words of one insider, started to 'defy the laws of gravity'. Boardroom pay has been escalating at such a rapid rate that becoming a director of a FTSE 100 company today virtually guarantees you multi-millionaire status. The top professional advisers they depend on – the

City lawyers, accountants and financiers who manage their business deals – can receive even more bloated rewards. Annual bonuses alone for the most successful City brokers and investment managers can outstrip the annual pay deals enjoyed by Britain's top executives. No fewer than nine current or former partners of the American investment bank Goldman Sachs are worth between £80 and £150 million each.[5] Today is an era when successful sports stars, entertainers, television celebrities, authors and chefs can also join the ranks of the multi-millionaires.

Rich Britain will tell the story of the rise of the super-rich in today's Britain. What lies behind the transformation? Has it peaked? Are there losers? It will argue that the wealth explosion at the top represents a permanent economic and social shift, the beginning of a new epoch, one that is fundamentally different from the more egalitarian post-war era, and one that carries profound implications for the type of society we are living in. The book will ask too if it matters if the wealth gap continues to soar. Would Britain be a less dynamic nation, and would we all suffer, without the lure of unprecedented personal fortunes?

In today's pro-rich climate, it is mostly seen as churlish and certainly old fashioned to question the rise of wealth at the top. To do so invites the risk of being accused of the 'politics of envy', not just from the right, as would be expected, but from much of the moderate left as well. Today, the wealthy are seen as largely deserving of their escalating fortunes. The modern wealth revolution is viewed as a sign of a new entrepreneurial spirit in Britain, the awakening of a long-awaited enterprise culture. The higher levels of personal enrichment are, it is claimed, being driven by rising levels of business skill, risk and leadership, which are benefiting us all.

Supporters of the wealth explosion also like to argue that today's wealth tables are much more meritocratic than in the past. Today, it is suggested, opportunities have spread, individuals can increasingly determine their own rank and modern wealth is more likely to be the product of ambition, hard work and self-improvement than privilege. According to this view, today's higher levels of inequality are fair because those at the top are more likely to get there by merit and ordinary people are increasingly able to join their ranks if they choose to do so.

The book will challenge the modern conventional wisdom about the merits of escalating levels of personal enrichment. It will thus take the risk of criticism for peddling the politics of envy. It will argue that the remarkably rapid increase in wealth concentration of recent times is not the product of more successful and effective risk-taking and entrepreneurial dynamism. Little of it is down to the emergence of a more meritocratic culture. New money is important but has only partially displaced the dominance of old wealth. Although inheritance plays a lesser role in the wealth stakes than in the past, a significant proportion of the wealth at the very top continues to derive from a shrewd choice of parentage.

While there has been an increase in the proportion of the self-made amongst successful entrepreneurs, most of them come from a relatively privileged background. New money is not, in general, a sign of a more opportunistic culture. The degree of social mobility from the bottom to the very top appears to be lower today than it was in the days when social privilege was accepted to be more entrenched.

Entrepreneurialism is vital to economic progress. Exceptional merit and effort undoubtedly deserve high and generous financial reward. A personal wealth explosion that was driven by the forging of a new economic resurgence, by reaching new heights of artistic and sporting achievement or by perceptive investment decisions would be widely and justly welcomed. But today's escalating rewards are not strongly linked to exceptional levels of skill, risk-taking and effort.

The continuation of the old landed classes in the wealth leagues is largely the product of upward movements in land and property prices, which stem from wider public policy decisions more than property improvement. Many of those sitting comfortably at the top of the rich lists have simply had to sit back and watch their fortunes soar. The extraordinary rise in corporate remuneration in recent years has little to do with superior business success but lots with the importing of American business habits into Britain and the ambiguous role played by institutional shareholders.

A common argument for claiming that the growing wealth gap does not matter is that personal wealth accumulation is said not to hurt anyone else. This is the essence of the argument used by Tony Blair, who has applauded the rise of a new wealthy super-class and has invited a good number of its members to tea at No. 10. As David Goodhart, editor of *Prospect* magazine, has put it, 'gap thinking is based on a defunct zero-sum idea of wealth creation. In a nineteenth-century mining village it was clear that the mine owner's wealth in a sense caused the poverty of the miners. Other than the odd sweatshop, that is not the case today . . . Bill Gates has not amassed a fortune of $150 billion by exploiting the poor of Seattle.' In fact, the arguments continue to rage about Gates, a man whose wealth is seven times

Ghana's GDP. Is he a technological and business genius who deserves his place as the world's richest man or an undeserving monopolist whose empire has been built through the ruthless destruction of his rivals, giving him the ability to charge premium prices for his software?

Some of today's personal fortunes are certainly the result of real wealth creation that harms nobody and benefits society as a whole. But many of them are the product of a carefully manipulated transfer of existing wealth from one group in society to another. Many of today's fortunes have been swollen still further by a burgeoning, lucrative and largely unchecked tax avoidance industry. Indeed modern entrepreneurship and tax avoidance go largely hand in hand. Highly paid tax accountants and lawyers are, in effect, engineering a redistribution, and a pretty massive one, from other taxpayers as a group. The continued wealth of the old land-owning class, resulting from rising land and property prices and rents, has been borne in part by increased burdens on small tenant farmers and leaseholders. Much of the finance industry is engaged in activities that involve the redistribution of existing wealth – towards themselves and their clients – rather than the creation of new.

Of course, there are examples of inspiration, skill and foresight. Some of today's rich are outstanding citizens, willing to share their personal achievements. But with some exceptions, there is little evidence that the new rich are the architects of a revolution in productivity or new technology that is underpinning a British economic revival, or that rising personal wealth has led to a revival of a philanthropic spirit. Boardroom decisions have been increasingly motivated by attempts to manipulate short-term share prices rather than achieve long-term and sustained business health. Investment decisions have too often been driven by frenzied and ill-advised speculation, such as that which fuelled the investment in small internet companies in the late 1990s. Multi-millionaire celebrities are the beneficiaries of a new commercialism in entertainment in which the 'winner takes all'.

The forward march of the super-rich has profound implications for Britain. It is changing the structure of the class system with the addition of a new layer, a mega-rich super-class, parallel to but different from the old upper class, which is a largely declining force. It is the central driving force of the sharp rise in inequality of the last two decades. Twenty-five years ago, Britain was one of the most equal societies in the developed world. While the United States tops the rich nation inequality league, Britain is now amongst the most polarised.[6]

Britain is now back to levels of pre-tax income inequality last seen in the 1940s, possibly earlier. Official figures for the share of wealth enjoyed by the top 1 per cent show inequality back to levels of more than a generation ago. And the very richest within that top 1 per cent are almost certainly enjoying wealth shares that take them back even earlier. Britain may not be back to the extreme levels of inequality that prevailed at the end of the nineteenth and beginning of the twentieth century, when a tiny proportion of the population, a mix of the landed aristocracy and the new industrial and commercial barons, held an even greater share of the nation's wealth and income. But in those times, the constraints on wealth-making were much weaker, monopolies could operate largely unchecked, the Inland Revenue was in its infancy, unions were few and regulations minimal. It was a society in the process of transition and that degree of inequality was eventually to prove unsustainable.

What is surprising is how, in today's much more mature democracy and complex and regulated economy, the top few thousand individuals are able to win such large shares of the economic wealth of the country. The question of extremes of personal wealth used to divide the political parties and the public. But recent times have seen the emergence of a new consensus that straddles the bulk of political and much popular opinion.

Rich Britain will argue that today's wealth revolution is less a justified reward for promoting a new economic, entrepreneurial and artistic leap forward than a large windfall gain stemming in the main from this shift in the political and cultural climate, one in which increasingly generous rewards, sometimes staggeringly so, have become acceptable. The gains can be seen as the financial equivalent of extras in cricket, welcome to the batting side but unearned, and much more damaging in their implications than in cricket.

The book will show how today's wealth explosion has strong roots in the parallel rush to personal wealth that began in the United States. Indeed, it is an almost uniquely Anglo-Saxon phenomenon. There are no real parallels in continental Europe. In America the remarkable growth in wealth at the top over the last fifteen years has been likened by one American expert to an 'economic megashift'.[7] Where America led, Britain has followed. The former ideological and cultural divide that used to distinguish attitudes towards personal enrichment and acceptable levels of inequality between the two nations has been closing sharply.

Since the Victorian era, society has chosen to distinguish between the deserving and undeserving poor, a distinction that continues to affect anti-poverty policy today. Yet such logic is applied only partially to the rich. Certainly, those who have added to the size of the cake through inspired economic and entrepreneurial leadership would in most people's eyes be seen as deserving of today's exceptional rewards. But the ranks of the rich are dominated by tycoons, investment bankers and business executives who, far from creating wealth, have taken advantage of today's much more pro-rich culture to seize a larger slice of the cake for themselves.

We might argue about who and how many fall into each camp, but meanwhile, the signs are that the very rich are likely to continue to prosper, that the steady rise in the extreme income and wealth divide may not yet have reached its peak. Corporate rewards are continuing to soar, the post-millennial stock market crash proved merely a dent in the upward march of the super-rich, big City bonuses are back.

It is possible that the tide will turn against the rich. The public may have been mesmerised by individual members of the super-rich club but in general take a lukewarm view of the growing income and wealth gap and may yet force an apparently reluctant government to intervene. Nevertheless, the broad sign is that higher degrees of wealth concentration are proving more acceptable than in the past. If so, Britain is almost certainly in the early stages of a new epoch, one that admires extreme personal fortunes, one much more accepting of growing inequality, one much closer to American than European social norms.

Far from a largely temporary phenomenon, the wealth explosion of the last two decades looks increasingly like a permanent shift and one still not complete. If so, it is the age of egalitarianism that lasted for two generations that may come to be seen as an aberration, a one-off age, a temporary interruption to a more natural state of deeper economic and social polarisation.

1

Let the children grow tall

'Let our children grow tall, and some taller than others if they have it in them to do so.'

(Margaret Thatcher, BBC radio, 1 March 1980)

In October 2005, the retail multi-billionaire Philip Green was invited to speak at a seminar on the future of private equity at Oxford University's prestigious Said Business School. His co-speaker was David Bonderman, an American venture capitalist and co-founder of the Texas Pacific Group, which owns a number of British firms from Burger King to Debenhams. At the end of their talk, the speakers were questioned by the 500-strong audience. One of the school's students asked the two men if they would be willing to consider investing in any of their ideas for new businesses. It was an audacious question which put both speakers on the spot and caused a ripple of laughter throughout the lecture hall. Green looked uncomfortable, hedged and then, after being pressed by the student, suddenly announced that he would be willing to invest £500,000 of his own money in the best idea. The audience had not expected such generosity and broke into spontaneous applause. A grinning Green turned to Bonderman and asked him to match his generosity, but this was not forthcoming.

For Green, one of the richest men in Britain, £500,000 is largely pocket money. A man who is currently paying himself some £3 million a day, he can earn that sort of sum in a couple of hours from his retail empire. As a known gambler, it is money he can easily afford to risk on a business punt. Green is also no stranger to big spending. A few months earlier, he had splashed out £4 million on his son's bar mitzvah, the Jewish coming of age. Stonemasons and craftsmen were flown out to the venue – on a private peninsula overlooking the Mediterranean between Nice and Monaco – to build a temporary synagogue big enough to seat 300 people. The guests were put up at the £1,000-a-night Grand-Hotel du Cap-Ferrat, a favourite celebrity haunt, while the musical highlight was provided by Beyoncé and her platinum-selling group Destiny's Child.[1] Three years earlier, he had spent £5 million flying out 200 guests to a five-star Cypriot hotel to celebrate his fiftieth birthday. Highlights at the three-day event included a special edition of *This Is Your Life* presented by Michael Aspel and a solid gold Monopoly set complete with diamond-studded dice from his wife, Tina, with the properties representing all his high street assets.

As contemporary parties go, Green's are far from the most expensive. In 2004, Lakshmi Mittal, the Indian-born international steel magnate, and another multi-billionaire, spent a record £30 million on his daughter's wedding at a seventeenth-century chateau in France. It lasted several days, was attended by 1,500 guests and included performances by Kylie Minogue and several Bollywood stars. His son's wedding in 1998 was no less spectacular. The events would not even have dented his bank balance – in 2005 he was estimated to be the richest man living in Britain.

The rich can be ranked either by their wealth or by what they own. On either basis, the secretive Roman Abramovich, a British resident, would land at or very near the top. Besides Chelsea football club, he owns a Boeing 737, a chauffeur-driven bombproof Mercedes-Benz and homes in Russia, Nice, St Tropez and Austria as well as his West Sussex estate, once owned by Australian media magnate Kerry Packer and which includes two polo pitches. He also has the choice of three luxury yachts. One, the £72 million *Pelorus*, has ex-SAS men amongst its forty crew plus a missile-detector system and mini-submarine; another, the £50 million *Grand Bleu*, has its own helicopter.

Even those with lesser degrees of wealth know how to spend it. When Chris Evans was wooing the young pop singer Billie Piper, he didn't send her flowers, he bought her a Ferrari. It had the right effect – they married a year later. If you don't need the real thing, there's a toy version. David and Victoria Beckham splashed out £45,000 for one for their son Brooklyn when he was barely out of nappies. In 2003, eleven England international footballers, amongst them Beckham and Michael Owen, invested in the ultimate dream holiday hideaway. They all bought luxury five-bedroom villas, each complete with private beach and swimming pool, on The Palm, an artificially created luxury island being built off the shores of Dubai in the

Arabian Gulf. The players are said to have paid £1 million for each of the villas. All 4,500 villas and apartments on offer were sold out within three weeks of going on the market, and at least a year before completion. So successful was the project that a second island is being built.

Ernest Hemingway famously responded to F. Scott Fitzgerald's assertion that 'the rich are different' with the retort, 'Yes, they've got more money.' But just how much 'more' do you need to make it into today's top wealth leagues? Some view the rich as those able to enjoy the privileges denied the great majority. Others say it is the level of wealth at which you can do more or less what you want without having to worry about the cost. In 1992, Greg Dyke, then running London Weekend Television, had his own take on what distinguishes the rich from the rest:

> I'm an old-fashioned sixties liberal who happens to find himself running a business . . . I'm going to end up rich, which is odd because I think I'm one of the few people in television who really doesn't worry about being rich. The one advantage of being rich is that it's 'fuck off' money. If you don't like it you can walk away.

Silicon Valley, in California, which led the technology revolution of the 1980s and is known as the 'Valley of the Dollars', is awash with ultra-rich residents who are free never to have to work again. They call it something similar – 'fuck-you money'. Britain has a different, only slightly more polite phrase for the well off who choose not to work – the 'idle rich'. Before the Second World War they used to be known as the leisured classes, the upper classes who lived off a mix of rent from land and property and the interest from their capital, and who enjoyed a lavish and often bohemian lifestyle.

To join the really exclusive set who 'can walk away' you would need to be amongst the ranks of those who, in the wealthy Conservative MP Alan Clark's memorable phrase, have sufficient capital 'to live off the interest on their interest'. Although most of today's very wealthy could give up work if they wanted to, live off their assets and do so pretty comfortably too, most of them don't, presumably because, although they have the choice, they appear to prefer work or more money or both to more leisure. In fact, the 'leisured classes' appear to be a dying breed.[2]

The poor are usually defined in relative terms – as those falling *below* an income level set at a fixed proportion of the average. On a parallel basis, the rich could simply be defined as those living *above* a particular income level.

There are two possible routes to selecting the appropriate level. First, it could be set at a fixed upper ratio of average incomes, although, just as in the case of the poor, this does not help much with where to set the line itself. Fifty times the average, for example, would mean a rich line of slightly over £1 million. Setting a line at a fixed proportion of the average would mean that the numbers of rich at any given time would depend on the extent of the distribution of incomes above the line. Extensive inequality would mean more rich than if incomes were more evenly distributed. Rising inequality over time would increase the rich count. On this basis the number of rich has been rising significantly in the last two decades.

A second approach might be to reverse an alternative method used to define poverty, as the minimum income level needed to be able to afford a bundle of *necessities*. The rich might then be defined as those able to afford a bundle of extreme *luxuries*. What should be included in such a bundle remains, of course, somewhat arbitrary. It might include a high-performance car, a second and third home, holidays in exclusive resorts and top designer jewellery and clothes, but what about a yacht or a jet? As the international technology giant Jim Manzi once explained the dilemma, 'there is only one difference between $5 million and $50 million – with $5 million you can do what the hell you like; with $50 million you can do what the hell you like in a jet'.[3] In the case of poverty, studies have attempted to assess what should be in a bundle of essentials but no systematic research has attempted to define a bundle of appropriate luxuries.[4]

There are no shortage of views about where the 'wealth line' should be drawn. Public opinion is somewhat divided. According to a BBC poll in 2003, a third of the public think £100,000 or less 'in ready cash' is enough to make you rich; 27 per cent pitched the threshold at somewhere between £100,000 and £1 million. Just over a quarter thought you would need a million or more to be rich today while only 3 per cent said £5 million or more (see Table 1.1).

It is doubtful if most of those in the half-millionaire or even millionaire camp would share these popular views and place themselves firmly amongst the rich. Indeed, while those on average incomes tend to set a modest income level as sufficient, the wealthy themselves tend to set a much higher threshold, typically high enough to conveniently exclude themselves.

The rich typically misrank their position in the wealth distribution. Such is their divorce from reality that when asked what the average income is, the wealthy tend to pick a sum that is much higher than the actual figure. In a survey of those worth between $1 million and $4 million in the United States in 2000, for example, only 9 per cent admitted to being wealthy – the pollsters didn't even use the word 'rich'. The rest said they were comfortable or 'very comfortable'. About half the respondents defined wealth as $5million or more.[5]

Table 1.1 How much 'ready cash' do you need to be rich in Britain, 2003?

Amount	% respondents
£5 million or more	3
More than £1m but less than £5m	9
£1 million	14
More than £500,000 but less than £1m	4
£500,000	8
More than £100,000 but less than £500,000	15
£100,000	8
Less than £100,000	25
Don't know	13

Source: BBC poll for BBC 5 Live, July 2003.

Ultimately, where we draw the line is a subjective matter. As social scientists have found with defining a poverty line, there is no scientific way of drawing up an objective 'rich line' and few, if any, academics have attempted to do so. A million pounds in 'ready cash' might be thought by most to get you into the rich camp. Indeed, although inflation has eroded the value and status of being a millionaire, those with that much 'cash and other liquid assets' are certainly in a pretty exclusive group – around one in 500 of the adult population.[6] But amongst the rich themselves and those who are paid to advise them, £1 million is small beer. It's not enough to get you noticed or come remotely close to financing the kind of lifestyles and the social, cultural and global demands that today's rich elite have come to expect.

In 2005, a report by Britain's most 'establishment' bank, Coutts & Co., claimed that today you would need £2.6 million to finance the lifestyle of a millionaire of twenty-five years ago. Then the magical seven-figure sum would have bought a lifestyle that included a five-bedroom house with two staff, two luxury cars, and an apartment and a yacht in the south of France. Now you would need to be a near trillionaire to enjoy the same. As Sarah Davies, Coutts's chief executive, explained, a millionaire used to be someone who was seen as mega-wealthy – a person who didn't have to work if they chose not and who was able to live a life of luxury. A million is obviously still a sizeable amount of money . . . However, while twenty-five years ago it would have been more than enough to comfortably live the millionaire's lifestyle a few times over, today it will only afford a small portion of the trappings.[7]

A million is also not enough to pull the top investment banks, which charge huge fees for managing their clients' wealth but which can barely be bothered with the mere millionaire. They rank potential clients according to their investment potential, and the admission price tends to be pretty high. With £30 million or more you would get safely into the 'super-rich' bracket and the various competing companies would battle hard to sign you up. Those with a more modest £10 million or so would still get a pretty big welcome. The US-based Bessemer Trust, which handles 10 per cent of America's top thousand chief executives, talks of 'substantial people' – those with a minimum of $10 million. Private banks prefer the very wealthy but will handle those with less wealth than this. They will end up with a more modest label, though. Typical terms for those with less would be 'very high net worth' for those with £5 million or more to invest and 'high net worth' for clients with £1 million or more.

Like the giant investment banks, *Rich Britain* does not attempt to draw up a definitive rich line, referring instead to a hierarchy of wealth, in which those with assets of, say, £50 million or more – the premier division – might be called the 'mega-rich'. It was a fortune of this size that was required for entry in 2005 to the top 1,000 list compiled annually by the *Sunday Times*, about one in every 45,000 adults. Those with wealth of between £5 million and £50 million – the first division – might then be referred to as the 'super-rich'. The number of people making up the premier and first divisions, those worth over £5 million, has been variously estimated at between 9,000 and 30,000. Those with between £1 million and £5 million – the second division – might then be called the 'merely rich'. This group is estimated to number a further 85,000 to 110,000 people.[8]

The status chase

One of the characteristics of today's rich is that, whatever camp they find themselves in, they rarely seem very satisfied with their lot. Many of them seem to be in a state of denial about their good fortune. In 2005, Rosie Millard, the former arts correspondent of the BBC, wrote an article for the *Sunday Times* complaining of being an 'impoverished professional' and £40,000 in debt despite owning, with her husband, four London properties worth some £2 million and a 'fabulously chic' Paris apartment.[9] Millard had written the confessional article to highlight the growing problem of middle-class debt, but in the process had, perhaps inadvertently, given the game away in her somewhat tongue-in-cheek parody of her own lifestyle, one that included a runaway spending habit on items such as expensive haircuts, designer clothes and make-up. She is a classic example of the modern-day phenomenon of even the pretty well off feeling poor, her 'plight' the product of believing she was entitled to a lifestyle that was in fact beyond her means – even if her means were beyond those of most of the population.

In the United States, the rich are also apparently finding it difficult to live within their means. Debt addiction is as much an issue for the very rich as the poor. Some borrow to pay for second or third holiday homes, racehorses or yachts. A survey of those worth more then $5 million found that 19 per cent had a second mortgage or home loan, 14 per cent had credit card balances and 11 per cent other loans.[10]

Millard and her television producer husband may not be in the super-rich or even the 'merely rich' camp, but well off compared with most of the population they certainly are. What they illustrate is a phenomenon that as people get richer, far from being satisfied with what they can now afford and moderating their consumer appetites, they do the opposite: they stretch and inflate the nature of need, discovering in effect a whole new range of wants. At its most extreme, as people get very rich they view what are to the rest of us extreme luxuries – the yacht, the penthouse suite, the private island – as essentials they don't seem able to live without. Even those near the top of the pile who can't afford these trappings of a modern wealthy lifestyle end up feeling poor and/or in debt. The sort of top fortunes available even in the recent past would not today be sufficient to pay for this expanded list of 'necessities'. This feeling of 'relative deprivation' is an experience that was once confined mostly to the poor but has increasingly been adopted by the rich as well. To the multi-millionaire, a mere million would barely secure the necessities of life; to nearly everyone else it represents unattainable and virtually unimaginable abundance.

What the rich and the near rich are experiencing is a form of wealth illusion – they seem to think they are poorer than they are. This is because they compare themselves not with those worse off than them, or even with their peers, but with those above them in the wealth stakes.

In 2005, Britney Spears is said to have spent some £26 million in one year on luxury homes in Florida, Manhattan and Arizona, a fleet of cars, and a lifestyle that included a private jet, exclusive jewellery and clothes and lavish partying. The wealthy do not all seek publicity, lead ostentatious lives, or complain about struggling to get by, even in the United States. Malcolm Glazer is a reclusive billionaire who refuses to give interviews. The 76-year old owner of Manchester United is desperate to keep out of the limelight and is known to eschew what he calls 'unnecessary luxuries' such as designer clothes. The co-founder of Microsoft, Paul Allen, owns one of the world's largest yachts with a deck the size of football pitch, but generally prefers to keep a much lower profile than his much better-known partner, Bill Gates. The international investor Warren Buffett, who owns great swathes of corporate America, is notorious for his careful living and his admonishment of extravagance. Yet even he has been seduced by the pull of the corporate jet, though initially with a conscience. He called his first jet *Indefensible*. When he became dependent on it he renamed it *Indispensable*.

Traditionally, the British and continental Europeans have been much more coy about the question of personal wealth. In April 2004, a Swedish business magazine, *Veckans Affärer*, claimed that the Ikea founder, Ingvar Kamprad, had overtaken Gates as the richest man in the world. Such is the significance of the claim, that Gates had been unseated after a decade at the top, that the story made international headlines. The furniture store, however, moved swiftly to deny the story. Kamprad's wealth had been calculated by adding up the value of Ikea's 186 stores, in thirty-one countries, while Ikea responded that Kamprad no longer owned the stores. The magazine retorted that the Kamprad family remained the effective owners through a network of complex foundations. In contrast to many of those topping the world's rich lists, Kamprad is renowned for his thrift. He drives an old Volvo, lives discreetly near Lausanne, travels second class by train. His idea of fun is cycling across rural Sweden. On the other hand, he has moved from high-tax Sweden to low-tax Switzerland and has deliberately set out to minimise Ikea's corporate tax bills by shrouding the business in trusts and holding companies.

Some British tycoons also lead quiet though rarely frugal lives, insufficiently flamboyant to get into the gossip columns. Many of those who are really taking the key decisions in Britain's biggest companies prefer to stay invisible. The new hedge fund multi-millionaires are renowned for the secrecy of their profession and their lives. As one City PR executive once explained, 'my job is to keep them out of the spotlight'. The Barclay brothers, with a business empire ranging from the London Ritz to the *Telegraph* newspapers, eschew publicity and fame. Indeed, such is their obsession with privacy, they once sued a BBC journalist who rowed out to film their mansion on the island of Brecqhou, which they own. The small island is off Sark in the Channel Islands and was uninhabited when they bought it – a perfect hideaway. After it became theirs, they adorned it with a mock-Gothic castle, designed by Terry Quinlan, the Prince of Wales's favourite architect. All in, the deal cost £30 million, but money had been no option. The building exudes wealth – the banqueting hall, overlooking the rocky wind-swept coast, is fully eighty metres long while the library ceiling is decorated with frescoes in the style of the Sistine Chapel.

Some have an ambiguous relationship with their wealth. John Caudwell, the self-made mobile phone billionaire, cuts his own hair with a powered clipper from Boots, buys his clothes from Marks and Spencer and food from his local cash and carry. On the other hand, he owns a thirty-acre estate, a helicopter and his own twin-engined plane, although, as he is quick to point out, it's not quite a jet.

In the post-war era, the rich largely shunned open extravagance. Wealth was to be kept behind closed doors. All that has changed. Then, wealth was associated with guilt. Today the only guilt around is 'why haven't we made more?'. In the post-war era it was not polite to talk about how much money you had. Now the rich like to boast about it. They are increasingly open about their success and want to flaunt it. The editor of *Tatler* describes the changes as 'seismic'.

> We have seen the tweed set go bling. That sense of inverted glamour by having a frayed shirt collar or threadbare jacket no longer holds. No more do guests take the rug off the floor to put on the bed for warmth in draughty country houses. Gone is the stinking estate car as a symbol of inverted wealth.[11]

Ostentation has also been encouraged by an often fawning public. As Ferdinand Mount describes it, 'adulation of the rich and famous is surely as fulsome as ever. In hotels, restaurants and aircraft – the sites of modern luxury – the new upper crust is fawned on as egregiously as old money in its Edwardian heyday.'[12]

When David Beckham took his wife to Paris for her 31st birthday, he hired a private Learjet with 'gold-plated bathroom' and Victoria's initial printed on the side and booked them into the Ritz hotel's £3,000-a-night Coco Chanel suite. The weekend cost close to half a million pounds. Before his spectacular fall, the naturalised British tycoon Lord Black courted the limelight with his own lavish multi-home, private-jet lifestyle. His personal household staff included chefs, senior butlers, under-butlers, chauffeurs, housemen, footmen and security personnel. As his wife, Barbara Amiel, once boasted, her extravagance 'knows no bounds'. She would regularly fly from Britain to Canada just to have her hair done. Her wardrobe ran to 100 pairs of Manolo Blahnik shoes and ranks of Hermès handbags. They entertained in exalted fashion. Their greed was fuelled by a desire not just to join in with but to outdo the American jet set.

The historian Paul Johnson recently wrote:

> Today, in terms of London or Parisien splendor, a magnate who has $300 million to his name can comfortably be considered among the super-rich and can conduct himself accordingly. But if he wishes to occupy such a position among the financial elite of New York or Palm Beach, he must have at least $1 billion. This, it is said, is the reason media titan Conrad Black had to go to such lengths to finance his lifestyle from the funds of his business.[13]

In 2003, Black was forced to resign as chief executive of Hollinger International, owners of the Telegraph newspaper group. In the £700 million lawsuit issued against the disgraced press tycoon, Hollinger International described Black's companies as using 'Hollinger as a cash cow to be milked of every possible drop of cash, often in a manner evidencing complete disregard for the rights of all shareholders'.

Status seeking is fuelling the process. The rich appear to be especially conscious of their relative positioning and appear to love to compete to outdo their peers in today's leapfrogging culture. There is the race for exclusivity. One of the most exclusive clubs in the world is F1 Clienti, set up by Ferrari for those who own a Formula One car, which comes complete with a dedicated Ferrari pit crew. The club currently boasts forty mega-rich members worldwide. A new store in Moscow offers the ultimate cachet – it only sells goods, from racehorses and private jets to paradise islands and artworks, that cost at least $1 million. Locals call it the multi-millionaire's supermarket.

Upstaging is commonplace. While *OK!* magazine paid David and Victoria Beckham £1 million for their wedding photos in 1999, Jordan and Peter André were able to get £1.75 million for theirs in 2005. Although Rio Ferdinand was already one of the highest-paid footballers in Britain – on £90,000 a week – he demanded a rise to £120,000 a week, not because he needed the money, but because he wanted the ultimate accolade of being the very highest-paid footballer in Britain. Although he was paid £400,000 a year as director general of the BBC, John Birt is believed to have been disappointed at missing out on the millions some of his former colleagues received when LWT was taken over by Granada.

Investment bankers are no longer content to just drink vintage Dom Perignon: in 2005, one senior banker sprayed £26,000 worth of 'Dompers' around the VIP room of the exclusive West End club Mo*vida. Commonplace in Monaco and St Tropez clubs, the champagne-spraying craze had finally spread to London and had become something of a rite of passage for highly paid investment bankers and hedge fund managers. At the burgeoning number of charity dinners, the super-rich love to openly outbid each other for the star prizes, which often involve days out with celebrities. At one dinner organised by the hedge fund industry, a participant said, 'It was one of the rare times you got to see how much money these people had, and they were loving the chance to exercise their competitive natures, by saying, "Not only am I richer than you, I'm also more generous." '[14]

To compete in this status-driven world, the incomes expected at the top are on an ever-upward spiral. Celebrity presenters demand and get more or less what they want. Chris Tarrant gets £1 million a year from hosting *Who Wants to Be a Millionaire?* on ITV, and this came on top of the reputed £1.5 million salary for his Capital Radio show, which he gave up in 2004. Carol Vorderman is paid £1 million for appearing on Channel 4's *Countdown*, for which she is required forty days a year. Top executives have increasingly come to expect and demand a tycoon lifestyle. High pay packets seem to have become a badge of honour. As one well-to-do columnist has written, 'my experience is that the rich themselves are extremely interested (and competitive) about wealth totals'.[15] As the highest fortunes race away, those left behind seek to catch up and overtake, fuelling an increasingly runaway process of salary hiking. Modern businessmen are renowned for their irritation at their earnings being outstripped by those of celebrities and sports stars. Far from being a term that describes the feelings of the poor towards the rich, the 'politics of envy' would appear to be an apt description of the feelings of many of the rich themselves towards their peers and those above them in the wealth stakes. Indeed, some seem to display an extreme version of the condition.

In the spring of 2000, Larry Ellison, the billionaire owner of Oracle, was in the middle of a global conference call in his office in Redwood City, thirty miles south of San Francisco. Before the call began, Ellison had given instructions that he was to be interrupted for only one thing, the moment he dethroned Bill Gates as the richest man in the world. Gates had held that position for the previous eight years and Ellison had long courted the idea of taking his place. That spring offered his best chance. Microsoft shares had plummeted in the wake of the sudden stock market crash in March of that year. At one point they had fallen so drastically that Gates's $100 billion fortune had halved. According to Oracle, for a few seconds Ellison came within a whisker of overtaking Gates, and by some reckonings he did. But then Microsoft's share price recovered and the opportunity was gone.[16] Ellison is not the only rich American who would love to topple Gates from his pedestal.

The publication of the annual *Forbes* list of the 400 richest Americans has become an annual ritual to see who has leapfrogged who. In Wall Street investment banks, traders, already on huge pay deals, are obsessed with their relative pay as well as bonuses. According to one insider at Morgan Stanley in the mid-1990s, 'each wanted to be paid more than his peers, not necessarily because the money was relevant to day-to-day life, but because it would signal that he had beaten the others'. Such competitiveness is rife across Wall Street. 'The money in fact meant very little. What's another few million when you already have fifty?'[17] Some traders unhappy with their bonuses have been known to try and 'get even' by hiring limousines at odd times, making drivers wait and billing the fees to their clients. Bonus day at the Wall Street firm First Boston is known as the 'Valentine's Day Massacre'. As one insider put it, 'by the time bonuses are paid, most salesmen and traders are so infused with greedy, revolutionary fervour that no matter what amount the firm actually pays them, they automatically think they have been screwed'.[18]

This frenzy is now equally endemic to the City. For City high flyers, the annual bonus can range from half to up to ten times basic salary, but, as on Wall Street, this doesn't always seem to satisfy those on the receiving end. In the late 1990s, as stock markets soared, and it was hard to fail, bonuses turned some of Britain's most highly paid successful traders, and even unsuccessful ones, into multi-millionaires, sometimes overnight. Those offered a mere million pounds, when others were getting several million, didn't always acknowledge their good fortune. As in the United States, explosive tantrums were and remain commonplace on bonus day. No issue is more divisive at an investment bank. There are tales of bankers angrily tearing up their bonus cheques and resigning on the spot.

The conspicuous consumption that has become increasingly common, especially amongst the new rich, is often as much for show as enjoyment. In 2000, Joe Lewis, a British financier living in the Bahamas and estimated to be worth £1.8 billion, paid £1.4 million for the privilege of a round of golf with the world's number one, Tiger Woods, who unsurprisingly proceeded to thrash him. In 2004, a Goldman Sachs banker bid £90,000 at a charity auction to play tennis with Tony Blair. The expensive yachts, helicopters, lavish parties and football clubs are in many ways little more than 'trophy assets' – super-rich toys that have become an essential part of the leapfrogging ritual that proves you have arrived. This applies maybe even to the wives. The Greek shipping tycoon Aristotle Onassis, it is said, married Jackie Kennedy as an act of conspicuous consumption. A beautiful, young and preferably blonde wife who spends her time buying expensive clothes is a must for the growing band of super-rich Russians.

Sometimes the rich have so much money they lose count of it. In 2004, a PA at the London office of American investment bank Goldman Sachs was found guilty of plundering the private bank accounts of two of her bosses to the tune of £4.5 million. For two years, Joyti De-Laurey and her family lived tycoon lifestyles. She bought a twelve-cylinder Aston Martin Vanquish and a Saab convertible, properties in Britain and Cyprus, a wardrobe full of top designer clothes, Cartier jewellery worth £300,000 and a luxury break at a hotel in Beverly Hills. The relatively low-paid PA held a chequebook for her bosses' private bank accounts and repeatedly forged their signatures. The fraud went unnoticed for two years and one of her bosses, Edward Scott Mead, only discovered the loss while making a donation to his former American college. In her defence, De-Laurey claimed that the money had been 'a reward for me' and was only 'pocket money' to them. She described the bank's culture as one of 'dog eats dog', and dismissed its staff as 'vultures'. 'No one person is worth all the money they are able to earn.' Top City and Wall Street financiers are usually very cagey about what they earn and the size of their bonuses. De-Laurey had not only copied the lifestyle of her wealthy bosses, she had lifted the lid on what one lawyer at the trial described as the 'fairytale wealth' of the Square Mile super-rich. Failing to miss the missing millions, the bosses were obviously able to live comfortably without them. When a highly embarrassed Mead was asked in cross-examination about the scale of his personal fortune, he confirmed that he had received about £50 million in shares when Goldman Sachs had floated on New York's stock exchange in 2000. He denied that he had received as much as a rumoured £10 million bonus for work on Vodafone's takeover of German rival Mannesmann in 2001. In 2005, he was estimated to be worth some £80 million.[19]

'Goldmine Sachs', as it is known, is no run-of-the-mill bank. Its employees have an overriding life goal – to make big money for their firm and themselves. And they are very successful at it. Its office in Fleet Street has a greater concentration of multi-millionaires than any other in Britain. This is partly because of the sums received by the partners when the firm floated in 2000. But it is also down to the sky-high fees the firm can earn from its specialist activities – mergers, acquisitions and corporate finance. Successful staff may have to work gruelling hours, but can expect to amass riches beyond the dreams of most.

Those riches can buy you a pretty exclusive lifestyle. Mead lives in Notting Hill and has five children. When he became unhappy with the local schools, with three other investment bankers he paid for a new school, Notting Hill Preparatory, to be built from scratch. Another former partner bought Eileen Righ, a remote Scottish island, which he reaches using one of his three private helicopters. He also has a house in Italy and a multi-million-pound five-storey town house in Belgravia.

Join the club

When Paul Getty was named the richest person in the world by *Fortune* magazine in 1957, he told his brother, 'I don't know how much money I have. I don't know how they would know.' Until recently most of the rich, at least in Europe, preferred to keep details of their true wealth private. Many still pay hefty fees to experts who help them both stay rich and hide what they are really worth. But, as wealth has escalated and public interest has soared, it has become increasingly difficult for those rich who would prefer to stay out of the limelight to hide themselves or their wealth away. Indeed, such is the continuing public curiosity that recent years have brought an expanded rich-gazing industry aimed at identifying who the rich are and how much they have. The result is a steady growth in the number of annual 'body counts' compiled by newspapers and magazines, which compete to provide a directory of the wealthy. Proprietors and editors are only too aware of the potential to boost sales through publishing detailed reports on Britain's rich.

The craze in fact started in Britain, with the first British millionaire counts being published by the *Spectator* magazine in 1873 and 1883. The first rich list in the United States was published by the *New York Tribune* in 1892. Then the motive was not curiosity, prurience or sales, but politics. American opponents of protectionism argued that import tariffs had turned thousands of American businessmen into millionaires. To refute the claim, the paper's publisher, who was fervently pro-protection, ordered the drawing up of a list of millionaires in America. It ran to 4,047, of whom 1,125 had become rich in industries protected by tariffs.[20]

In 1918, a new business magazine called *Forbes* compiled a list of the thirty richest Americans.[21] Then sixty-four years later, in 1982, *Forbes* started its annual list of America's 400 wealthiest families. The magazine sold out within hours but the list didn't please everybody. One person credited with two million shares in Campbell Soup turned out to have only two. The comedian Bob Hope said of his $200 million valuation, 'If I had that kind of money, I wouldn't have gone to Vietnam, I would have sent for it.'[22] The list was and still is limited to 400 names because 'the Four Hundred' was a familiar shorthand term for high society during the 'Gilded Age' in 1870s and 1880s America. This was a period when huge fortunes of up to $100 million, an unprecedented level, were being accumulated first through the railway boom and then through oil and steel. Mrs William B. Astor, the wife of one of the richest of the group of multi-millionaires, used to hold regular social events for those 'who matter' and only 400 people could fit into her personal ballroom on New York's Fifth Avenue.

Shortly after *Forbes* started up its annual list, the city editor of the *Sunday Telegraph*, Ivan Fallon, and a colleague, Dr Philip Beresford, were having lunch in Claridge's with Tiny Rowland, the controversial head of Lonrho and himself a member of the mega-rich. Rowland suggested a similar list in Britain. Easily convinced, Fallon and Beresford set to work by phoning potential candidates. Unfortunately for the paper, two of those contacted were dukes. One of them, the Duke of Devonshire, an aristocrat and one of Britain's biggest landowners, summoned the paper's editor, John

Thompson, to his club, White's, where he was suitably rebuked. The Duke of Atholl, also contacted by the paper, made it clear to the paper's then owner, Lord Hartwell, that he could forget shooting grouse across the duke's 147,000 Scottish acres if his name appeared in the list. Hartwell had been made a life peer in 1968 and was himself a leading figure in London society. A similar complaint came from the Sainsbury family, which had been warned by Scotland Yard that publishing such a list would put them at risk of kidnap.[23] The establishment pressure worked and the idea was quickly dropped.

Some years later, Fallon and Beresford both left to join the *Sunday Times*. The paper's owner, Rupert Murdoch, and the then editor, Andrew Neil, were both devoted Thatcherites. They not only spotted the financial potential for the newspaper, they were antagonistic to what they saw as the continuing power of a British establishment based on old money and class. They had no qualms about publishing details of Britain's rich and indeed had nothing to lose from establishment threats. Nevertheless, the lesson had been learned and the work began in total secrecy. The list was compiled through secondary sources rather than direct contact and other staff were kept in the dark. The first the entrants knew of it was when the *Sunday Times* duly published its first list of the 200 richest Britons in 1989. It contained a few blunders, such as including a bankrupt and someone who had died eight months earlier, but still proved a great boost to circulation. According to Beresford, sales rise by some 14 per cent on rich list day.[24]

Spurred on by the success of the *Sunday Times*'s lists, other Sunday newspapers now publish their own. Indeed, it has now become something of an annual race among the Sundays to be first with the list, with publication date a closely kept secret. Other publications also love their own charts: *Broadcast* magazine has published its list of the richest 100 people in the media since 1999; *Heat* publishes a list of Britain's top music earners; and the London *Evening Standard* has its own 'City Rich List'. In 1995, the *Sunday Times*'s list was extended to 500 and then three years later to 1,000.

These lists provide great interest for a public seemingly never satiated by intrigue and gossip about the rich and famous. Nevertheless, the difficulty of getting access to all sources of wealth is such that the calculations will always be estimates. The result is some amusing and sometimes embarrassing inconsistencies. In their 2003 list, the *Mail on Sunday* announced a new British billionaire – the Kensington-based property developer and art collector David Khalili, worth more than £2.5 billion, and the man who once owned the most expensive house in Britain, a mansion in Kensington Park Gardens. Khalili sold it in 2001 to Bernie Ecclestone, the Formula One boss, for £65 million, and he sold it to Lakshmi Mittal in 2004. This was enough to put Khalili into the top five wealthiest people in Britain. Yet this was, in fact, the first time he had appeared in the *Mail*'s list even though it had started in 1999, and even today it is difficult to acquire that kind of fortune in one year. The *Sunday Times* meanwhile ranked him as 133rd, on a par with the Queen, and estimated his fortune at a mere £500 million.

Initially the annual ritual of being ranked and evaluated by a bunch of newspaper journalists did not go down well with many of those listed. On publication of its first list, the *Sunday Times* received all sorts of threats over inclusion and accuracy. The aristocracy, perhaps the least popular of Britain's rich elite, have always been especially hostile. They would generally prefer their fortunes and their financial arrangements to remain hidden from excessive public gaze. For them, occasionally opening up their stately homes is enough.

A preference for secrecy is not confined to the aristocracy. The late steel tycoon Jack Walker, echoing the fears of the Sainsburys, described the first list as 'a beggars' and burglars' charter'. Peter de Savary, the property developer, has made the occasional appearance and likes to make phone calls beginning, 'Hi, number 65, this is number 44 here.'[25] Gavyn Davies, a former partner with Goldman Sachs and former chairman of the BBC governors, was rather more coy when approached by the paper: 'I think it's nosy and irrelevant and also I don't know the answer. Sorry.'[26] The new rich are not always so shy. The porn king David Sullivan wrote to the *Sunday Times* enclosing his accounts and declaring himself grossly undervalued in the 1990 list at £60 million. In 1991, he was upgraded to £100 million. Some even send in building society details showing millions held on deposit.

For years, the Reuben brothers, David and Simon, who had built a fortune founded on aluminium mining in Russia and Afghanistan in the early 1990s, guarded their privacy and were keen to hide the extent of their wealth. Then in 2003 they set up their own website with details of how they built their fortune. In the same year they threw a private cocktail party in a magnificent villa overlooking Cannes to which they invited many people who they had never met before. As a result of their new openness the brothers raced up the *Sunday Times*'s rich list, rising from number 253 in 2002 to number 5 in 2003. Their 2002 fortune of £131 million was re-estimated at £2,100 million. The brothers, who were born in Bombay but moved to Britain as teenagers, had recently diversified their empire into property, acquiring amongst other things Millbank Tower in Westminster – former home of the Labour Party. According to friends, they decided to disclose the extent of their wealth in order to become accepted as serious players in the world of British business, as have others such as the Barclay brothers and Philip Green.

In 2005, according to the *Sunday Times*, there were forty billionaires in Britain (see Table 1.2), up from twelve in 1990. The top two were both foreign born – Lakshmi Mittal and the Russian oligarch Roman Abramovich, both of whom have chosen to settle and live in Britain. In October 2005, Abramovich sold Sibneft, the Russian oil company he controlled, for £7.5 billion, which would have greatly increased his fortune to close to that of Mittal. The Duke of Westminster took third place. Fourth was Hans Rausing, a Swede who moved to Britain in 1982. He made his fortune from his milk carton business, Tetra Laval. Fifth on the list was Philip Green, who had quadrupled his wealth in three years.

Other billionaires included the Virgin boss, Sir Richard Branson; Bernie and Slavica Ecclestone, with an estimated £2.3 billion from Formula One motor racing; and Lord Sainsbury, the supermarket chain owner and Labour minister. There were four aristocratic billionaires, whose inherited wealth is made up largely of property, land and art. As well as the Duke of Westminster – whose fortune of £5.6 billion comes from owning 300 acres of prime land and property in Mayfair and Belgravia, the most highly valued streets in Britain, and who has never been out of the *Sunday Times* top ten since it started – they include Earl Cadogan, who owns more than 1,000 acres of Chelsea, and Viscount Portman, with 110 acres of prime shopping sites around Oxford Street including the freehold of Marble Arch, land originally given to his family by Henry VIII.

Below the billionaires came a group of 460 with fortunes of between £1 billion and £100 million. Sprinkled amongst the entrepreneurs, business executives and those who had inherited a fortune were a dozen rock stars, names such as Sir Paul McCartney, worth £800 million; Madonna, worth £235 million; and Eric Clapton, worth £130 million. Other high-profile names included Lord Lloyd Webber (£700 million); Mohamed al-Fayed, the controversial owner of Harrods, the Paris Ritz and Fulham football club (£450 million); and Catherine Zeta-Jones and Michael Douglas (£170 million between them).

Table 1.2 The billionaire count, Britain, 2005

	Name	Worth (£bn)	Source of wealth
1.	Lakshmi Mittal	£14.80	Steel
2.	Roman Abramovich	£7.50	Oil, investments
3.	The Duke of Westminster	£5.60	Property
4.	Hans Rausing and family	£4.95	Food packaging
5	Phillip and Christina Green	£4.85	Retailing
6	Oleg Deripaska	£4.38	Aluminium
7	Sir Richard Branson	£3.00	Transport, mobile phones
8	Kirsten and Jorn Rausing	£2.58	Inheritance, bloodstock, investments
9	David and Simon Reuben	£2.50	Property, metal trading
10	Spiro Latsis and family	£2.40	Banking, shipping
11	Bernie and Slavica Ecclestone	£2.32	Motor racing
12	Charlene and Michael de Carvalho	£2.27	Inheritance, brewing, banking
13=	Mahdi al-Tajir	£2.10	Oil, investments, bottled water
13=	Sri and Gopi Hinduja	£2.10	Industry, finance
15	Joe Lewis	£2.00	Foreign exchange dealing
16	John Fredriksen	£1.89	Shipping
17	Lord Sainsbury and family	£1.71	Supermarkets
18	Earl Cadogan and family	£1.65	Property
19	Sergio Mantegazza and family	£1.54	Travel
20	Roddie Fleming and family	£1.50	Banking
21	Eddie and Malcolm Healey	£1.45	Property, kitchens
22=	Nadhmi Auchi	£1.40	Finance
22=	Mary Czernin and the Howard de Walden family	£1.40	Property
24	Michael Moritz	£1.35	Finance
25=	Leonard Blavatnik	£1.30	Industry
25=	Clive Calder	£1.30	Music
25=	Richard Desmond	£1.30	Publishing
25=	Sir Terry Matthews	£1.30	Telecommunications
29=	John Caudwell	£1.28	Mobile phones
29=	Bruno Schroder and family	£1.28	Finance
31	Philippe Foriel-Destezet	£1.27	Recruitment services
32	The Aga Khan	£1.25	Head of the Ismaili people
33=	Sir David and Sir Frederick Barclay	£1.20	Media, retail, property
33=	Viscount Portman and family	£1.20	Property
35	Lady Grantchester and the Moores family	£1.16	Retailing, football pools
36=	Paul Fentener van Vlissingen	£1.10	Inheritance
36=	Michael Lemos	£1.10	Inheritance
36=	Sir Ken Morrison and family	£1.10	Supermarkets
39	James Dyson	£1.05	Household appliances
40	Roger and Peter De Haan	£1.02	Leisure

Source: *Sunday Times* Rich List, 2005, 3 April 2005. For definitions, see the Appendix.

At less than £100 million were a number of new celebrities, entertainers and television presenters, there because they can command increasingly colossal fees. They included the comic Rowan Atkinson, the film star Sir Sean Connery and the actor Sir Anthony Hopkins. David and Victoria Beckham were worth an estimated £75 million in 2005. Like other young sporting superstars, David Beckham's wealth comes not just from his club earnings, massive as they are, but also from huge sponsorship and advertising deals. He has lucrative deals with Gillette, Vodafone and Adidas. Although Beckham is the only footballer in the top 1,000 list, such is the potential of the top-flight footballer that Coutts & Co. regularly sends out brochures headed 'Expert Wealth Management for private clients who are professional footballers'. Coutts counts a fifth of Premiership footballers as clients. It also caters for a third of the millionaires created through the National Lottery since 1994, of whom there are more than 1,000.

Following the hike in executive and City salaries in recent years, company executives, bankers and City investment managers have enjoyed a growing presence in successive lists. Michael Spencer, the 49-year-old boss of Icap, one of the world's largest money brokers, was estimated to be worth £372 million in 2005. The 2005 list also included nine current and former partners from investment bankers Goldman Sachs and a number of hedge fund managers with over £100 million. The hedge fund industry, which sets out to make money when the stock market falls as well as rises, has seen some spectacular fortunes in recent years, provided you call the markets right. Corporate and City millionaires would also feature strongly amongst the 'super-rich', with fortunes of between £5 million and £50 million. Sports stars, rare amongst the top 1,000, would be more abundant in the super-rich and 'merely rich' camps with wealth levels of between £1 million and £50 million.

Trickle up

In the space of two decades or less, Britain has experienced an explosion of personal wealth, one of the fastest rates of personal enrichment on record, bringing a sharp rise in the number of people in the mega-rich, super-rich and 'merely rich' clubs, together with a surge in the level of their wealth holdings.

Whatever income or wealth threshold we take – £1 million, £5 million or

£50 million – more and more Britons have been rising above it. Experts predict that the explosion is set to continue, with the number of people worth more than £5 million in liquid assets – cash, shares and bonds – predicted to rise at an annual rate of nearly 8 per cent between 2005 and 2009.[27] The very rich have also become much richer. The *Sunday Times* top 200 were worth £172 billion in 2005, up from around £70 billion in 1990.[28] As shown in Figure 1.1, the level of wealth required to gain a place in the *Sunday Times* top 200 has been rising sharply from £50 million in 1990 to £250 million in 2005.[29] The climate could hardly be better for the rich than it is today. As the journalist Max Hastings has said, 'it seems remarkable that any high roller these days resorts to fraud to enrich himself. It is possible to bank such huge sums legally that criminality seems redundant.'[30]

Figure 1.1: The level of wealth required to make it to the richest 200 in Britain, 1990–2005

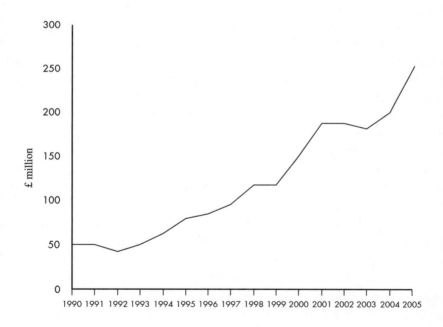

Source: *Sunday Times Rich List*[31].

The wealth explosion of recent times has been a largely Anglo-Saxon phenomenon. It has been especially dramatic in the United States, where the number of billionaires grew from 12 in 1982 to 313 in 2004, a 25-fold jump.

Adjusted for inflation, the aggregate wealth of America's top 400 increased from $169 billion in 1982 to close to $1 trillion in 2004 (i.e. $1,000 billion) – that's a sixfold increase in two decades.[32] One commentator has described the process of enrichment at the top of American society as 'the most colossal redistribution of wealth in modern world history'.[33] Britain's own revolution, although a little more modest than in the United States, has still been remarkable. By contrast, it is a phenomenon that has largely bypassed continental Europe.[34]

Of course, the rich, old and new, do not always enjoy a continuously upward ride. Many of the mega-rich, from Lord Sainsbury to Bernie Ecclestone, suffered heavily in the dramatic collapse in share prices from April 2000, which led to a major, if temporary, downgrading of their paper wealth. As shares plunged so did many fortunes. Some went bankrupt. Nevertheless, while some lost, often heavily, from the millennial implosion, the rich as a group continued to prosper. The combined wealth of the top 1,000 in Britain rose more than 60 per cent between 2000 and 2005.[35]

Worldwide, the effect of the downturn was to slow the rise in global wealth but not reverse it. Between 1999 and 2004, the number of people worldwide with financial assets worth more than a million dollars grew by nearly a fifth to reach 8.3 million people. The rise in Britain was more than double this rate.[36] In general, rich Britons survived the market turmoil and sinking share prices of the early years of the new century more successfully than most of their foreign counterparts.

The fact that the collapse in share values at the turn of the millennium barely dented wealth holdings overall reveals a remarkable resilience amongst today's very rich. The heavy losses made by some were more than offset by the gains made by others. Many of the rich, often guided by their wealth management companies, proved adept at clever and in some cases bold management of their money. Entrepreneurs often protected their assets by selling businesses; company directors and celebrities negotiated bigger pay cheques and fees. While share values fell, property prices soared. Wealthy aristocrats such as the Duke of Westminster continued to thrive. While City bonuses fell initially, top salaries kept rising. Today, wealth may not be totally secure, but in general once they have acquired it, most hang on to it.

The spectacular rise of a new mega- and super-rich enjoying higher and higher levels of wealth and income adds up to a profound social revolution, which has reversed one of the most significant economic and social trends of the post-war era – the gradual decline followed by stability in the level of wealth and income concentration. We are now in the midst of a new chapter in the history of wealth concentration and inequality in Britain.

This history has three distinct phases. The first began in the late nineteenth century, a period that brought a great surge in the number and scale of personal fortunes, and with it an extraordinary level of inequality. That phase was brought to a fairly abrupt halt by the crash of 1929. It was followed by a second sustained phase, a wholly different era of equalisation that lasted for close to two generations. During that phase, much of the gain from growing prosperity went to middle and lower income groups. A process of 'trickle down' was at work. We are now in a third, perhaps transitional phase, one that has seen a reversal of the trend towards greater equality, and a sudden spurt in the wealth gap. We are now in a period of 'trickle up', with more and more of the gains from growth since the late 1970s going to the rich and especially the very rich.

What these dramatic trends show is that we have entered a second 'Gilded Age' in both Britain and the United States, a return to the late Victorian era when great fortunes were being made on both sides of the Atlantic. The factors driving these historical shifts are examined in the next chapter.

2

A licence to make money

The idea that money doesn't buy you happiness is a lie put about by the rich,
to stop the poor from killing them.

(Michael Caine)

In the run up to the general election of 2001, Tony Blair was grilled on
Newsnight by Jeremy Paxman about his views on inequality. 'Prime Minister,
is it acceptable for the gap between rich and poor to widen?' quizzed Paxman.
Blair wriggled and Paxman repeated the question many times before giving
up. The nearest he got to a clear answer was: 'I know it's not your question
but it's the way I choose to answer it. If you end up going after those people
who are the most wealthy in society, what you actually end up doing is in fact
not even helping those at the bottom end.'

It was a remarkable answer, not the response that any previous Labour
Prime Minister would have given. It reflected the completion of a
transformation in the cultural and political climate towards the wealthy and
wealth-making that had begun with the election of Margaret Thatcher in
1979. Thatcher wanted to turn Britain into a nation of risk-taking
entrepreneurs and set out to remove what she saw as state-imposed breaks on
personal enterprise. Blair has embraced that revolution in full. He first
signalled his intentions while leader of the opposition. In his introduction to
the 1997 Labour manifesto, Blair wrote that he had 'no time for the politics
of envy'. This was more than a symbolic gesture or vote-seeking rhetoric. It
was a key turning point in Labour's central philosophy.

Blair later expanded on what he meant – he didn't care what David
Beckham earned, and he wanted a society that encouraged 'levelling up'
rather than 'levelling down', one that allowed the rich to flourish but one that

also protected the poor. Stephen Byers, trade secretary from December 1998, said that wealth creation was now more important than wealth distribution. Peter Mandelson put it more crudely. He once told the CBI that New Labour was 'relaxed' about people becoming 'filthy rich'. New Labour sympathisers have joined in to argue that the 'wealth gap' doesn't matter.[1] It was only twenty-five years earlier that Labour's then Chancellor of the Exchequer, the moderate Denis Healey, had adopted a somewhat different rhetoric with his famous threat to the rich that Labour would make their 'pips squeak'.

The size of the gap between the rich and the poor has been one of the most contentious and bitterly disputed issues in politics for more than a century. Today it has suddenly become much less controversial. A new consensus has emerged that rising inequality is more acceptable than it was. Many think it is desirable. Others say it is unavoidable. To challenge the new conventional wisdom invites the risk of being accused of being mean spirited, out of touch, of being divorced from reality. Even on the left it has become something of a taboo subject. It is the widespread acceptance of growing levels of personal wealth, and the growing polarisation that goes with it, that is perhaps one of the defining characteristics of the shift away from the social democratic values that used to dominate post-war politics and opinion.

The issue has also become a sensitive one amongst New Labour insiders. In August 2004, the Institute for Public Policy Research (IPPR), a left-of-centre think-tank with close connections to New Labour, produced a report, *Injustice in the UK*, which showed that although poverty had been falling, the gap between the top and bottom had been rising from the 1980s – and had continued to do so since Labour came to power in 1997.

It was not long before the counter-attack began. A few days after publication, John Rentoul, a left-of-centre political commentator and former deputy editor of the *New Statesman*, wrote an impassioned article for the *Independent* condemning the report.[2] Rentoul dismissed the view that inequality had been rising under Labour as an 'urban myth', questioned the ability of government to influence such trends and suggested that the IPPR should be told 'to shove it'. Rentoul, who had written the first biography of Blair, had himself written a book on inequality in 1987 that was a strong condemnation of growing inequality under Thatcher.[3]

A few days later the *Guardian* suggested cryptically that Downing Street was turning to its 'praetorian guard' to defend its record and that maybe the Prime Minister's strategy about Labour's apparently poor record on inequality seemed to be denial.[4] The implication was that Blair may not have cared about inequality but he was sensitive to the charge that Labour had made it worse. It was also significant that this was not an argument between the right and the left about the course and desirability of inequality but within the left itself.

So what does the evidence say about the course of inequality and of top incomes and wealth over time and under Blair's tenure? Figure 2.1 shows the trends in the share of net income received by the top 1 per cent since the late 1930s. The shares fell for both groups until the late 1970s and then started to rise continuously until 1999. Net income inequality (as measured by the shares at the top) in 1999 was above levels seen at the end of the 1940s, possibly even earlier. The share of income received by the top 1 per cent, for example, stood at 10.2 per cent in 1999 compared with 6.8 per cent in 1949 and 12.6 per cent in 1937.

Figure 2.1: How the rich have fared since 1940
Net incomes shares – after income tax – for the top 1 per cent, 1937–1999

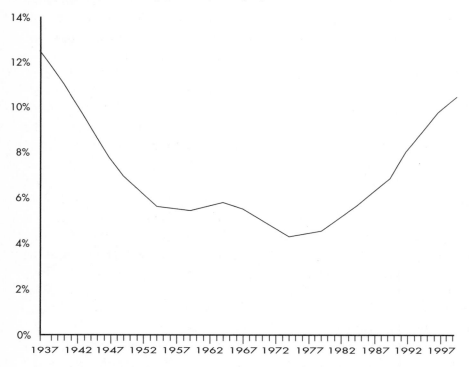

Source: A. Atkinson and W. Salverda, 'Top Incomes in the Netherlands and the UK over the Twentieth Century', *Journal of the European Economic Association* (2005), vol. 3, no. 4, 883–913.

Figure 2.2 shows in more detail what has happened to incomes (at individual percentiles) over the more recent period from 1979 to 2003/4. This shows just how far, and how quickly, the rich have succeeded in reversing their fortunes. They have been charging ahead over the last twenty-five years, with income increases for the richest groups outstripping those enjoyed by all other groups. It is this rise that has been fuelling the increase in income inequality of the last two decades. In the decade to 2003, for example, average earnings of the lead executives of FTSE 100 companies rose by more than six times those of British employees as a whole. In the twenty years to 1999, the richest 1 per cent saw their share of gross income double from 6.5 per cent to 13 per cent.[5]

In contrast, income levels at the bottom end of the distribution have been rising more slowly than the average. As a result, although relative poverty fell consistently from the early 1960s until the late 1970s, it went on to rise dramatically in the 1980s and more slowly in the early 1990s, but then stabilised and has been falling since 1996/7.[6] Even so, current levels of poverty are still not back to the levels seen in 1979 and are well above those of most other richer nations.

These changes in the level of poverty reflect the wider changes in

Figure 2.2: How the rich have got richer
Real income growth by percentile point, 1979–2003/4

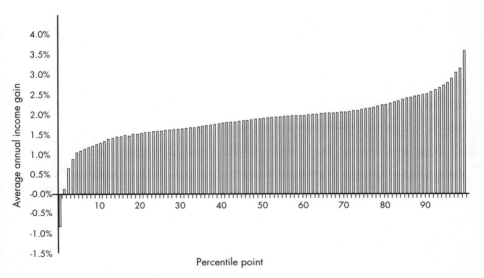

Source: Institute for Fiscal Studies.

inequality. The income gap grew rapidly throughout the 1980s under Thatcher's governments and then levelled off during the first half of the 1990s under John Major. As to the hotly contested issue of Labour's record, inequality grew during Blair's first term and by 2004 had fallen back a little, but only enough to offset the rise after 1997, not to reverse the trends of the previous fifteen years. As the Institute for Fiscal Studies (IFS) has concluded, 'despite a large package of redistributive measures, the net effect after seven years of Labour government is to leave [income] inequality effectively unchanged and at historically high levels'.[7]

The effect of these trends is that the UK has been rising up the international league table for inequality and has been closing the inequality gap on the United States. Indeed, in the period from the late 1970s to the mid-1990s, the UK had the fastest growing income inequality of all advanced economic nations, including the United States. The increase in inequality in the UK between the mid-1990s and 2000 also outstripped that in most other countries.[8]

Figure 2.3: How wealth has become increaingly concentrated
Share of marketable wealth enjoyed by the top 1 per cent and bottom 50 per cent, UK, 1976–2002.

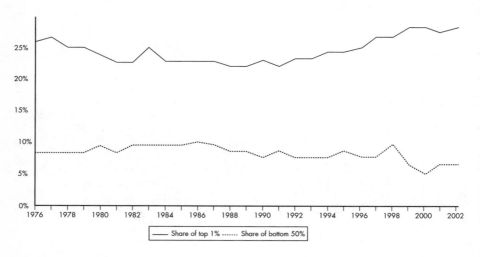

Based on marketable wealth, which includes liquid assets, including stocks and shares, property and other saleable assets but not pension rights.

Source: HM Revenue and Customs.

Wealth – which is much more unequally distributed than income – has followed a slightly different pattern since the late 1970s. Like income, the wealth gap fell for most of the twentieth century and continued to do so until the late 1980s, when it reached its minimum. The gap then levelled off and has been rising again since the early 1990s. According to the latest official figures, shown in Figure 2.3, in 2002 the top 1 per cent owned 23 per cent of 'marketable wealth', up from 17 per cent in 1988.[9] While the share of the nation's wealth at the top has been rising, that of the bottom 50 per cent has been shrinking from 10 per cent in 1986 to an even smaller 6 per cent in 2002.[10] The share of wealth enjoyed by the top 1 per cent is higher, and that of the bottom half smaller, today than it was a generation ago.

The fact is that Britain has been slowly moving back in time – to levels of income inequality that prevailed more than half a century ago and to levels of wealth inequality of more than thirty years ago. Moreover, the statistics almost certainly understate the extent of wealth at the very top. According to Robert Chope, director of the IFS, 'it is like looking through thick fog'. If official data allowed a more detailed analysis of trends in the share of income and wealth enjoyed by the top half or quarter per cent, we would almost certainly see their share at levels last seen even longer ago. Over the last two decades we have been turning the clock back. Exactly how far is a matter for statisticians to argue about, but the direction of change is not in dispute.

There are of course a variety of explanations – economic, technological, social and political – for this backward drift and the sharply rising shares of income and wealth enjoyed by the very richest groups in society. These differing explanations are all important, but the central argument of this book is that there is one overarching change that lies behind it – a fundamental shift in our cultural and political attitudes towards the very rich. Without this change, inequality would not have risen at the rate that it has.

The fluctuating fortunes of the rich and the poor, and the gap between them, can be traced to the way in which the political and public climate and wider economic conditions interact. Governments can leave the issue of distribution alone or intervene to raise the floor or cap the ceiling. In the nineteenth century, the state largely left things alone and the last decades of the century brought a sharp increase in the number of those with exceptionally large fortunes. The brakes were first applied in the opening years of the twentieth century. This brought some protection for the poorest, but did little to thwart the progress of the very rich. Indeed, the spendthrift extravagance of the 'roaring twenties' contributed to the 1929 crash. This led to the first great reckoning for the rich, with repercussions that lasted for more than a generation. The levels of inequality prevailing up to that time had, eventually, proved unsustainable. In the two or three decades after the crash, some top personal fortunes shrank, the brakes were applied more firmly and the wealth gap narrowed.

The 1970s brought another turning point. Political and public support for welfarism had cooled as economic difficulties mounted, and under Thatcher the brakes on inequality were loosened. During the 1980s, Britain's wealthiest began their upward march to new heights, a process fuelled by the importing of American values, business methods and tax policies. In the 1990s, stock markets boomed, interest rates fell, top salaries soared, property values rose. Economic, political and cultural conditions were back in harmony for the rich. The stock market boom may have turned to bust in March 2000, just as it had in 1929, but this time the consequences for the wealthiest were much less severe.

The great levelling

The historical high point for the super-rich came in the late nineteenth century, when a combination of a lack of government regulation, low taxes, weak unions and the maturing of the industrial revolution combined to bring Britain's first significant personal wealth acceleration. After 1870, the pace at which fortunes could be made accelerated sharply. The number of fortunes recorded as being worth over £2 million on death stood at two in the thirty-year period from 1810 to 1839, nine between 1840 and 1879, and then grew to twenty-two in the period from 1880 to 1909.[11] As the numbers of very rich grew, their composition changed. The proportion who were landowners fell from around seven-eighths at the beginning of the nineteenth century to around a half by its end. The new rich of the time were building their fortunes less from manufacturing than from commerce and finance.

The political ideology of the time remained one of laissez-faire, a belief that economic progress depended on a largely free market. Attempts to tackle poverty were limited to the prevention of destitution of the very poor through a draconian system of workhouses, the provision of food and shelter in return for work. But pressure was building to tackle both poverty and inequality in a more coherent way. After trade unions became legal in 1825, union membership grew rapidly. In 1884, the Fabian Society was founded by socialist thinkers such as George Bernard Shaw dedicated to creating a more equal society. In 1900, the Labour Party was formed. It is from these latter decades of the nineteenth century that the egalitarian ideas that were to become a much more central driving force of social and economic policy after the Second World War were essentially born. Despite this and the economic progress achieved in the latter decades of the nineteenth century, the distribution of wealth remained stubbornly unequal.

In 1906, the Liberal Party won the general election and launched a programme of profound social change. They introduced the first system of national insurance, aimed at providing a basic minimum income when unemployed, sick and retired, a policy that was highly controversial at the time but which became the foundation of the modern welfare state. David Lloyd George's 'people's Budget' of 1909, introduced only after a prolonged and bitter political battle, was the first to introduce a set of graduated income tax rates, with the introduction of a 'supertax' – a tax surcharge on incomes over £5,000. This was a considerable sum at the time, covering some 11,000 taxpayers, and was the equivalent of around seventy times average income. The principle that a fair tax system should be progressively related to 'ability to pay' had come from an unlikely source. It had first been suggested by the patron saint of free-market economics, Adam Smith, in his remarkably influential book *Wealth of Nations*, published more than a hundred years earlier: 'It is not unreasonable that the rich should contribute to public expense not only in proportion of their revenue but in something more than their proportion.'[12] Throughout the nineteenth century, however, the idea had been savagely opposed by successive governments. What finally made it possible in 1909 was the transformation in the political and public climate.

The 1909 Budget not only targeted the income of the rich, but their wealth holdings as well. Lloyd George had once depicted the landed elite as 'idle, greedy, parasitical, self-interested profiteers, as men who enjoyed wealth they did not create while begrudging help to those less fortunate whose labours had helped to make them rich'.[13] He was also one of the first to recognise the distinction between earned and unearned wealth. He saw inheritance as one of the key sources of unearned wealth and in 1909, estate duties, which had been introduced in 1894 by Sir William Harcourt at relatively modest rates, were doubled. There was also a new tax on unearned increments in land values. These developments were the first explicit acceptance that the distinction between the 'deserving' and 'undeserving' poor should be applied to the rich as well. In effect the Budget was an attempt at a redistribution from the 'undeserving rich' to the 'deserving poor' and it did not go down well with those who had to pay the higher taxes. The measures were bitterly but unsuccessfully fought by the aristocracy, as the principal targets of the tax hikes were the landed rich. The former Prime Minister the Earl of Rosebery, a member of the rich class himself, denounced the changes as 'not a Budget but a Revolution, a social and political revolution of the first magnitude'.[14] In contrast, across the Atlantic, Andrew Carnegie, one of America's richest men, hailed the introduction of graduated death duties in the UK. Carnegie, who perhaps pioneered modern philanthropy, took the view that passing on wealth to one's descendants, over and above a modest provision, is good neither for them nor for the state. In defending his views, he said,

> Men who continue hoarding great sums all their lives, the proper use of which for public ends would work good to the community, should be made to feel that the community, in the form of the state, cannot thus be deprived of its proper share. By taxing estates heavily at death, the state marks its condemnation of the selfish millionaire's unworthy life.[15]

These changes may have dented the fortunes of the rich, but they continued to thrive right up until the end of the 1920s. The 'roaring twenties' was a period when a small elite of the young and rich, many of them firmly in the idle camp, chose to flaunt their wealth in a parade of extravagance. The hedonism was catalogued by gossip columnists and contemporary authors and, as the scandals broke, gorged on by an eager public confused between expressions of envy and intrigue on the one hand and shock and outrage on the other. Evelyn Waugh's novel *Vile Bodies* presented a whirl of parties, wild living and philandering unspoilt by any daily grind of work or awareness of the real world.

The partying did not last. The 1929 stock market crash, triggered to some degree by a parallel but more significant orgy of economic extravagance on the other side of the Atlantic, brought much of the fun to an abrupt halt. The crash was to prove a decisive turning point in the history of the fortunes of the rich. Not only did many of the wealthy classes suffer big losses in their fortunes, the political climate towards personal wealth and wealth-making turned much colder.

The crash, the subsequent recession and then the Second World War transformed public and political attitudes to wealth for a generation and more. The forty years from the mid-1930s until the mid-1970s brought about the single most sustained period of equalisation in British history, a period known as the 'great levelling'. It was an era during which rewards for the most successful were more modest, expectations were checked and there was much less flaunting of wealth. The rich knew their public place and, mostly, preferred to keep quiet about their good fortune. At least initially, the gap between the rich and the poor narrowed and the kind of rewards that are obtainable today would, for the most part, have been unacceptable to public opinion then.

This equalising process – at its greatest in the period between the end of the 1930s and the mid-1950s – was the product of three main forces. First, the new post-1929 political climate, which was much less sympathetic to the rich and to personal wealth-making. Second, the impact of the Second World War with its combination of full employment and higher tax rates on profits and high incomes. Third, the policy agenda of the reforming post-war Labour government.

The retreat from the hands-off government of earlier times was one that mostly transcended political divisions; post-war governments, Conservative and Labour alike, though with different degrees of emphasis, accepted the importance of a state-managed system of welfare aimed at reducing poverty and creating a more equal society through a process of modest redistribution from the top to the bottom. If the nineteenth century was an era with no floor and no ceiling on personal incomes and wealth, the aim now was not just to raise the floor but also to cap the ceiling. The new consensus, and public mood, had been built out of the experience of the post-1929 recession and the Second World War. The intellectual climate had changed too. The egalitarian case fashioned by moderate socialist thinkers, from R. H. Tawney in *Equality* to Anthony Crosland in his social democratic bible *The Future of Socialism*, gelled with the spirit of the times. The political ascendancy moved to the left. The principle of higher taxes on the rich and the importance of redistribution were embraced by the public, the Labour leadership and even leading Conservative patricians who accepted the tenets of 'noblesse oblige'. In the thirty years after the war, public spending and taxation rose, finally reaching a peak in the mid-1980s. Politicians justified higher taxes on 'unearned income', and taxation on income, capital gains and inheritance became steadily more progressive until the 1970s.

The period can perhaps best be described as the age of 'welfare capitalism', an era that showed a new concern with the distribution of wealth as well as with its creation.[16] The very rich, a mix of aristocrats, businessmen and entrepreneurs, kept a mostly unobtrusive profile. As one respected observer noted, 'to many foreigners in the fifties and sixties, the British, from dons to dustmen, seemed stubbornly united in their lack of interest in money'.[17] This did not mean an end to fortune building. Although the climate was much more lukewarm to personal wealth-making on any scale, new fortunes were being created in the boom conditions of the 1950s and 1960s. Property development and the swelling demand for new offices brought fortunes for developers such as Harold Samuel, Joe Levy and Harry Hyams. Hyams built the Centre Point skyscraper of offices on a tiny plot on the corner of Charing Cross Road and New Oxford Street, a prime site in central London, and deliberately kept it empty during the property boom of the 1960s in order to increase its value.

Fortunes were also being made at the time by takeover tycoons including Charles Clore and Sir Isaac Wolfson.[18] In 1969, the *Daily Express* published a list of Britain's wealthiest individuals and families. The list was topped by Garfield Weston, the Canadian-born food and restaurant king, who was credited with holdings of £200 million; the glass-making Pilkington family (£200 million); Lord Cowdray, with interests from Shell to Penguin Books (£150 million); Sir John Ellerman (£150 million); and the Moores brothers, owners of Littlewoods football pools (£125 million). Nevertheless, the best evidence is that there was a decline in the number of the very wealthy between the 1930s and the late 1950s and that the numbers started to creep up again only from the 1970s.[19]

Although the key reason for the decline was the change in the political and social climate, a process of wealth redistribution within the family was also taking place.[20] This was one of the principal means of estate duty avoidance and had the effect of reducing wealth concentration at the very top by shifting wealth to the tier immediately below. Another equalising force within middle England was the spread of popular wealth especially through the extension of home ownership. The period also saw the steady rise of the middle classes, an increasingly well-educated group with more secure incomes and a serious political force able to secure a larger share of the pile for itself. Along with the emergence of full employment during and after the war, government policy also had the effect of boosting the incomes of the poor.

It was an era too when the lifestyles of the rich were transformed. Gone were the public displays of extravagance of the 1920s, gone were the servants and the extremes of aristocratic high living. The idle rich were still around, though not in such numbers and not with such high levels of wealth, but they chose to keep themselves and their wealth more in the shadows. This was perhaps especially true of old wealth. From the 1930s depression onwards, the rich ended up playing quieter roles. Partly this was induced by the decline in the value of their fortunes. Partly it fitted the temper of the times. In 1963, at the Royal Variety Show, John Lennon asked people in the cheaper seats to clap and the rest to 'rattle your jewellery'.

The levelling was not to prove a permanent revolution. Slowly but surely since the late 1970s the rich have made a dramatic comeback, with their lifestyles returning to the front pages and fortunes being made at a record-breaking rate. This dramatic and relatively sudden shift has its roots in the changing political and ideological climate of the 1970s. In 1974, the Wilson government set up the Royal Commission on the Distribution of Income and Wealth, chaired by Lord Diamond, in part to appease the unions and the left for Labour's back-tracking over a wealth tax which they first promised and then dropped. While confirming that Britain had become a more equitable society than before the war, the Diamond commission coincided with the high point of British welfarism.[21] From this point onwards, rising economic difficulties put pressure on welfare spending and public attitudes towards some recipients of benefits grew colder.[22] In 1976, an influential book by two Oxford economists, Roger Bacon and Walter Eltis, *Britain's Economic Problem: Too Few Producers*, blamed Britain's recurring economic problems on a lack of wealth creators.

The mood of the time was one of economic despondency. A generation of new right thinkers, advocates of free enterprise, emerged, pinning the blame on what they saw as the self-defeating collectivist ideology of the post-war era and the lack of an entrepreneurial spirit. They came too with a ready supply of solutions to apparent economic and social malaise – less state regulation, lower taxes especially on capital and on the rich and a shift to anti-inflationary policies through tighter control of the money supply. One of those influenced by the new revisionist thinking was Margaret Thatcher, who set out to end what she saw as a British malaise of antagonism to personal ambition and wealth creation.

During the 1980s, controls on banks and their lending and investment practices were dismantled, most state-owned monopolies were privatised, and corporate and top income tax rates were slashed. Thatcher was driven by an ideological belief in the power of individualism and entrepreneurialism, a power that may have been displayed in Britain's earlier history but which she held had been withered by decades of excessive state interference. She believed that individual effort and enterprise was good for society and was to be encouraged and rewarded. Thatcher was also driven by a belief that the old establishment, based largely on privilege and class, was a drag on enterprise and should be replaced by a new meritocratic elite based on talent and not birth. She set out to build a freer and less regulated society. And in so doing, a licence to make money had been granted.

A year after her election she was joined by a powerful soul-mate in the form of the new President of the United States, Ronald Reagan. Reagan was committed to the same values, the freeing of the economy from state regulation and the encouragement of wealth-making. As he put it, 'what I want to see above all is that this remains a country where someone can always get rich'. He too had been influenced by a powerful group of neo-conservative thinkers, believers in 'supply side' economics, many of whom ended up as White House advisers and who were behind the new President's three-year programme of tax cuts. In 1984 an article in *Money* magazine pronounced that being rich 'happens to be in fashion'.[23] The 'fashion' was encouraged by what Vance Packard called 'a crusade of easing constraints on the entrepreneurial rich individuals and their companies'.[24]

The 1980s were to provide a great bonanza for the wealthy on both sides of the Atlantic. Top salaries soared. Taxes at the top fell. The biggest gainers were those involved in finance rather than manufacturing – City dealers, property developers, investment fund managers, commercial lawyers and bankers. In 1989, the *Sunday Times* published its first rich list and soon other newspapers followed. 'The signs of money worship multiplied. Newspapers fattened with business supplements. TV channels competed with money programmes . . . Tycoons, after years of discretion, became the subject of best-selling memoirs or biographies.'[25]

The new spirit of the times was captured in films, novels and plays – Caryl Churchill's *Serious Money*, Martin Amis's *Money*. The new market reverence was also reflected in an apparent erosion of the limits that had governed acceptable business and political behaviour. In Britain, business scandals hit the headlines with monotonous regularity – Guinness, Blue Arrow, Robert Maxwell, British Airways. Although rarely exposed or prosecuted, insider dealing seemed the norm rather than the exception. Executive salaries and perks continued to soar during the recession of the early 1990s, usually in reverse relation to performance, while business leaders continued to preach moderation to their employees and the nation.

What started in the 1980s continued into the following decade and beyond the turn of the millennium. Although only a few have benefited from the modern get-rich-quick ethos, it seems to have set a new standard and goal for society as a whole. Today money-making is back in fashion. In his last book, *Who Runs This Place?*, published just before his death in 2005, Anthony Sampson, who had chronicled changes in British society over forty years, wrote that the key change to the British psyche over the previous twenty years had been a new obsession with money and money-making: 'The colour is the colour of money. The new elite is held together by their desire for personal enrichment . . . while the resistance to money-values is much weaker.'[26]

The all-pervading obsession with money has contributed to a new 'grab now' spirit, a world in which old values are being displaced in the rush to the fast-track fortune. The wealthy are mostly less willing to give to charity than they were; despite falling rates of taxation on the very rich, the tax avoidance industry is booming; salary levels have become ever upwardly elastic. Material well-being has come to dominate our lives. Fast cars, fast living and fast jets have become the pinnacles of success. The money-moving and -making professions are the most sought after for top graduates. Making money has become more of a pull than the ethos associated with public service. The world's poorest are being denied access to drugs because pharmaceutical companies are focusing their resources on diseases suffered by the wealthy. Money and the market are encroaching on more and more aspects of life that once were largely uncommercialised, from leisure and sport to health care. 'Commerce has invaded pleasure with a vengeance.'[27] Nowhere is the invasion of the money culture more pervasive than in sport, where for example television sports rights are seized by the highest bidder and top footballers seem more interested in how much they earn than how well they play.

This obsession has also infected the top echelons of the Labour Party. Some Labour Cabinet ministers – most, though not all, of whom come from non-wealthy backgrounds – have become obsessed with becoming wealthy or living a wealthy lifestyle. Peter Mandelson could not resist buying a house in Notting Hill that he could not afford without a generous loan from a fellow minister. The Blairs themselves love spending their holidays in the lavish holiday homes of the international wealth set including Silvio Berlusconi. Because of the steady flow of expensive jewellery and gifts from the Italian Prime Minister, the Italian newspaper *Corriere della Sera* has dubbed the couple the 'Sultans of Bling'.[28]

Charlie Whelan, former press adviser to Gordon Brown, told the *Mail on*

Sunday that Cherie Blair was 'obsessed with money'. During a conversation between Tony Blair and Brown about MPs' salaries, according to Whelan, the Chancellor insisted that the Cabinet, including the Prime Minister, should have a pay freeze. 'You can tell Cherie, then,' retorted Blair.[29] In June 2005, Mrs Blair was heavily criticised for cashing in on her husband's position when she earned £30,000 for a ninety-minute speaking engagement in the United States. Her highly lucrative speaking engagements are apparently necessary to pay the mortgage on the £3.65 million house they bought in London's Connaught Square. Critics believe that her and successive Cabinet ministers' obsession derives from their growing association with what the *Guardian* columnist Polly Toynbee has called the 'upper stratosphere of wealth and power', which makes them lose sense of what is normal.[30]

The effect of the new mood on financial rewards at the top has been dramatic. At first, top salaries, perks and bonuses in the City, in business and in some key professions started to creep upwards slowly enough not to be more widely clocked. Then they just accelerated. It is not just City lawyers and dealers and company executives that have joined the bandwagon. Sven Goran Eriksson, England's football manager, negotiated a contract worth in excess of £3.5 million a year, the highest international manager's salary in Europe and way above those of his predecessors. Professional footballers have demanded and been awarded similar hikes in pay and benefits, as have film stars, television celebrities and chat-show hosts. It is these hikes that have been stretching the distribution of incomes upwards. Once the income distribution looked like a pyramid – now it is a long thin upward spire at the top.

The Robber Barons

Much of the transformation of Britain has its roots in a parallel cultural shift in the United States. Indeed, the history of wealth in Britain and the United States has followed a remarkably similar pattern, though with one key difference – scale.

The last three decades of the nineteenth century saw a similar surge in personal wealth accumulation in America. Writing in 1873, the satirist and novelist Mark Twain dubbed the period the 'Gilded Age'. At the turn of the century, top American fortunes were up to five times those of their British counterparts. They have stayed above British levels ever since. In 1914 the oil magnate John D. Rockefeller became the world's first dollar billionaire, largely as a result of the growth of the US automobile industry, which provided him with a huge new market for petroleum.[31]

The Americans were also much more likely to build their fortunes through industry – railways, oil, steel and automobiles – than commerce or land. Those worth $100 million or more at the turn of the century included several rail magnates such as William Vanderbilt and E. H. Harriman, the steel manufacturer Andrew Carnegie, and James B. Duke, whose fortune came from tobacco. But if Rockefeller, Carnegie and the other manufacturers built the industrial age, J. P. Morgan and the Mellon family financed it.

The creation of such vast fortunes was enabled by the survival-of-the-fittest political canon of the time. According to this ideology, a form of social Darwinism, the new multi-millionaires were economic pioneers who were the embodiment of the American dream, not just enriching themselves but creating a more powerful American economy in the process. 'Monumental wealth was widely considered a just reward for those presumed responsible for the United States becoming the richest and mightiest nation.'[32] Taxes were frowned on.

Nevertheless, the new tycoons were soon embroiled in controversy for their ruthless tactics. Rockefeller exploited his power, colluded with railways to gain preferential freight rates, bribed state legislators and engaged in industrial espionage. He had one goal: to destroy his rivals and create an oil monopoly. In 1883, Rockefeller faced demonstrations both from his own staff, who had had their wages cut, and from protestors working for competitors he had driven out of business. The demonstrators burnt an effigy of him while chanting 'the most hated man in America'. His tactics of buying up rivals and putting others out of business by manipulating market prices ensured that by the end of the century he had a near 100 per cent oil monopoly. In the early 1900s, the oil magnate, then in his nineties, had to face prosecution hearings for illegal business activity from price-fixing to collusion. Rarely has the American public come to so revile a self-made entrepreneur.

In a book published in 1934, the tycoons and speculators such as Morgan, Cornelius Vanderbilt and Jay Gould were dubbed 'The Robber Barons'.[33] These men had certainly built their fortunes in a climate when regulation was more or less non-existent, when bribery of officials and congressmen was widespread, when business ethics were undeveloped and when labour abuses and stock manipulation were endemic. To some they were unscrupulous and opportunistic, men who had built their fortunes through corruption. To others they were heroes.

Often prompted by their wives and children, the new magnates spent millions on yachts, mansions, jewellery, servants, art collections and in many cases on mistresses and divorces. Similar indulgence and opulence was apparent in Britain as well. In 1899, the economist Thornstein Veblen invented the term 'conspicuous consumption' to describe the extravagant and ostentatious lifestyles enjoyed by the small elites of the largely leisured classes on both sides of the Atlantic.[34]

The baronial estates and lavish parties of the turn of the century alternately fascinated and revolted ordinary people, an ambivalence that has remained to this day. Surveying the competitive ostentation of the time, and the envy it promoted, Twain wrote to a friend, 'Money lust has always existed, but not in the history of the world was it ever a craze, a madness, until your time and mine.'[35] Criticism mounted against such ostentation, particularly when it was contrasted with the urban squalor that was the lot of the majority of Americans. William Vanderbilt's response to such comparisons was 'the public be damned'.

Class tensions mounted. While the American conscience liked to see itself as free of the inequalities prevalent in Europe and especially Britain, writers began to draw unflattering comparisons with the disparities that disfigured that continent. Concern also mounted about the extent to which America was becoming a plutocracy, a nation run by and for the rich. The giant corporations had certainly gained de facto control over many aspects of government. In 1906, no fewer than a third of the US Senate were multi-millionaires, all bar two of them Republicans.[36] Indeed, the Senate was known as the 'millionaires' club' at the time.

As in Britain, social reformers began to question the virtues of untrammelled free enterprise and the immense concentration of wealth and power it was generating. Mainstream reformers, such as the Supreme Court Justice Louis Brandeis and the newspaper publisher Joseph Pulitzer, helped to promote a new vision of an America free of plutocracy and free of poverty. In 1902, the progressive Republican Theodore Roosevelt became the first President to directly challenge the excesses of the Gilded Age, 'the malefactors of great wealth', as he put it. He questioned the survival-of-the-fittest philosophy, highlighted political corruption and introduced new anti-trust legislation aimed at controlling and breaking up large monopolies.[37]

His successor, the Democrat Woodrow Wilson, was equally dedicated to taming the power of money and questioned whether labour was getting its fair share of the rewards. His first two years in the White House from 1912 produced two significant amendments – the sixteenth and the seventeenth – to the US constitution. These respectively authorised a federal income tax for the first time and required popular election of senators. After a decade of political infighting, an inheritance tax was first introduced in 1916.

Despite the new political rhetoric, the rich continued to prosper during the 1920s, as they did in Britain. A new Republican administration proved a bonanza for the rich with the dismantling of government restrictions and the slashing of taxes, which unleashed another era of serious money-making. Looking back in 1931, the novelist F. Scott Fitzgerald described 1920s America as the 'most expensive orgy in history'.[38] As in the next period of personal wealth creation from the late 1980s, most of the gain from the new prosperity went to the top 5–10 per cent of US families. It could not and did not last.

Echoing events in Britain, the Great Crash of 1929 not only destroyed some fortunes but ushered in a new political and social era. The United States experienced its own 'great compression' and for largely similar reasons. In a spectacular reversal of fortunes, public attitudes turned against the wealthy elite, the belief in untrammelled markets waned and the Republican Party, itself heavily interconnected with the wealthy, lost the grip on power they had held for most of the previous seventy years. In 1933, Franklin D. Roosevelt, the newly installed Democratic President, launched a direct attack on 'the unscrupulous money-changers' and on 'an unjust concentration of wealth and economic power'.[39]

The changed political climate, new economic regulations and higher income and inheritance taxes transformed the fortunes of the richest. Sharing the wealth became the new common cause. The share of wealth enjoyed by the very rich started its first serious decline.[40] In the post-war decades, the wealthy became less secure, less admired and less powerful. America in the 1950s and 1960s was a middle-class society in which the vast inequalities of the Gilded Age had gone, and wealthy businessmen played a quieter role and could no longer control the political system as they had in earlier decades. The evidence too is that the biggest fortunes shrank – up until the late 1970s, the very wealthiest Americans were simply not as wealthy as the Robber Barons of seventy years before.[41] The lavish spending and profligacy of the Gilded Age had also long gone, the result of higher taxes, waning fortunes and a much more sober social climate. War, taxes and recession had taken their toll. It was a remarkable turn around.

Corporate life was associated with conformity. The pay of the best-paid corporate chief executives was much lower in the 1950s than half a century earlier – and indeed half a century later.[42] As one sociologist described the United States in the 1950s, 'the crazy millionaire is dead, and a subdued non-conspicuousness seems to be spreading over our styles in leisure and consumption practices'.[43] Conspicuous consumption was frowned on. Henry Ford gained notoriety for spending $100,000 on a coming-out party for his daughter in 1959.[44] The squandering may have continued, but it was less frequent and less evident.

Today's America could hardly be more different. In the last twenty years, personal wealth has achieved a status it once held and lost: the means of enriching all through encouraging growth, and thus to be celebrated. Beginning in the 1980s, openly displayed extravagance has returned to levels last seen in the Gilded Age and the 1920s. The reservations about wealth, its roots, benefits and display that had characterised earlier decades have largely gone. The rich may have gone underground for a while but today, they are back in full public gaze. The American wealth historian, Kevin Phillips, describes the transformation as 'an *inversion* of the 1950s in moral, philosophic and wealth terms'.[45]

The process began in the 1980s. In that decade, top executives lived like kings. They enjoyed corporate jets, often complete with gold-plated bathroom fittings; helicopters stocked with alcohol and fitted with televisions; chauffeured limousines; lavish apartments; maids; and private country clubs, all paid for by their companies. Donald Trump, the New York property developer, together with his former wife, Ivana, turned themselves into celebrities by emblazoning the family name across the hotels they owned in Manhattan and openly flaunting their wealth with their extravagant yachts, homes and shopping trips. Trump's phallic towers were an overt expression of his power and money. Henry Kravis, the arch deal-maker of Kohlberg Kravis Roberts, and his fashion designer wife, Carolyne Roehm, were fixtures at black tie events and rarely out of the society magazines. Kravis and Roehm's Fifth Avenue apartment had two Renoirs on the walls. A uniformed servant walked their dog. 'Today to be counted seriously rich in America, you must own a Van Gogh, a Cézanne or, at the very least, an early Picasso.'[46]

Ross Johnson, the chief executive of the giant food and tobacco conglomerate RJR Nabisco, insisted on a corporate aircraft fleet, known as

RJR Air Force, which was used not only by board directors for business but to ferry friends and celebrities around as well. At its peak, it comprised eight corporate jets. After the dramatic and notorious buy-out of the company in 1988, the new owners, Kohlberg Kravis Roberts, found that whenever Johnson took a trip in one of the firm's jets, he was followed in a separate plane by a certain G. Shepherd. The mystery passenger turned out to be Johnson's Alsatian, Rocco.[47]

The new ethos was captured in novels such as Tom Wolfe's *The Bonfire of the Vanities* and Oliver Stone's film *Wall Street*, built around the theme of the corrupting power of a driving passion for money. As the film's central character, Gordon Gekko, put it, 'greed is good. Greed is right. Greed clarifies, cuts through and captures the essence of the evolutionary spirit.' In 1989, Michael Lewis, a trader with one of Wall Street's leading investment bankers, Salomon Brothers, published his inside account of the firm and its activities in *Liar's Poker*. Fiction this was not, but real life in the raw – a tale of hysterical greed and obsession all encouraged and enabled by vast earnings. As Lewis described it, 'that was somewhere near the middle of a modern gold rush. Never before have so many unskilled twenty-four year olds made so much money in so little time as we did this decade in New York and London.'[48]

The new psyche – an acceptable lust for wealth and its trappings that heralded a lucrative and benign era for wealth-makers and their entourage – was well summed up by a 1986 episode at Salomon Brothers. John Gutfreund, the head of trading, described by *Business Week* as the 'King of Wall Street', challenged his chief bond trader, John Meriwether, to one hand of 'liar's poker' in front of the bond trading team. The game is one of bluff in which participants hold a single dollar bill each and attempt to outguess each other about the serial numbers on the bills. The first player might bid say 'three sixes' – guessing that the serial numbers of the bills held by all players contain at least three sixes – and subsequent bids have to raise this guess to three sevens or four of a kind, escalating until one player 'challenges', at which point the players disclose their notes. It requires nerves of steel. As Gutfreund put it to Meriwether, 'one hand, one million dollars, no tears'. By 'no tears' was meant that the loser was meant to suffer real pain but not whine about it. In the end the game was not played. Gutfreund backed down when Meriwether raised the stakes to $10 million, though it wasn't a lack of personal wealth that stopped them.[49]

The closing of the cultural divide

America has always dominated the world wealth leagues and continues to do so. As shown in Table 2.1, the two richest individuals in the world in 2005 were Bill Gates of Microsoft and Warren Buffett, the investor, with estimated fortunes of £24 billion and £23 billion respectively. The scale of such wealth is perhaps difficult to comprehend. To put it into perspective, the UK's total wealth adds up to some £5,344 billion (£5.3 trillion). This means that collectively some 46 million adult Britons are worth only 220 times the wealth of Gates.

Gates co-founded Microsoft, the giant international company that provides the operating systems for 93 per cent of the world's desktop computers. His more obscure co-founder, Paul Allen, was twelfth while the company's chief executive, Steve Ballmer, is another billionaire in the world's top fifty. Buffett has made his money through very shrewd investing. The richest family in the world were the Waltons, owners of Wal-Mart, the world's largest retailer. Between them they were worth some £47 billion. Sam Walton, who started with very little, was America's richest man when he died in 1992. He opened his first store, Wal-Mart Discount City, in Rogers, Arkansas in 1962. His eldest son, Robson, controls the family's 38 per cent stake in Wal-Mart, which has 3,200 stores in the United States and nearly 1,200 stores abroad. Wal-Mart accounts for a tenth of all American retail sales and bought a stake in Britain with its acquisition of Asda in 2000.

Table 2.1: The World's Richest, 2005

Name		Worth (£bn)	Source of wealth	Country
1.	The Waltons*	47.1	Retail	USA
2.	Bill Gates	24.2	Software	USA
3.	Warren Buffett	22.9	Investments	USA
4.	Karl and Theo Albrecht*	17.7	Retail	Germany
5.	Forrest Jr and John Mars*	16.2	Confectionery	USA
6.	Lakshmi Mittal	14.8	Steel	UK
7.	Carlos Slim Helu	12.4	Telecoms	Mexico
8.	Prince Alwaleed	12.3	Investments	Saudi Arabia
9.	Barbara Cox Anthony and Anne Cox Chambers	12.2	Media	USA
10.	Ingvar Kamprad	12.0	Retail	Sweden

* denotes family wealth
Source: *Sunday Times*, 3 April 2005.

Six 'British' names appeared in the world's top fifty in 2005 – Lakshmi Mittal, Roman Abramovich, the Duke of Westminster, Hans Rausing, Philip Green and Oleg Deripaska. Mittal and Abramovich have become British residents; Rausing is in fact Swedish by birth but has lived in Britain for the last twenty years. While American names dominated the list with seventeen of the fifty places, British names held the second largest number of positions, with Italy filling four places and Germany three.

Despite their parallel wealth histories, there has until recently been an ideological and cultural gulf in attitudes across the Atlantic towards the very rich, towards wealth and wealth-making. For most of the last 100 years, Britons have held a more aloof and ambiguous attitude to wealth. Americans have always been more pro-market and pro-rich, viewing the accumulation of large fortunes as a reward for effort and skill. Today they tolerate large differences in wealth mainly because most would like to become rich themselves. As the *Economist* has put it, 'America is still a place where most people react to seeing a man in a Ferrari by redoubling their own efforts to be able to afford one, rather than by trying to let down his tyres'.[50] Although, as shown in Chapter 6, the belief that America is a fully opportunistic and meritocratic society is a myth, it is a belief that is deeply embedded in the American psyche, even during the era of the 'great compression'. What distinguished that era from the great wealth-making period that preceded and has now succeeded it is a matter of scale not principle.

Britain may not have closed the wealth gap at the very top with America, but the cultural and aspirational gap has been narrowing sharply. Both nations are experiencing what some have called 'a second gilded age'. Attitudes towards the accumulation and flaunting of wealth in the UK are increasingly aping those that have become central to American culture. Part of the explanation for the growing wealth polarisation of recent times is that Britain has been moving away from European social norms and adopting those that have long characterised American society. Much of the recent wealth explosion in Britain can be traced to the arrival of American financial institutions in the City and to the importing of American attitudes and customs – the hiking of corporate salaries and perks, the introduction of share option packages, the pro-market culture, the relaxing of attitudes towards corporate and capital taxation. British businessmen and City dealers want to emulate the flamboyance of their American counterparts. The bonus free-for-all now commonplace in the City began with the entry of American investment banks into the UK. Top corporate executives, investment brokers and celebrities are demanding and receiving rewards that permit more and more lavish lifestyles and the more extreme symbols of wealth.

Britons today have a more tolerant attitude towards at least some of the rich and the young especially have a much more aspirational culture about wealth. They are more willing to accept the flaunting of wealth than they were in the post-war era. This change has been driven by the cultural shifts that began to emerge in the 1970s and the growing visibility of the rich. It is displayed in the popularity of magazines such as *Hello!* and *OK!*, our heightened fascination with celebrities and high-profile businessmen, the success of the national lottery and the popularity of television programmes such as *Who Wants to Be a Millionaire?* and *The Apprentice*, the American reality television programme that was reinvented for a British audience. The success of the British series is all the more remarkable for the fact that it would not have been made even a few years before.

Today, British attitudes towards wealth and its gap lie closer to pro-enterprise American values than the more pro-welfare European ones. In Britain, the debate about inequality and wealth-making no longer splits the main political parties. Labour has turned its back on the egalitarian agenda of earlier decades, preferring to tackle poverty alone by raising the income floor of the poorest. Britons seem to have embraced the emergence of liberal capitalism more openly than Europeans on the continent, though the evidence is that they remain wary of excessive inequality and of the more dominant plutocratic tradition in the United States.

Meanwhile, the rich – old and new, domestic and foreign alike – are continuing to take advantage of the favourable climate. It is no accident that the British wealth leagues contain a significant number of foreign 'tax exiles'. Britain is widely seen abroad as an international tax haven. Some of the explosion in wealth has been the product of Britain's generous tax treatment of foreign-born multi-millionaires, with HM Revenue and Customs rules deliberately bent to encourage rich foreigners such as Roman Abramovich, Lakshmi Mittal and Hans Rausing to take residency here. So many of Russia's super-rich have chosen to live in London that *Forbes* recently dubbed the capital 'Londongrad'. The estate agent Savills estimates that a third of buyers at the multi-million top end of the London housing market are Russians.

But an uncomfortable issue remains. Is it right to accept today's escalating levels of personal enrichment and growing concentration of wealth at the top without question? Is the modern tycoon, businessman or financier really worth so much more than their predecessors in earlier decades when they seemed sufficiently motivated and content with their apparently more modest lot? Have we bred a new generation of entrepreneurs and business leaders with such exceptional skill, drive and leadership – sufficient to justify the much higher rewards they are earning?

The next chapter will look at Britain's entrepreneurial record. Can the escalation of wealth at the top be explained and justified by a new surge of exceptionally successful entrepreneurial activity?

3

The Midas touch

In the 1990s there was no increase in human greed, just an increase in the
opportunities for greedy behaviour.
(Alan Greenspan, chairman of the Federal Reserve, 2003)[1]

In July 2005, Richard Desmond, the proprietor of the *Express* newspaper
titles, announced that he was paying himself a 'chairman's remuneration' of
some £52 million, that is, the equivalent of £1 million a week. It hardly raised
an eyebrow. Although it was certainly hefty by historical standards it was not
by contemporary ones. Three months later, in October 2005, the high street
retailer Philip Green paid himself a dividend of £1.2 billion from his Arcadia
shops, which he had acquired three years before. This generated a lot more
interest – it was, after all, the highest private dividend on record.
Furthermore, it came on top of a dividend of £460 million he had paid
himself the year before. The previous record dividend was in fact £1.1 billion
paid in the autumn of 2004 by Lakshmi Mittal to himself. What Mittal,
Green and Desmond all have in common, apart from their nose for business
and their places at the top of the rich lists, is that they are owners of private
companies.

There are several routes to great wealth. It is possible – just – to get rich by
a combination of frugal living and wise saving, even on a relatively modest
income. In 1972, for example, a London bus driver, a Mr Rowse, died
leaving £62,388. He had no children, never took a holiday and lived off just
the bare necessities.[2] The biggest fortune accumulated in this way appears to
be that of the retired American tax clerk who, through modest living and
careful blue-chip investment, converted a $5,000 nest-egg into $22 million
over fifty years.[3] Such examples are rare, however, and generally not much

fun, it would appear. Winning the lottery, marrying money or being born to rich parents are all, generally, a lot easier.

Entrepreneurship is a much harder route to great wealth, but for the lucky or especially talented ones it also brings the greatest and fastest fortunes. Amongst the forty billionaires in the *Sunday Times* rich list for 2005, more than half could be called tycoons, who have created a personal fortune, although not always from scratch, through entrepreneurial and business activity (see Table 1.2). Entrepreneurs also account for a sizeable proportion of centi-millionaires.

Entrepreneurial success undoubtedly requires a range of exceptional personal skills. As the economist Josiah Wedgwood, himself a descendant of the self-made pottery entrepreneur, put it in 1929, successful entrepreneurs need to 'take great risks, and [have] exceptional luck or exceptional talent'.[4] It helps, of course, to have all three. There is no doubt that past and modern entrepreneurs from Viscount Leverhulme to Richard Branson have shown bucketloads of business acumen along with great vision, determination and self-belief.

Luck has certainly played its role in some of the great fortunes. The property speculators such as Harry Hyams who built acres of new office space in central London in the 1960s were helped to their fortunes by a convenient combination of a surge in demand for offices just at the point at which the then Labour government imposed a ban on further office building. Sir James Goldsmith, the financier, sold most of his considerable assets shortly before the 1987 stock market crash. *Time* magazine put him on the front cover under the headline 'The Lucky Gambler'. John D. Rockefeller became very rich through his capture of the market for oil products, the result of a mix of ruthless competition and creative marketing. But what turned him into the world's first billionaire was almost certainly the invention of the motor car, which hugely increased the demand for his oil. Bill Gates may have been saved from the anti-trust court ruling to split up Microsoft by the election of George Bush in 2001. The Russian oligarchs such as Roman Abramovich were mostly in the right place at the right time.

Despite their diversity, what binds the entrepreneurs at the top of today's wealth pile is that they appear to be richer, much richer, than their pre-decessors of thirty years and more ago. So why is it that current entrepreneurs appear to be accumulating bigger fortunes than in comparison with the post-war era? Is it that we have bred a new generation with exceptional skill, talent and drive? Is it that the modern tycoon has uncovered new secrets of business success? Has the rate of scientific breakthrough moved up a level? The answer is almost certainly no to all of these. If they were the case we would be seeing an historic rise in the rate of economic progress as well. Today's escalating personal fortunes are not, in general, down to greater risk taking, superior talent or better luck. There is no reason to believe that today's business tycoons are more gifted than their predecessors or that they are willing to take much bigger gambles.

A vibrant entrepreneurial and innovative culture is vital to economic progress. Exceptional merit and dynamism undoubtedly deserve generous reward. The successful entrepreneur, especially one who is self-made, is widely seen as the most deserving of Britain's rich. People who can build a fortune from scratch or turn a poorly performing company around are rightly admired not only for their personal achievement, but for their wider contribution to job creation or protection, economic growth and in some cases national prestige. But there are no strong reasons to believe that today's escalating rewards are closely linked to historically and internationally exceptional levels of skill, risk-taking and effort.

Beginning with the administration of Margaret Thatcher, recent governments have attempted to promote more of an enterprise culture in Britain, and with some success. Business studies has become one of the most popular subjects in school and university, business schools are booming and entrepreneurial aspirations have undoubtedly been growing. Increasing numbers of the young declare that they want to become their own boss. But there is no evidence that these rising aspirations have yet been translated into an improvement in the quality of entrepreneurship. New business start-up rates have marginally improved over the last decade and there has been a steady rise in the number of businesses and of the self-employed, but the rate of business failure has remained pretty static. Britain is relatively low in the international entrepreneurial league, with one in twenty-five of the population starting a business compared with one in ten in the United States, although we are slightly above the European average.[5] Another recent study found that Britain had a relatively low rate of innovative activity within firms compared with France, Germany and Spain.[6] Our record on productivity is also poor – Britain ranked fifteenth in the thirty richest countries for productivity growth.

The key difference is not yet that we have superior entrepreneurs compared with the past, but that the personal returns from risk-taking, investment and talent can be greater, often much greater, today than they used to be. This is because modern entrepreneurs are operating in a very different economic and political climate that can offer higher individual premiums for success and, sometimes, more precipitous falls for failure.

The first difference is that markets have been transformed by growing affluence, improved transport and the dismantling of international cultural and trade barriers. The policies of economic liberalisation and deregulation of the last two decades have opened markets up: brands once confined to national boundaries are increasingly global. Throughout history, founding entrepreneurs have been able to convert their ideas into personal fortunes. Inventors who not only come up with a product but build the company that makes it continue to rank amongst the most successful entrepreneurs, but today's pioneers can often accumulate fortunes that tower above those of the past.

Hans Rausing is a multi-billionaire because he invented the Tetra Pak milk and fruit juice carton, which is much cheaper to produce than glass and allows drinks to stay fresh without refrigeration. But his wealth is not just down to the invention of a ground-breaking product. He has also benefited from the advent of the global mass market. The milk carton is now used in almost every home in the western world. To take another example, Bill Gates is worth upwards of $40 billion partly because he has created a monopoly for his Microsoft computer software operating system, but also because of the massive world market for computers. Microsoft's core business, the Windows operating system and the Office software, brings in a staggering billion dollars' profit a month. In another area, television has transformed and commercialised entertainment and sport. Today billions of people around the world can watch football and tennis stars, and their fees have soared as a result. The emergence of the mass world market has opened a vast door denied to earlier wealth seekers, who had to be content with the potential of their own country or continent.

A second factor is that markets often mature much more quickly than in the past, with much higher levels of product penetration. In little more than a decade from its first appearance, the mobile phone reached near saturation point in Britain with 80 per cent of consumers owning one. In the last decade, worldwide sales have exceeded 800 million. Nokia, the market leader, sold 128 million handsets in 2000 alone. There has been similar demand for new technology-related products, from the home computer to video games, which have all achieved relatively rapid popularity.

Of course, entrepreneurs have made money through being in at the start of rapidly expanding markets in the past. This was true of the early railway contractors such as Thomas Brassey, and the Vesteys and Sainsburys, who pioneered the manufacture and distribution of food. The popularity of the supermarket made a huge fortune for Sir Jack Cohen of Tesco. Nevertheless many of these successful markets, including the washing machine, the deep freeze, even the ubiquitous television, were much slower to mature than their equivalents in electronics and computers today.

Thirdly, although many of the world's big fortunes of the last 200 years can be linked to breakthrough inventions, from the steam engine and the camera to the pacemaker and the photocopier, the route to entrepreneurial wealth is no longer heavily dependent on building a business from scratch, as it was prior to the Second World War and even the decade beyond. Of course, many modern entrepreneurs continue to make money this way. Richard Branson's success is down to the creation of a very successful brand name. James Dyson's invention of the dual cyclone vacuum cleaner in 1993 has enabled him to build a fortune of over £1 billion in a decade. Stelios Haji-Ioannou has made his money by founding the budget airline easyJet.

Increasingly, though, the big money is less in blockbuster new products and the founding of new companies than in modifications to existing products, improved processes and astute marketing. Henry Ford did not invent the motor car but rather a greatly superior way of manufacturing it through the mass-production assembly line. Philip Green has made his fortune by making some of Britain's existing high street stores much more profitable, partly through a ruthless squeeze on suppliers to cut costs but also by cutting overheads and 'quickening the pace' of decision-making. Michael Dell and Sam Walton (of Wal-Mart) are the Henry Fords of computers and food respectively. Their companies have risen to the top of their industries through much more efficient ways of getting ordinary products to consumers. They have not brought a new product to market or built a new industry but have still created value and big shareholder returns.

At the heart of the rising wealth levels of recent times has been the expansion of the role of financial deal-making. Financiers have always played a significant role in the making of the great fortunes. Despite Britain's role as the pioneer of industrialisation, it was bankers, merchants and financiers who built the biggest fortunes at the end of the nineteenth century. While landed wealth remained significant, non-landed wealth was more likely to be found amongst those involved in London-based commerce and finance than amongst northern industrialists and manufacturers. The number of millionaires from commerce and finance totalled 158 in the period from 1809 to 1939 compared with 100 from industry and manufacturing.[7] In the years immediately before the First World War, the richest Britons outside the titled landowners were almost certainly Lord Rothschild, a banker; Charles Morrison, a banker and warehouseman; Lord Overstone, a financier; and John Ellerman, a shipowner and financier.[8]

Today, the opportunities open to financiers are greater. In many ways, the modern process of wealth-making is a product of the growing trade in money, divorced from actual production, service delivery or even banking. This has become possible through the nature of modern financial invest-ment, in which financial deregulation and the growth of world markets have turned financial speculation into the biggest growth industry in the world. The returns can be high while the risks can be limited and even then are often borne heavily by others.

As Paul Volcker, the chairman of the Federal Reserve for most of the 1980s, describes it, 'it seems to be easier to make money in some sense, with paper chasing paper, than in investing in real goods and services'.[9] During the last twenty years, the accumulation of personal wealth has been closely linked to financial deals, to predatory raiding, to property and business speculation, all driven by the financial revolution that began in the 1980s. As one US financial insider put it,

> prior to this decade the only way to really make huge amounts of money was to be essentially very productive. In the eighties you didn't have to be. You could make a billion dollars, as some people did, simply by shuffling pieces of paper, or by helping a raider take over a company and break it up.[10]

The final explanation, and an especially significant one, for the explosion in the size of fortunes being made by modern entrepreneurs has been the growth of the importance of private equity. The last five years in particular have seen an acceleration in the rate at which former publicly owned companies have been taken private. In the retail sector, for example, Debenhams, Bhs, New Look, Selfridges and Arcadia were all being run by corporations in the late 1990s. By 2005 all had been taken into private ownership. This is a highly significant development. Taking companies private, as we will see, has been the source of the accelerating wealth enjoyed by many of those who have emerged at the top of the rich lists in recent years.

Measuring up

So how do today's entrepreneurs measure up against the great moguls of the past – for example the inventor of the water frame, Richard Arkwright; the cotton magnate Sir Robert Peel the elder; the soap manufacturer William Lever; and the chocolate manufacturer Joseph Rowntree? Or indeed those of more recent years, such as the successive generations of the Sainsbury family; Jack Cohen, who created Tesco; and Simon Marks and Marcus Sieff, who built Marks and Spencer into Britain's largest and most popular fashion retailer? Britain certainly has popular contemporary tycoons who have created wealth, jobs and opportunities just as in the past. Founding entrepreneurs such as James Dyson, and John Caudwell, who set up the Phones4U retail chain, are rich by virtue of the market value placed on their companies. Most of them are seen as worth their place at the top.

But this is far from true of all those who have topped the wealth leagues in recent decades. Tiny Rowland, chairman of Lonrho in the 1970s and 1980s, used a variety of accountancy tricks to help build the company, originally based in mining, into an international empire. In 1973, the Prime Minister, Edward Heath, denounced him in Parliament as the 'unpleasant and unacceptable face of capitalism'. Thirty years later, the same description was applied by the managing director of BMW UK to the 'Phoenix Four' – the four venture capitalists who had acquired Rover from BMW for £10 and ran it with the aid of substantial public money. The owners were initially hailed as saviours of the company, and more specifically of the Longbridge assembly plant, but when it went bankrupt in November 2004, leaving the workforce without work and in most cases pensions, the four were accused of being primarily concerned with lining their own pockets, having continued to pay themselves generously while pumping money into their own pension funds. Sir Digby Jones, the director general of the CBI, summed it up: 'If you, as four people, take £40 million out of the company – quite legally, honestly, openly and transparently – on your way to burning £600 million in cash and end up putting 6,500 people on the dole, I think your behaviour has been appalling.'[11]

Robert Maxwell, who ended up owning the *Daily Mirror*, was a consummate gambler who illegally stole the company's pension fund before mysteriously disappearing off the side of his luxury yacht. His contempt for the people around him was displayed by his habit of urinating from the top of the Mirror building upon passers-by. One of Britain's most notorious entrepreneurs is the property developer Nicholas van Hoogstraten. Sometimes dubbed the 'devil's landlord', Hoogstraten is renowned for the contempt he holds for his tenants, accusing them on one occasion of being 'scum'. In December 2003, the entrepreneur was released on appeal by the High Court after spending a year in gaol for manslaughter. He also has strong ties with Zimbabwe, where he holds the largest stake in the country's biggest coalmine and in one of its major commercial banks. He once branded the white farmers evicted by Robert Mugabe as 'white trash'.

When Richard Desmond bought the Express Newspaper Group for £125 million from Lord Hollick in November 2000, there were cries of outrage across the political and journalistic establishment. A man who had made much of his money through pornography was not seen as a suitable person, at least in some quarters, to own one of the country's oldest newspaper titles. The wealthy Russian oligarchs such as Roman Abramovich, who has chosen to relocate to Britain, are rich because of the way they took advantage of the privatisation rush initiated by Boris Yeltsin. Far from being the men who discovered the oil, laid the pipelines, built the refineries, took the risks, they have effectively inherited the wealth created by earlier generations mainly through being a small, favoured and influential, group of insiders who successfully subverted plans for the wealth to be shared.

Even founding entrepreneurs can prove controversial figures. Richard Branson's genius, and popularity, has as much to do with his brilliant self-promotion and high-profile stunts – posing naked on his autobiography, his attempts to beat the round-the-world balloon record – as his business acumen. Not that Branson doesn't make enemies – on occasions he also gets nominated for the most disliked man in Britain. This may be an example of British schadenfreude or an awareness that his business dealings may not always be as straight as his carefully constructed image would have us believe. He certainly made himself unpopular with the press when he attempted to sue the journalist Tom Bower for libel. Bower had written an article for the *Evening Standard* about Branson's bid for the National Lottery, but Branson chose to sue the individual, not the paper. The paper's editor, Max Hastings, funded Bower's defence anyway, but it appeared like a return to the earlier scare tactics applied by James Goldsmith and Maxwell.

Branson likes to promote himself as the acceptable face of capitalism, the 'consumer's champion', a man you can trust for fair dealing. He once boasted, 'There is nothing phoney about my idealism . . . I had a genuine belief that I should be using my skills and the resources at my disposal to "do good".'[12]

Yet his business record is certainly not without its blemishes. Lynne Barber, the acerbic *Observer* columnist, once described him as a 'suit disguised as a sweater'.[13] In 1972, some two years after Branson had started making big profits from his first serious business venture – selling cut-price, mail order pop records, he was charged with tax fraud, spent one night in gaol and had to pay back taxes of £40,000 and a fine of £20,000. He had stumbled across a lucrative way of avoiding paying purchase tax. Branson later justified his evasion as youthful rebellion: 'I have always enjoyed breaking the rules.'[14] Despite his claims to run socially responsible companies, Branson is believed to employ every legal trick in the book to minimise his corporate tax bills. Most of his companies are based offshore, which is usually a sure sign of tax avoidance. His complex labyrinth of some 250 companies makes it very difficult to assess his real worth.

Branson defends his use of tax havens as a way of keeping his competitors guessing, but his unwillingness to allow his business affairs to be subjected to the usual public scrutiny has raised suspicions in some quarters. Some of his companies are substantially financed by tax avoidance schemes, legal as they are. A scrutiny of the accounts for Virgin Atlantic, for example, suggests that the deferred tax liability is worth considerably more than the shareholder investment. Without the use of such avoidance, it is likely that the Virgin empire and Branson's personal fortune would be noticeably smaller.

Indeed, as we will see in Chapter 9, modern entrepreneurship and tax avoidance seem to have become increasingly synonymous. Rupert Murdoch's media empire has paid hardly anything in tax in the UK since the late 1980s. Mohamed al-Fayed, Lakshmi Mittal and Hans Rausing have all used a range of tax loopholes to enhance their personal fortunes – all perfectly legal if you can afford the massive fees that tax accountants and lawyers charge and which have helped some of them to join the rich lists themselves.

Many companies and business leaders would not stand up to detailed scrutiny of their financial affairs. Indeed, many of the most colossal fortunes have been built through arcane financial manipulation, especially in the United States. The 1980s saw one financial scandal after another emanating from Wall Street and involving new financial devices such as derivatives, leveraged buy-outs and junk bonds as well as insider trading. One of the most vilified at the time was the immensely wealthy and powerful Henry Kravis of Kohlberg Kravis Roberts, perhaps the ultimate corporate raider and the pioneer of the leveraged buy-out, in which a public company's shareholders are all bought out using the company itself as collateral. By the end of the 1980s, Kravis had built a huge personal fortune through the controversial restructuring of one major American corporation after another. His company controlled so many businesses that it ranked in the top ten US corporations.

In 1987, Ivan Boesky, the stock speculator, was sentenced to three years in prison for insider trading. Two years later, Michael Milken, then one of America's richest men, was indicted on almost 100 counts of securities fraud and racketeering. He was sentenced to ten years in gaol but served only twenty-two months. Boesky's and Milken's activities were well summed up in the title of the book – *Den of Thieves* – which charted their and others' rise and fall. As its author, James B. Stewart, described it, 'this is the full story of the criminals who came to dominate Wall Street, how they achieved the pinnacle of wealth, power and celebrity, and how they were detected and brought to justice'.[15] Milken specialised in junk bonds – the bonds of less creditworthy companies that offered high interest rates. From 1975 to 1986, $71.5 billion of junk bonds were issued. Such bonds were one of the main sources of the huge sums of quickly borrowed money that such corporate raiders as Kravis and James Goldsmith used in the 1980s to finance their hostile takeover bids. Yet 'junk' is exactly what many of the bonds turned out to be – by 1988 around a fifth had defaulted. Most of Milken's clients were left bankrupt.[16]

Britain has had its fair share of rogue entrepreneurs. One of the men who came to symbolise the greed culture of the 1980s was Roger Levitt. Nicknamed 'the man with the golden grin', he was an investment broker in the City. Sporting a trademark Groucho Marx moustache and smoking a Havana cigar, he had long been in the habit of hoodwinking investors by exaggerating the profits his investment funds were making. Among those taken in were the pop singer Adam Faith, the thriller writer Frederick Forsyth and the film director Michael Winner. When his group collapsed in 1990 with more than £30 million in debts, he left 18,000 investors high and dry. Levitt was eventually convicted of fraud. Similarly, in the 1990s, Ted Ball, the head of Lansing Leasing, an apparently flourishing London car-leasing enterprise, took to doctoring his accounts when he ran up big losses. Eventually, his firm went into liquidation with debts of £50 million and Ball was gaoled for corruption.

The Canadian-born Conrad Black, who took British nationality to become a British peer, treated Hollinger International, the owner of the *Telegraph* newspapers, more like a private fiefdom than a public company, and was accused of raiding its finances to pay for a lavish international lifestyle until the company directors pulled the plug. In November 2003, he was forced to resign as chief executive of Hollinger International, for, allegedly, serious financial irregularities. In 2005, he (along with three associates) was charged with fraud, including the abuse of corporate perks, by a US attorney who described his actions as 'the grossest abuse'. In 2005, Refco, one of the world's biggest futures brokers, came close to collapse when its British-born president, chief executive and chairman, Philip Bennett, was accused of perpetrating a giant fraud over several years, of hiding away over $500 million of bad debts from investors and of having public accounts that could not be relied on. It was a spectacular, sudden and unpredicted collapse.

Casino-capitalism

The modern entrepreneur typically plays a very different role from the moguls of the past. Today they are more likely to have made their money not from building firms and products from scratch or adding value by introducing new processes but through financial raiding and deal-making that involve less risk and arguably create less new wealth, in some cases none at all.

In the 1990s, Philip Green became renowned as a 'bottom-fishing' opportunist who made huge sums of money buying up existing companies, stripping their assets and selling them off. He and his backers – the Barclay brothers and the Scottish entrepreneur Tom Hunter – were behind the purchase and the dismantling of the giant Sears conglomerate, originally created by the legendary Charles Clore, which owned the mail order business Freemans and a range of high street stores from Dolcis and Miss Selfridge to Wallis and Richards. The consortium put together by Green organised a hostile takeover of the firm and sold all of it off in a matter of months, making in the process a profit of more than £200 million. It was from that time that he became known among his detractors as 'Conan the Barbarian'. It was this ability to make money through asset-stripping that built a reputation that persuaded a handful of giant banks to finance his successful bids for Bhs and then Arcadia, companies that he made profitable by hands-on management. Nevertheless, Green's wealth has been built through the acquisition and transformation of existing companies, not the creation of new ones.

Other British deal-makers who have made contemporary fortunes in a similar way, if not on the same scale, include Luke Johnson and Hugh Osmond. Johnson, the son of columnist Paul Johnson, the one-time socialist turned right-wing ideologue, is a very different 'entrepreneur' to the nineteenth-century industrialists who created a product and brand, built a company from scratch and stayed deeply rooted in managing the company they founded. Johnson has made his money largely through financial engineering, 'circling the business pages like a carrion crow, picking at bits of companies, gobbling pieces up, looking for opportunities'.[17] He makes money from paper transactions, setting up shell companies and undertaking reverse takeovers, and describes himself as 'an entrepreneur of sorts'.[18]

Throughout the 1990s, 'Hughie and Louie' became leading members of the 'business brat pack', pulling off a succession of lucrative, high-profile deals. In 1993 they snatched control of Pizza Express and turned the under-performing chain into a much more profitable operation. Johnson then repeated the move with Belgo, the moules-et-frites chain, and took stakes in the celebrity-studded Ivy and Le Caprice restaurants and in companies in sectors as diverse as tyres, teeth and wedding dresses. The business partnership between Johnson and Osmond eventually collapsed in a bitter public row when they started buying shares in each other's companies. The *Sunday Times* puts Johnson's wealth at £80 million.[19] Of course, some deal-making and restructuring activity is highly productive. Johnson and Osmond greatly improved the fortunes of Pizza Express, while Green has turned both Bhs and Arcadia into much more profitable companies.

Today, some of the biggest fortunes can be linked to financial speculation, to hot money circulating the globe in search of the 'quickest buck'. The last decade has seen a dramatic shift in the way British joint stock companies are owned. Even in the late 1990s, most large companies were dominated by traditional UK-based institutional investors representing pension funds or managing large savings accounts, groups that tended to take a long-term view of a company's performance. But subsequent years saw the arrival of a set of more volatile investors. Some of these new-style investors are super-rich private individuals only interested in making short-term profits by speculating on the share price. But most are financial institutions, often American based, with a very different outlook from the old pension company investors.

This is illustrated well by the flow of speculative money before and during Green's £11 billion bid for Marks and Spencer in the summer of 2005. Even before Green declared his hand, close to a third of M&S shares were held by American institutions. They typically had little or no interest in the long-term future of the company – they were waiting for an opportunity to sell up and cash in. In the six weeks after Green's announcement, there was a huge turnover in M&S shares: close to three-quarters of the company's 2.2 billion shares changed hands.

Those buying in were mostly speculative institutional investors looking for a quick killing, many of them consisting of hedge funds – the ultimate short-term investments. Many of these investors were American, betting on cashing in on the difference between the buying price and the 400p per share Green would offer if he were to turn his phantom into a formal bid. One of New York's speculative traders, a thirty-something, fast-talking guy called Harry, had put a good deal of his own hot money into the company that week and declared that 'rabid dogs now own Marks & Spencer'.[20] This was capitalism 2004 style – characterised by the flow of global 'loose' money looking for a potentially lucrative home, money that increasingly has a powerful influence on the fate of many British companies, as illustrated by Malcolm Glazer's dramatic and controversial takeover of Manchester United in May 2005.

Felix Rohatyn, a senior director of Lazard bank in New York, has described the process:

> The fact that money just carooms round the world at infinite speeds has made it possible for people to speculate on a huge scale with very little money of their own committed to it . . . the returns on those kinds of speculation were always bigger than if you had really had to go to work and build a factory or develop a new product.[21]

Those running hedge funds – private pools of capital that invest long or short – are in essence speculators, often flush with investment money and interested in one thing only: making big money through speculative share activity, while also funding mergers and takeovers and in some cases, taking public companies private. The rise of the hedge fund, an arcane, mysterious and largely unregulated operation understood by few, reflects the increasingly short time horizons of the modern investor, the obsession with jam today. Hedge fund managers bet on the movement of share prices. They 'hedge' their bets by, for example, identifying shares they think are overvalued and betting they will go down in price. Often they don't even own the shares they are speculating with. They 'borrow' a bunch of them (for a fee) and agree to give them back at a later date. They then sell them at the current price and re-buy them when, as hoped, they have gone down in price, pocketing the difference.

The average length of time for which shares are held has been falling sharply over the last two decades. Churning rather than long-term holding is now the norm. This new emphasis on short-term, fast-buck-generating deals is making it much more difficult for the patient organisation-building on which enduring companies and long-term wealth creation are founded and which was the way in which many large and successful British companies were originally built. In the United States, hedge fund owners are variously known as the 'Midas men' or the 'attack dogs'. It is no coincidence that those running such funds, both in the UK and in the USA, have been climbing up the wealth ladder. Their profits, however, estimated to be in the order of $21 billion in 2005, have come from correctly anticipating market movements rather than reshaping the fundamentals of the business world – redistributing rather than creating wealth. As one of the industry stars admitted, 'when I first went into the City, I could not believe that anyone would want to pay me so much for creating nothing'.[22]

The arrival of this new breed of tycoon – the corporate raider and speculator – was made possible by the growth of shareholder capitalism after the First World War. The raiders who emerged in the 1950s were essentially financiers who saw the potential to make quick profits by restructuring companies. A similar kind of predatory activity had last been prevalent in America in the late nineteenth century. Then it had been initiated by the great industrial barons such as John D. Rockefeller, Andrew Carnegie and Cornelius Vanderbilt, who used ruthless corporate tactics and mergers to take on their competitors and build the giant near-monopolies that made them the world's first centi-millionaires. The reason why the personal wealth made from the industrial revolution was so much greater in the United States than in the United Kingdom was partly down to the sheer scale of the market in the United States, but also down to the slowness with which Britain exploited the potential of the limited liability joint stock company.[23]

Throughout the nineteenth century, most British industrialists preferred to keep their firms as relatively small family-run affairs or partnerships, rather than set up as joint stock companies. By the turn of the century, Britain had no fewer than 2,000 cotton firms. John Maynard Keynes joked that there was 'probably no hall in Manchester large enough to hold all the directors'.[24]

In contrast, the United States built giant and often near-monopolistic firms through merger and takeover, most of them joint stock companies, which undoubtedly contributed to its growing industrial power and the new giant personal fortunes. The ruthless corporate tactics behind the building of the giant US fortunes was seen in some quarters as acceptable economic behaviour, the application to business of the Darwinian principal of 'the survival of the fittest'. The philosopher Herbert Spencer likened business to the modern equivalent of war and the tycoons, later described as 'robber barons', were seen in some quarters as similar heroes to the early adventurers and buccaneering sea captains such as Francis Drake and Sebastian Cabot of the sixteenth and seventeenth centuries. Eventually, however, brakes were imposed on the growing concentration of power through the anti-trust laws passed around the turn of the twentieth century.

For the next fifty years, such predatory behaviour and the application of the 'laws of the jungle' to business were seen as unacceptable in the new economic and political climate. As a result firms were able to expand without external threat. But in the 1950s, a new group of businessmen started to question the orthodoxy. Watching from the sidelines, they spotted the potential of making money by moving in on companies that had apparently grown fat and complacent. But there was a taboo against predatory takeovers, which were viewed as socially and economically destructive. That taboo was first broken in Britain in the 1950s by the financier Charles Clore, the man who pioneered the hostile takeover bid, becoming infamous as a corporate raider in the process. No one else had dared to try. Put in simple language, he would buy up a company, often against its will, close down or dispose of the bits that weren't making enough money and sell off any property freed up in the process. Many people lost their jobs while Clore made a killing. Like the raiders who followed him, Clore was driven by a cavalier need to break the rules, and became a much reviled man. The then Labour Party leader, Clement Attlee, once referred darkly to 'nature red in tooth and claw – particularly Clore'.[25]

Throughout the 1960s and 1970s hostile takeovers became more common. Most of the activity was being initiated by a small group of financiers including Clore, Jim Slater, James Goldsmith, James Hanson and Gordon White. What united these men was a tendency to reckless action – they were mostly disaffected right-wingers who were out of tune with the post-war politics of consensus. They became known as the 'Mayfair set' because of their regular attendance at John Aspinall's Clermont gambling club in London's Berkeley Square and all made huge personal fortunes through 'bombardments of mobile money'.[26] None of them were conventional entrepreneurs. They didn't make anything, build a company from scratch or introduce more productive methods. They accumulated their wealth through financial deals that involved dismantling and reconstructing existing companies. All of them were gamblers. Goldsmith himself had a habit of using the language of the casino – when he moved anywhere, he was 'moving his chips'. Some dubbed them the 'casino capitalists'.

One of the first to spot the potential was Slater, who, in the early 1960s, formed a company, Slater Walker, with the young Tory MP Peter Walker. The first company Slater bought up was Cork Manufacturing, a public company that made cork seals and gaskets for an international market. At the time it was being run by Colonel Andrew Coote, a relative of the founder some seventy years before. When first approached by Slater about a takeover, Coote told him to 'go to hell'.[27] But Coote and the City establishment, also appalled at what they saw as an outrageous and ungentlemanly act, had no power to prevent Slater buying up the company shares and taking control. After taking over, Slater sold off land and factories to property developers and used the money to pay off his debt and finance the next bid.

Slater's lead was followed by Hanson and White. They started in Britain in the 1960s but then switched to America, where in the 1970s they started to take over a number of unglamorous but cash-rich businesses, such as brick and tobacco firms. The new raiders soon started to strike fear in both British and American boardrooms. They would suddenly grab the corporations by their necks, buy up their shares, take them over and turn them upside down. It was all made possible by the deregulation of markets, the dismantling of controls and the expanded access to borrowing.

The man who exploited the potential most decisively was Goldsmith, another member of the Mayfair Set. He was educated at Eton, where he gambled heavily and gained his ruthless and combative streak. The day he left the school he went to see the headmaster, who he had often clashed with, and offered him a present of a recording of *The Marriage of Figaro*. As the delighted headmaster went to take the present, Goldsmith dropped it – deliberately. As one financial journalist described him, 'he was not the sort of man not to kick a man when he's down'.[28]

Goldsmith built a large financial empire in the 1960s and 1970s, moved to America in the 1980s and made a series of dramatic raids on big corporations. His most audacious strike of all was against the giant Goodyear tyre and rubber company. Goodyear was a typical paternalistic company of the time, a believer in corporate social responsibility, a big local employer and a provider of recreational and social facilities in its base town of Akron, Ohio. Together with Hanson, he started buying shares in the company, accusing it of neglecting its core business of tyres and of building a bloated corpocracy run by a complacent and lazy board. The company responded in kind, accusing Goldsmith of inhumanity and greed, of behaving like a shark, of trying to destroy the company's ethos and values. After an increasingly acrimonious and public battle for control, one which was referred to a congressional hearing on monopolies, Goldsmith was eventually forced to back off and agreed to sell back his shares to Goodyear, but at a tidy profit of $90 million. And all for a few weeks,' work. The company saw it as a victory. 'We sent that slimy bastard back home,' as Tom Sawyer, an Ohio congressman, put it.[29] But Goldsmith's view of the company was vindicated. To remain profitable, the company was forced to slim down, to sell off some of its subsidiaries and to lay off staff and senior managers.

Goldsmith was not alone in exploiting the potential to make huge profits out of the restructuring of American industry. The deal that most came to symbolise the greed and power-mongering of the period was the dramatic buy-out of RJR Nabisco, the giant tobacco and food conglomerate, in 1988, and documented in the best-selling book *Barbarians at the Gate*.[30] The winner of the bidding war, a nail-biting game of corporate poker played for immensely high stakes, was Kohlberg Kravis Roberts. The $25 billion deal – the most expensive in history and heavily dependent on junk bonds – involved a river of money so great that for a month it greatly distorted the American money supply figures. This was paper shuffling at its most extreme. The fees enjoyed by the winners were enormous even by Wall Street standards. The firms involved, from Drexel Burnham and Morgan Stanley to Merrill Lynch and Kohlberg Kravis Roberts itself, pocketed between them some $800 million in fees, all for a few weeks' work.[31] This was the quickest of all the 'quick bucks' of the time.

The redundant chief executive, Ross Johnson, walked off with $53 million, while Ed Horrigan, head of the tobacco arm, walked away with $46 million.[32] The level of debt accrued to finance the deal meant a massive shake-up for the company. The aftershocks of such a seismic financial event went on for a decade and eventually led to a cut in the workforce of 40 per cent. Johnson was vilified in the press as the man who enriched himself at the expense of the company he ran and remains loathed to this day in the town most affected, Winston-Salem, North Carolina.[33]

Whether the hostile activity of the time was beneficial is a matter of hot dispute. Defenders argue that financial Darwinism was necessary to overturn the bloated, over-perked and self-serving networks that ran some companies, and separate the weak from the strong. To their opponents, the actions of the takeover tycoons were seen as immensely destructive, bringing a new wave of insecurity to staff and management alike. The journalist Paul Johnson, then on the left and never a man to mince his words, described the architects at the time as 'squirming, social scum, typical of the rottenness that is poisoning British society'. Most of the deals at this time were not hatched in boardrooms but in private clubs and restaurants. It was no coincidence that the Savoy Grill in the Strand, a favoured haunt of the rich and the famous, was known as the 'Deal Makers' Arms'. The takeover pioneers were brilliant businessmen but not great industrialists – they cared little for the companies they bought. Financial engineering created no new products. It often destroyed rather than built. Companies were cracked open like piggy banks because the parts were worth more financially than the whole. As the author of *Barbarians at the Gate* put it, 'this was wealth created by tearing apart companies rather than building them up, by firing or downsizing companies rather than by hiring them'.[34]

Economists have debated whether the winnowing of the time led to strengthened overall economic performance. Supporters claim it forced companies to ensure they were sufficiently lean to withstand hostile activity. Others say there is little evidence that the process increased British productivity or economic growth. Instead it may have hastened the decline of British manufacturing. Many small communities dependent on local firms for employment suffered immensely. There are two quite different models of capitalism at odds here. As Anthony Sampson has put it, 'companies clearly often needed shock treatment to make them more competitive; yet they were still expected to have social responsibilities, including fair wages, contributions to charity and concern for the environment, which diminished their short-term financial competitiveness'.[35]

What drove the deals was not a crusade to re-energise American and British industry, but the pursuit of personal enrichment through the staggering fees and pay-offs involved. As a result, the fates of companies were being determined often by a handful of individuals – bankers, traders, lawyers – barely connected with the company or having any knowledge of its workings and usually for reasons that had little to do with the health of the company. They had no interest in wider responsibilities, the 'national interest', the future viability of the companies they targeted or their employees. Lord White used to boast that he had never set foot on the shop floor of any of the companies that he had bought. As James Hanson has acknowledged, the name of the game was to get hold of 'tomorrow's money today'.[36]

Although there have been some success stories, the threat of hostile takeover has been a real problem for the UK economy. It pressures directors into making dividend payments even at the expense of cutting investment, merely to prevent the share price falling and increasing the risk of takeover. Many deals have ended with the breaking up of companies, including Marconi and ICI, destroying rather than creating value. They have mostly been driven by the demands of the investment banks in search of fee income and fat bonuses. Some corporate raiding makes no business sense at all. Malcolm Glazer's highly controversial 2005 takeover of Manchester United was neither in the public nor the club's interest and has simply saddled the club with enormous debts. The deal certainly enriched the club's principal shareholders – the Irish investors J. P. McManus and John Magnier – but on the wider impact only time will tell.

The undisputed effect of most of the corporate raiding and financial restructuring of the last decade and more has been to enrich those behind the activity: the bankers, stockbrokers, corporate accountants and lawyers as well as the front men. Huge executive bonuses nearly always follow. And then there are the fees picked up by the City. In 2000 alone, it was estimated that 2,000 people in the Square Mile received bonuses of at least £1 million for a year's work. And these were not entrepreneurs who were putting their livelihoods on the line to create wealth by taking big business risks.

A swarm of locusts

If the takeover kings of the 1970s and 1980s were able to build some of the biggest fortunes of the time, they have typically been replaced in contemporary rich lists with a new breed of entrepreneur made possible by the private equity revolution that began in the late 1990s. Dubbed 'the new kings of capitalism' by the *Economist* magazine, they have, in essence, found a new way of building fortunes that outclass even those made by the early predators.[37]

Philip Green is a classic example. He has in many ways copied the activities of the corporate raiders like Clore and Hanson but ended up much richer than all of them. Indeed his fortune is of the order of five to ten times as large. Part of the reason is that, in the case of Bhs and Arcadia, he has rolled up his sleeves and become a very hands-on tycoon, taking the day-to-day responsibility for his companies with the aim of cutting costs to the bone.

But the key explanation for Green's multi-billionaire status is that he is at the forefront of the recent surge in the rate at which publicly owned companies have been taken private. Together with his wife, he personally owns over 90 per cent of his two companies. The gains from the cost savings and the boost to profits that he has engineered have accrued almost entirely to him, as indicated by the extraordinary £1.7 billion of dividends from Bhs and Arcadia that he paid himself in 2004 and 2005.

Green has built his fortune by buying up under-performing companies, often on the cheap, pumping them full of debt, stripping them down, refinancing them and making a pretty tidy profit in the process. He is hardly the first to have spotted the potential of buying up companies in trouble, companies that successive managements had failed to make work and that the shareholders were only too pleased to dump. But although he is not alone, he is the single best example of the scale of wealth emerging from the public-to-private deals of recent times. It is a trend that is slowly changing the way British business operates and is making those involved very rich indeed. In retail alone, companies that have been taken private since the turn of the millennium include not just Bhs and Arcadia, but Harvey Nichols, Heal's, Hamleys, Homebase, Halfords and Kwik-Fit. Other well-known names that have been taken private include William Hill and the AA. The management teams and funders involved in several of these deals have ended up with big windfalls from taking the firms private.

The trend has been driven in part by the mathematics of acquisition and the fall in share prices – and interest rates – since 2000. If share prices fall below the underlying value of a company it can become prey to predators, who know they can make money by snapping it up and taking it private.

Since private buyers finance their purchase through borrowing rather than issuing shares, the much cheaper credit of recent times has also made public-to-private deals much easier to finance.

Nevertheless, the central factor behind the trend has been the rush to get rich. Private equity can and does create big fortunes and is one of the forces behind the surge in the wealth of the super-rich of recent years. It is perhaps the modern day equivalent of the gold rush. It is leading to a much greater concentration of wealth and financial power at the very top and is certainly how many modern day billionaires and multi-millionaires have been financing their tycoon lifestyles.

The private equity revolution has been driven both by individual entrepreneurs and a number of private equity companies that have emerged since the late 1990s. Most of the latter are highly secretive, names such as Apax, BC, Candover, CVC Capital and Permira in London, and Blackstone and the Texas Pacific Group (which owns Gate Gourmet, Burger King and part of Debenhams) in the United States. These are run not by public figures like Green but by faceless accountants and financiers who are mostly desperate to keep out of the limelight, and who employ separate management teams to run the companies once they have been acquired. The partners who run the firms, such as Damon Buffini of Permira, Mike Smith of CVC and Martin Halusa of Apax, are certainly lavishly paid – at a 'gravity-defying' rate, according to the *Economist*.[38] Smith is estimated to be worth £250 million by the *Sunday Times*, jumping into the 2005 list from nowhere. It is a trend that has been accelerating, with private equity now accounting for a fifth of the workforce outside the public sector. In 2004, private equity firms accounted for more than half of all merger and acquisition activity in the UK. Indeed, the UK is the world's leading private equity market, which has been slowly eating away at the edges of the shareholding model that made the earlier business generation rich.

Private equity firms and publicly listed companies are a world apart. The private firm offers a very different, more cut-throat form of capitalism. It lacks transparency and is often less favourable to staff but has become an increasingly attractive option for those uncomfortable with the constraints of running a public company. Obligations on public companies are there for a reason – to prevent incompetent, reckless and even fraudulent or exploitative business practice. Private entrepreneurs, in contrast, are free of such constraints. They can run their companies for short-term gain or for the long term. Private companies are required to provide much less information about their activities, sales and profits, do not have to answer to shareholders and are much more difficult to scrutinise. Green's companies, for example, are listed offshore and owned through a Channel Islands holding company, Taveta Investments Ltd, incorporated in Jersey. What information is available about them is almost entirely at his disposal.

There are real questions about the wider economic and social merits of the rush to private equity. It has almost entirely involved the trading of existing companies, not the creation of new ones, and thus brought about a transfer of wealth between existing wealth holders. Private companies are free to pursue their business objectives as they see fit and this can result in the unbalanced pursuit of short-term goals, including the maximisation of cash flow – necessary to pay off debt – sometimes to the detriment of longer-term, more sustainable goals. The first call on the cash flow of a private company is the repayment of debt, which can often be hefty. Some critics fear that the piling up of debt by the new takeover firms is at risk of turning into a bubble. Private companies in general also feel less responsibility to a company's history, their values and their staff.

The arrival of private equity is certainly provoking controversy. In memory of the impact of the asset-stripping Mayfair set, modern takeovers often involve hundreds of lay-offs, the selling of the 'family silver' – land and properties – and much tougher deals for suppliers. This would have been more difficult in public companies and the result has sometimes – though not always – been staggeringly high returns on the initial investment, all accruing to a handful of people. The formerly mutual Automobile Association, eventually sold on to CVC and Permira in July 2004, faced the loss of 900 jobs. Halfords also faced big job losses when taken private. The Phoenix Venture Holdings group was blamed for the collapse of MG Rover with the loss of over 5,000 jobs. When Gate Gourmet, the private catering company that supplies British Airways with in-flight meals, was taken over by its new private equity owners, the US company Texas Pacific, its somewhat crude attempts to cut labour costs soon led to a bitter dispute with its workforce, mainly low-paid Asian women.

Some firms have certainly showed improved performance under the 'new kings', with Bhs, Burger King and Millets often quoted as examples. Question marks remain over others. Private equity firms insist that they are more than just financiers, and that they also bring better management. But the jury is still out on this. The lavish returns achieved on deals in recent years have mostly stemmed from the power of financial gearing – the use of borrowed money – than from smarter management. In Germany some British private equity firms were heavily attacked in the summer of 2005 by the chairman of the country's then ruling Social Democratic Party with views reminiscent of the feelings about the early activities of the Mayfair set: 'They remain anonymous, they have no face and descend like a swarm of locusts on a company, devour it then fly on.' In the UK the new predators have been criticised for buying on the cheap, selling off a company's prized assets and still being able to sell a firm within a year or two for a massive profit. One leading fund manager – Justin Urquhart Stewart of Seven Investment Management – has dubbed them 'vulture capitalists'.[39] What remains unclear is how far they have created value for anyone but the people who run them. Although the targets are often highly inefficient firms, some doubt if the process has had any real impact on overall growth. Some leading figures in the industry are only too aware of the risks of being seen to be too exploitative of their new power. As Sir Ronald Cohen of Apax has put it, 'the biggest threat to our business is not from within. We have demonstrated we can perform and survive. The biggest threat is attracting criticism for being part of the widening gap between rich and poor.'[40]

The real measure of success is whether profitability can be maintained. Some private companies have generated better returns than when they were public companies but not all have performed as well as Green's Bhs and Arcadia. Just how risky to entrepreneurs, staff and customers alike private ownership can be is starkly illustrated by the collapse of Allders. Philip Green's former chief executive at Bhs, Terry Green, a man determined to emulate his former boss and make his own personal fortune, came badly unstuck when he took over the chain in 2003 only for it to go bust in early 2005. Terry Green and hundreds of staff lost their jobs, and there was serious uncertainty about the future of the staff's pension rights. Although the chain was not in good shape when he took it over, he appeared to misjudge its problems, trying to do too much too quickly in the view of many observers.

The madness of crowds

Terry Green is hardly the first to come unstuck. Today's successful entrepreneurs can make more money then ever before, often by taking fewer financial risks than in the past. None of this means that the accumulation of big fortunes is free of risk or that all new entrepreneurial activity is productive. The newsagent Arundbhai Patel was estimated to have a fortune of £50 million in 1989, but the following year his company went into liquidation. Andy Campbell was awarded Glasgow Development Agency's Young Businessman of the Year as a result of his new computer games company, Red Lemon, which he co-founded in 1996. By 2000, Campbell was estimated to be worth £10 million by the *Sunday Times*. Two years later, the company went into liquidation. As he later told an interviewer, 'it's like Monopoly money. It's not tenners in your hand. You can be a paper millionaire but it could disappear tomorrow.'[41] And in his case it did.

Campbell was the victim of the much tougher market conditions that ensued at the turn of the twenty-first century. The FTSE 100 lost close to half its value between 2000 and 2003. Over the same period no fewer than 218 of the world's 476 billionaires saw their fortunes fall, while four former billionaires were wiped out completely.[42] Although the brunt of the falls were carried by technology and especially internet shares, others with extensive shareholdings also found their wealth dissipated.

Amongst the greatest losers from the crash were the new, mostly young internet entrepreneurs, many of whom lost their paper fortunes almost overnight. The rise of the internet entrepreneur was seen by some as a sign of the birth of a new enterprise culture in Britain. If so, it was both short lived and a harsh warning sign of the dangers of an unguarded rush for wealth. In the two years before the millennium, hundreds of small companies had been created to exploit what seemed at the time the unlimited potential to make big money out of the internet. The new entrepreneurs borrowed initially from friends and family to set up companies, often run from home, that offered sports goods, global fresh fruit, the best deals in last-minute holidays and even gambling, all on-line.

The owners were typically young, in their twenties and thirties, green when it came to business, brash and very ambitious. All hoped to become very rich. Most of them did for a short while, but few survived for long. Share values in Britain and across the globe had enjoyed the longest bull run in living memory. It could not last. Values peaked in March 2000 and then fell more or less continuously for three years. Those most heavily hit were shares in the new economy, the new internet, software and telecom companies that had sprung up during the technology revolution of the late 1990s. In 2000 there were sixty-two dotcom entrepreneurs in the *Sunday Times's* 1,000. By 2003 there were fourteen.

In 1999, 26-year-old Emma Edelson, supported by her father, Manchester United director Michael Edelson, set up Oxygen Holdings, an internet incubator designed to help entrepreneurial students start up their own businesses. Backed by some impressive names such as the media heiress Elisabeth Murdoch and her husband, the PR guru Matthew Freud, who both joined the board, the company was an instant hit. When the company came to market in February 2000, its share price rose an astonishing 2,775 per cent. At its peak in those heady early months of 2000, Oxygen was valued at £240 million. But the success was short lived. Within months its share price had collapsed from 60 to 2 pence.

Beenz.com was a loyalty programme awarding internet users points across websites that had signed up. Before long, its thirty-year-old founder, Charles Cohen, had a company worth £200 million and employed 300 staff. As the internet boom started to falter so did Beenz, whose clients were other internet companies. According to Cohen, 'our market just dissolved. We would sign contracts with a company on a Friday and call them on Monday only to find they had gone into liquidation.'[43]

Of course, there have been other similar investment crazes and wild overvaluations of equities before – the South Sea Bubble and the great railway boom and bust of the 1840s, for example – and on most occasions stimulated too by new industrial or technological breakthroughs. But this one was different for two main reasons. First was the sheer scale of the inflation involved. Many companies saw their value rise a thousand, even two thousand times, only to collapse back to virtually nothing when the bust came. The frenzy created hundreds of dotcom millionaires and multi-millionaires but most of this was paper wealth that lasted mostly only for a matter of months.

The second reason was the element of mass participation. The boom was promoted by venture capitalists and bankers, who, in search of quick returns and bonuses, seemed willing to fund half-baked business plans and untried managements. They were soon joined by PR firms, brokers and financial advisers, who wanted part of the action and started to believe their own hype that information technology would cut costs and fatten profits on a permanent basis. Swept along by the feverish over-marketing and the short-term gains being made, more and more jumped onto the bandwagon while more and more speculative money poured in. Savers – large and small alike

– also poured money into the new technology and internet funds, which followed the same pattern – first up and then down.

At the time at least some knew that it was a fantasy. Borrowing from a similar wording from Alan Greenspan in 1996, the Yale economist Robert Shiller had warned early in 2000 that such 'irrational exuberance born out of herds, hype and triumphalism' could not last.[44] Charles Kindleberger, in his book *Mania, Panics and Crashes*, describes the process leading to the bursting of a financial bubble: 'At a late stage, speculation tends to detach itself from really valuable objects and turn to delusive ones. A larger and larger group of people seeks to become rich without a real understanding of the processes involved.'[45] As far back as 1852, the British writer George Mackay had put it more bluntly in his own prescient book on market bubbles, which he called *Extraordinary Popular Delusions and the Madness of Crowds*. He observed: 'Men, it has been well said, think in herds. It will be seen that they go mad in herds, while they only recover their senses one by one.'

Some rode the storm better than others. Scores of companies crashed in spectacular style. Some owners were astute, or lucky, enough to sell out just in time. Sports Internet, a site providing sports news and on-line betting, was sold by its owners, Chris Akers and partner Peter Wilkinson, to BSkyB for £301 million in the summer of 2000. The timing was impeccable. Just days later, the technology market imploded. The owners netted £15 million. Wilkinson came up with the idea for Freeserve, the internet provider, built another fortune through internet services and was placed at number 182 in the 2005 *Sunday Times* list with a fortune of £269 million. Some of those that just survived, such as lastminute.com, run by its high-profile founder Brent Hoberman, eventually bounced back.

Some internet sites at the time, such as dotcomfailures.com and FuckedCompany.com, were set up apparently merely to wallow in the carnage and to predict the next dotcom demise. Most of the internet pioneers, from those who lost it all to those who made it through the storm, today take a more circumspect view of their experience. The phrase 'no God-given right to make money' seems to sum it up well.[46] Some saw the slump as less of a rerun of the 1929 crash than the modern telecom equivalent of the railway mania of 150 years before. The fear that the crash would lead to a full-blown recession on the 1930s scale never materialised, partly because politicians and central bankers had learned the lessons of 1929 and partly because consumers carried on buying and borrowing.

March 2000 was a painful experience for those jumping on the new entrepreneurial bandwagon. It demonstrated all too clearly that enterprise can be a risky venture. Modern business is not always so risky, however. Amongst those who have ensured that joining the multi-millionaire ranks is a largely one-way bet are the managers running large public companies.

4

Because I'm worth it

If you pay peanuts, you get monkeys.

(Jean-Pierre Garnier, chief executive, GlaxoSmithKline)

In recent years, a new phenomenon has been breaking out in British boardrooms. Directors of plcs have been becoming less than enamoured with their lot. They are finding it tougher to find top boardroom talent, they are subject to too many regulations, they are too closely scrutinised. 'Running M&S is like living in a goldfish bowl, only less peaceful,' howled one senior retail executive.[1] One of the subjects they like to protest about is their pay. Many are said to watch with envy at entrepreneurs running private companies who have been climbing the wealth ladder with little of the public attention or disapproval that plc bosses sometimes face. Sir Digby Jones, director general of the CBI, has spoken of the fear that 'talented management will find the world of private equity more attractive than the constantly critical, often unfair and less well-paid world of the listed company'.[2]

Chairmen and chief executives of top British public companies may find themselves lower in the wealth pecking order than some of those who have chosen the private company route, but on pay they have little cause for complaint. Indeed, in the last few years, boardroom pay has been escalating at an unprecedented rate. In the four years from the millennium, the pay, including bonuses and long-term incentive plans, of top executives at the UK's biggest companies more than doubled. Over the same period, the FTSE 100 index fell by around a third while average earnings increased by only 13 per cent. A total of 230 directors of FTSE 100 companies were paid more than £1 million in 2004, up from 130 in 2001. In 2004, the average remuneration of a top 100 chief executive was £2.5 million – some 113 times that of an average UK worker.[3] Twenty years earlier it had been less than twenty-five times as high.

And then there are the perks. A typical package would include a chauffeur-driven car, a team of secretaries, free lunches, complimentary tickets to Wimbledon, Lord's and Ascot, a free London pied-à-terre, pension arrangements that guarantee a more than comfortable retirement and access to the company jet.

Top boardroom executives have not only hit the jackpot on pay and perks. There's also the 'signing-on' fee and the 'golden goodbye'. Generous football-style joining fees are now routine. When Stuart Rose was rapidly hired as chief executive of Marks and Spencer in 2004 to fight off the takeover bid from Philip Green, he was paid a fee of more than £1 million just to put his foot in the door, even though he was unemployed at the time, and would almost certainly have taken the job without one. Signing-on fees of £1 million or more at top 100 companies are now commonplace.

It also pays to get fired. While Rose was arriving through the front door at M&S, those forced out by the boardroom coup that brought him in – Luc Vandevelde and Roger Holmes – banked more than £2 million between them. In 2003, Michael Green, the former chairman of Carlton, topped the league for 'golden goodbyes' with a pay-off of £1.79 million. He also received highly controversial long-term incentive payments of £6 million. Both came at the end of a year in which Carlton shareholders had campaigned for his exit following a series of expensive blunders. The former chairman of the company's remuneration committee insisted that the payment had to be made as a 'matter of law, not of fairness'.

Amongst the most controversial of recent pay-offs was that of Brian Gilbertson, chief executive of the mining company BHP Billiton. In 2003, Gilbertson was ousted after an internal boardroom row, and walked off with £9 million in pay, bonuses and a golden handshake, even though he was at the company for a mere six months. During 2002/3, ten executives received pay-offs of more than £1 million after they quit or were pushed. As one cynic has described the process, if you get a huge sum to join and then another huge sum to leave, you hardly need to make much money in between.

Getting to the top of a FTSE 100 company may not get you into the billionaire camp, which is still largely the preserve of entrepreneurs and aristocratic landowners, but it certainly guarantees you multi-millionaire status and with a much lower level of personal risk than that faced by entrepreneurs trying to build a business. Indeed for the great majority of corporate bosses, the risk is close to zero. Climbing up the corporate ladder can also bring a near-tycoon lifestyle. In his short career at the top of retail, Rose has accumulated a fortune in excess of £30 million, all in the space of a handful of years. Rose is a man who likes the good life and is a regular at celebrity restaurants such as the Ivy and Mayfair clubs like Harry's Bar. For leisure he owns a private plane, a Rockwell Commander, a fast, single-engined four-seater that he takes over to France for lunch. He enjoys an extensive rare wine collection, owns a house in Suffolk and an apartment in Mayfair and even before he joined M&S had a personal chauffeur. Once described as a 'corporate James Bond', he is rarely to be seen in anything other than a £2,000-plus Savile Row suit.

His accumulated wealth has come from a series of pay-offs from his early jobs at Burton, Argos and Booker and then from the windfall options he received when, as chief executive, he sold Arcadia to Philip Green in 2002. During the course of the negotiations, Green sang 'If I Were a Rich Man' over the phone to Rose, his way of joking that Rose stood to make a small fortune if the deal went through. Indeed, the deal left him some £25 million better off. He had been at Arcadia for two years. To be fair to him, he is not one of those to complain unduly about his lot.

The 'one-way road'

The increasingly explosive question of corporate pay first started to stoke public interest in the mid-1980s when Richard Giordiano, then the chief executive of the industrial gases company BOC, became the first director to receive a £1 million salary. But Giordiano was American, and American directors expected to be paid more. In 1987, Ralph Halpern, chairman of the Burton Group, was forced by public outcry to cut the level of share options he awarded himself from £8 million to £2 million. As 'greedy bosses' increasingly provided great headlines, newspaper coverage forced the BT chairman, Iain Vallance, to give a mid-recession bonus of £150,000 to charity in 1991.

Three years later, the question of corporate greed exploded into the headlines again when the directors of newly privatised industries such as Cedric Brown, the chief executive of British Gas, started to award themselves great hikes in pay. The privatisation of the utilities from telecommunications and gas to water and electricity was to provide a remarkable bonanza for their directors. When a number of them appeared before the House of Commons Employment Committee in 1995, their defence was that they deserved the increases because they had delivered. The reality, of course, was that as monopolies they had to do little more than they did before they were privatised. Even John Major was driven to describe their pay and share packages as 'distasteful'. Sir Charles Powell, Margaret Thatcher's foreign policy private secretary, who became a director of Trafalgar House, was scathing: 'They have not had to be entrepreneurs, but just to tighten the screws and reduce the costs. It is a one-way road.'[4]

Such was the growing outcry about corporate excess that no fewer than three separate committees were set up to examine the issue in an attempt to defuse the ongoing rows. First, in 1992, Sir Adrian Cadbury, chairman of Cadbury-Schweppes, was appointed by the London Stock Exchange following the concern over a number of serious financial collapses including Asil Nadir's Polly Peck and the Bank of Credit and Commerce International. Cadbury published a code of practice, which included a provision that the remuneration of directors be set by independent non-executive directors. Non-executives are part-timers, usually working up to ten days a year, who hold no actual executive or management function in the company. Independent of executive responsibility, they are there, at least in part, to ensure good practice on pay, accountancy and governance.

Then, in January 1995, with mounting public disquiet, the CBI set up a special committee to examine executive pay under Sir Richard Greenbury, the head of Marks and Spencer. The Cadbury recommendations had done little to quell the critics, who now hoped that shareholders would be given more muscle to intervene. It was not to be. Although the Greenbury report tightened the rules governing disclosure, requiring individual salaries to be declared, for example, it otherwise did little to improve on Cadbury. The corporate world retained its broad licence to do more or less what it wanted. While still sitting, Greenbury allowed his own pay to rise from £779,188 to £903,900.[5]

Three years later, yet another committee, under the chairmanship of Ronald Hampel, chairman of ICI, produced a new consolidated code. Thus the voluntary codes governing remuneration and drawn up by industry insiders were slightly tightened throughout the 1990s. Even the sternest of critics accepted that these had led to some improvements including the disclosure of directors' remuneration deals in annual reports. It was indeed the changed rules on disclosure that opened up the books and brought the revelations on pay and perks that were so eagerly seized on by the press.

Few disagree that business success deserves to be rewarded. Most of the rows about pay reflect the fact that, in determining remuneration, performance is mostly an irrelevance, with pay reflecting the stranglehold of directors, rather than their skill and contribution. In 2004, for example, the second highest-paid boardroom in Britain was Tesco's, whose members together took home some £31 million. Tesco is, of course, a highly successful British company, but this pay-out was 70 per cent more than that awarded to BP's board, an equally successful company that is five times as big and makes four times as much profit. In 2005, a new chief executive of Burberry was appointed on a salary (£15 million over three years) that outstripped that of much larger companies such as British Airways and Rolls-Royce. As the *Guardian* summed it up, 'the inescapable conclusion is that logic doesn't apply to boardroom pay'.[6]

In 2002, the Labour government made a rare intervention in the field by ruling that companies should, for the first time, publish an annual report on directors' pay and put it to an advisory vote at the company AGM, a move that led to a spate of shareholder protests. One of the most prominent took place at the AGM of the pharmaceutical giant GlaxoSmithKline (GSK), held at the Queen Elizabeth II Conference Centre in central London in May 2003.

While company AGMs are usually formal and self-congratulatory events with anodyne speeches and luxury biscuits, this one boiled over in acrimony, with shareholders and directors locked in bitter battle over the company's policy towards the pay of its US-based chief executive, Jean-Pierre Garnier. The stage had been set for a show-down at GSK – Britain's third largest company – when the Association of British Insurers (ABI) issued a 'red code' to its report on the remuneration policy of the company. The ABI represents the big insurance companies, which together control about a quarter of the stock market, and makes recommendations to shareholders. A red code is direct advice to shareholders that they should vote against the pay policy at the AGM. The row was not so much about Garnier's actual pay, a pretty generous £3.6 million nonetheless, but more about the promise of £22 million if he were fired.

No less than 51 per cent of shareholders voted against the deal, and a further 10 per cent abstained. Never before had shareholders voted so decisively against company policy. The day after the revolt, a clearly riled Garnier, who lives in Philadelphia rather than the UK, where GSK is based, responded, 'I'm not Mother Teresa. This is a very competitive business.' And two months later he complained that he was 'pretty much at the bottom of the pile' in terms of pay. This is not strictly true. Yes, Garnier was not the highest-paid executive in Britain at the time. Nevertheless, according to one survey, he was eleventh on the list of best-paid chief executives in 2002 and had risen to third place by 2004.[7]

The shareholder protests against Garnier and GSK are far from unique. Escalating boardroom pay since the stock market crash had been causing rising anger for some years amongst institutional investors, the primary owners of the companies, who had been forced to witness what seemed like undeserved and gratuitous rewards at a time when the value of their investments had been plummeting. Shareholders grew increasingly concerned that under-performing chief executives could still award themselves staggeringly generous deals even when their corporate strategies appeared to be failing. Yet they were largely powerless to prevent it.

From the spring of 2003, the institutional shareholders, led by the ABI and the National Association of Pension Funds, took advantage of their new powers to launch an unprecedented collective protest against company pay policies. In that year, the ABI produced eighty-five reports on companies' annual performance. Thirteen of them were coded red, an indication of serious concern about corporate governance at the companies. Another thirty were coded amber. Key concerns related to the weak qualifying targets set for share options and other performance pay-outs and the lack of independence amongst the non-executive members. As a result of these warnings, more than twenty companies endured protest votes in excess of 20 per cent against their remuneration reports. Prior to 2003, most resolutions at annual meetings tended to do little more than ratify company recommendations.[8]

Rows about pay are not unique to FTSE 100 companies. In 2005, Lord Hollick, the Labour peer and party fundraiser who had in the early 1990s arranged for senior staff to be paid bonuses in gold bars as a perfectly legal tax avoidance measure, found himself embroiled in a high-profile spat while chief executive of United Business Media, the company he had founded.[9] Hollick wanted to pay himself a special £250,000 bonus merely for arranging a smooth handover to his successor, as if this was not part of his normal job. The decision led to uproar amongst the company's shareholders and, with three-quarters voting against the bonus, Hollick was forced into a humiliating climbdown and eventually paid the money back.

Defying gravity

British chief executives have been taking their cue from across the Atlantic. Indeed, it is recent corporate practice in the United States that has been one of the most decisive influences behind corporate pay inflation in Britain. Pay rates at the top may have been surging in Britain but, at least until recently, not as much as in the United States. In 1980, chief executive pay packages stood at forty-two times average pay in 1980. By 1990, the ratio had risen to eighty-five. But, during the 1990s, pay went into overdrive, so that, by 2000, chief executives were earning some 530 times the average.[10]

During the 1990s, the United States, along with the rest of the world, had seen one of the longest stock market bull runs in history. As the apparently resurgent US economy seemed to defy the laws of the business cycle, some economists and political leaders talked of a new economic paradigm as if the world had changed forever and company chief executives started to be treated as superheroes. In 1980, only one issue of *Business Week* featured a chief executive on its cover. In 1999, the number was nineteen. Few turned an eye as the executives started to translate that new public reverence into personal reward, and at a staggering rate.

Central to these rises was the dramatic expansion of the stock option, which at first was seen as a way of linking the interests of owners and managers by setting a new objective of maximising the share value of the firm. Stock options operate by giving an executive the right to buy a given amount of stock at a certain price at a later date. The rise of the stock option and what became known as the new goal of 'shareholder value' had a dramatic effect on the way executives ran companies. The most effective way of upping the share price, at least in the short term, was by 'downsizing' and the 1990s saw huge lay-offs of staff. 'By 1993, it was clear that the quickest way to add 5 points to your stock price was to lay off 50,000 workers.'[11] By 2001, more than half of America's top 200 chief executives had 'mega-options', which by now had grown to an average value of more than $50 million. As a result, executives were able to build personal fortunes on a scale previously enjoyed only by top entrepreneurs.

Nobody worried too much about the astonishing hike in rewards during the long boom of the 1990s. But as the decade progressed, evidence of abuse started to emerge. Many companies began to re-price their senior executive's stock options at a lower level when the stock price fell. As one commentator put it, 'it is hard to think of a better example of what is wrong with corporate

America. When the firm's stock price does well, the people in charge make out like lottery winners. When it plummets, they get another set of chances to win.'[12] Graef Crystal, a former executive pay consultant and author of the book *In Search of Success: The Overcompensation of American Executives,* called the process of combining a volatile stock market with the re-pricing of options the creation 'of a money machine, an antigravity device which guarantees that the senior executives will get super-rich'. Joseph Stiglitz, the Nobel prize-winning economist, was even more direct: 'In less polite circles, we might speak of stock options as corporate theft – executives stealing money from their unwary shareholders.'[13]

Stock options soon started to operate in a perverse way, giving misleading signals to investors about the true condition of the company and working against long-run strength. 'More and more firms were resorting to accounting skulduggery, exaggerating their revenues and understating their costs.'[14] Indeed, it is likely that the profits boom that had fuelled the continuing bull market in stocks had, for many companies, peaked in the late 1990s and that firms had been inflating their revenue figures to hide it. In many ways, the much vaunted economic miracle was more con-trick than miracle.

Nevertheless, this 'orgy of self-enrichment', as one critic called it, suited the climate of the times.[15] With the deregulation of financial markets during the Reagan era, what checks and balances were in place were diluted. Malpractice should have been spotted and thwarted by the army of professional auditors, accountants and non-executive directors whose role it was to act as informal regulators. But being signed up themselves to lucrative deals, these organisations and individuals had an interest in keeping the myth going.

The interests of non-executives and executives were often closely aligned in the 1990s. In many if not most cases, company directors were appointed directly by the chief executive and were often close friends. It is said that the reason Michael Eisner, chief executive of Disney, was so well paid was because 'the 16-man board includes his personal attorney, an architect who designed his house, the president of a university to which he donated funds, the head of the school attended by the Eisner children, two former Disney executives and a former senator who was consultant to the company'.[16] In many companies non-executives had stock options as lucrative as those held by executives.

The laxity was to end in disaster for American business. In the autumn of

2001 Enron, the energy-trading giant, went bankrupt. Some 10,000 employees lost their jobs and their health care and pension arrangements along with them while investors lost millions after revelations that the company had been fraudulently hiding debt and losses worth billions of dollars from their accounts.

At its height Enron was America's seventh largest company. But it had got there through the use of clever creative accounting, or, put another way, corporate fraud. With the apparent connivance of its auditing firm, another top American company, Arthur Andersen, it had been hiding debts offshore and inflating its profits through a series of fake transactions. Arthur Andersen's responsibility, as the company's independent auditor, was to spot and prevent such malpractice, a responsibility it failed to exercise. When the rigging of the accounts started to become apparent, Enron collapsed in dramatic fashion.

Enron was just the start. A few months later came WorldCom, the American telecom giant, found to be up to very similar accountancy tricks. They had classed $9 billion of dollars in basic expenditure on items such as paying other telephone companies for connecting calls as capital investment. By this ruse, they could record it as depreciation and so inflate their profit figures. During 2002, household names collapsed one after another. Senior executives from several of the disgraced firms were led in handcuffs from the courts and paraded across television and newspapers. Arthur Andersen, one of the world's five biggest accountancy firms, was also brought to its knees by the scandal.

As companies were exposed, so were their bosses. The former head of the conglomerate Tyco, Dennis Kozlowski, was renowned for lavish spending on the company account, treating his job as one giant perk. Remarkable too was the fact that, as these bankrupt companies were heading for disaster, their bosses continued to enrich themselves. Kenneth Lay, the founder and chief executive of Enron, quietly exercised his stock options shortly before the company collapsed, bringing him more than $200 million. Gary Winnick, chairman of the communications company Global Crossing, the international fibre optic network operator, sold shares worth a staggering $734 million just before the company went under. These once publicly feted men – dubbed the 'barons of bankruptcy' by the *Financial Times* – were lining their pockets in full awareness that their employees and small investors were about to be stuffed.[17] While lucrative deals may sometimes have been the just reward for success, these were unambiguously rewards for failure, and colossal ones at that. One critic described the cashing in of share options at the time as a 'titanic redistribution of wealth achieved by corporate leaders'.[18]

Business America had been caught with its pants down. The scandals of the late 1990s outdid even those of 1980s Wall Street, a decade of high-level fraud, insider dealing and tax evasion. In the 1980s, it is arguable that at least some of the personal fortunes generated by restructuring activity involved a degree of necessary economic reorganisation. Greed may have driven the process, but some, if not all, of the upheaval made industry leaner and was thus in the interests of shareholders. The exploding self-interest of the next decade had no such defence. The self-enrichment of leading chief executives was almost universally damaging to the firm, the shareholders, the staff and the economy. It led firms to ruin, and impoverished employees and small shareholders alike. Those behind the scandals had come to believe that they were untouchable, that they were somehow above the law.

The scale of the scandals had a dramatic impact in the United States and across the globe. They probably delayed American and thus world economic recovery. Anger and revulsion mounted against high-profile executives such as Bernie Ebbers, chief executive of WorldCom, and Kozlowski, both of whom were subsequently convicted of high-level fraud and larceny and given long gaol sentences. Addressing the Senate Banking Committee, Alan Greenspan said that 'an infectious greed seemed to grip much of our business community'. By 2005, there had been almost 500 indictments and 317 convictions for fraud ranging from illegal manipulation of the balance sheets to artificially improve performance, as at Enron, to the use of companies as personal piggy banks, as in the case of Kozlowski.

There are striking earlier parallels. 'Self-dealing', the practice of making oneself rich at the expense of others, was at the roots of most of the scandals of the Gilded Age in nineteenth-century America, when companies, especially railways, used to siphon off the money of outside investors. After the 1929 crash, leading Wall Street figures were routinely humiliated in court and ridiculed in Congress, accused of widespread insider dealing, stock price manipulation and diversion of funds for personal use.

The crackdown on Wall Street following the Great Crash had introduced a whole raft of new and tougher regulations on corporate freedom, on banks and on stock-trading rules. In the 1990s, many of the controls introduced in the 1930s had been dismantled or weakened. But, as the evidence of extensive financial chicanery emerged, President Bush was forced to introduce a whole new swathe of tougher government regulations. Congress passed a controversial new law that increased the penalties for fraud, required greater independence of corporate directors and introduced a new regulatory board to discipline rogue accountants. Chief executives were forced to personally vouch for the accuracy of their accounts.

It might have been thought that the outcry and subsequent legal crackdown, together with the wider call for greater moderation, would have caused US corporate bosses to rein themselves in. But it was not to be. Evidence of self-serving business dealing has continued to emerge. In 2005, the FBI revealed that it was working on more than 400 cases of fraud, twice the number in 2003. As one top psychologist explained, some high-flying entrepreneurs develop a sense of superiority bordering on narcissism that seems to encourage them to 'usurp special privileges and extra resources that they feel they have an entitlement to over and above ordinary people'.[19]

While many top salaries stabilised between 2000 and 2003, and fewer monster stock options were granted, they have been replaced with other, equally lucrative, forms of reward from escalating cash bonuses to crediting pension plans with years of unserved 'service'.[20]

In March 2004, Warren Buffett, a stern critic of excess rewards, launched a stinging attack on continued 'corporate greed' in the United States. Writing in his famous annual letter to shareholders, Buffett said, 'In judging whether corporate America is serious about reforming itself, CEO pay remains the acid test. To date, the results aren't encouraging.' One example of the return of lavish deals was the $113 million paid in 2005 to Philip Purcell, the boss forced out of the under-performing Wall Street bank Morgan Stanley. His replacement was given a 'golden hello' worth $77 million. At Hewlett-Packard, the former chief executive walked off with a $42 million pay-off after being forced to resign while her replacement walked in with a $20 million golden hello and a $22 million annual salary. The boss of Pfizer will receive an annual pension of $6.5 million after he retires. Enron may have been 'the private sector's Watergate' but it has not stopped the bandwagon.

The 'ethical vacuum space'

The criminality exposed after 2000 was not confined to corporations. Also engulfed were a number of high-profile investment banks, several of which were found to have been deliberately promoting technology stocks, knowing them to be over-valued. In its issue of 14 May 2001, *Fortune* magazine carried a picture of Mary Meeker on its cover with the headline 'Can we ever trust Wall Street again?' The magazine accused Meeker, a 'superstar' stock analyst with Morgan Stanley and a strong advocate of online commerce, of compromising her position as a stock picker to win investment banking business for her firm.[21] Henry Blodget, an internet stock analyst at Merrill Lynch and one of the most enthusiastic promoters of dotcom shares, continued to make wild predictions of future share values of companies such as Amazon to clients even when the bubble was at its most overblown. He was later revealed to have described the very stocks he was promoting as 'junk' and 'crap' in internal e-mails. Blodget was paid $12 million in 2001. In 2003, he was fined $4 million and banned for life from the securities industry. Merrill Lynch was revealed to have urged Blodget on.[22]

What had been exposed was that much of the equities research establishment was talking up companies as long as they put juicy investment banking contracts their way. Wall Street firms were in effect touting tech stocks without revealing that they were collecting investment banking fees for selling them. Few of the Wall Street giants appeared to be giving objective advice. Ten major financial houses, from Goldman Sachs to Lehman Brothers, paid fines collectively of $1.4 billion imposed by the US regulators for feeding misleading stock market research to investors to drum up business and fees.[23]

This is hardly the only dubious and exploitative practice adopted by the world's giant and powerful financial services industry, one often characterised by even higher rewards than those found in corporations. At a US Senate hearing into abusive trading practices in 2003, one Republican senator from Illinois described the American mutual fund industry as 'the world's largest skimming operation'. He went on to describe the $7 trillion business as a 'trough from which fund managers, brokers and other insiders are steadily siphoning off an excessive slice of the nation's household, college and retirement savings'. He was referring to a range of abuses, including illegal trading, in which some favoured professional clients were being given special treatment at the expense of ordinary investors, failures to give entitled discounts and mis-selling.

Excessive fees are common. One former British banker has described the financial services industry as 'bloated and parasitic'. An oligopoly controlled by a handful of giant firms, the Square Mile can and does impose fat margins. The fees charged by the industry are known as 'the croupier's take' and overcharging is arguably widespread. One estimate of the take suggests that between 1984 and 2000, the average return for mutual fund investors in the United States was around 5 per cent per annum against an overall market return of more than 16 per cent. 'In other words, during the greatest ever bull market, a combination of the croupier's take and poor investment decisions cost the mutual fund investor more than eleven per cent a year in lost returns.'[24] Similar differences would be found in the UK. The *Evening Standard*'s City editor, Anthony Hilton, described the runaway profits and salaries that are the norm in investment banking as 'perhaps the biggest case of market failure the world has ever seen'.[25]

In his classic book *The Great Crash, 1929*, J. K. Galbraith referred to the way in which wealth is siphoned off in this way as a form of 'undiscovered embezzlement', which he shortened to 'the bezzle'. Galbraith argued that the bezzle grows during boom times like the 1920s, when the losers don't notice, and gets exposed during the crash, when they do. Or as Warren Buffett, the billionaire chairman of Berkshire Hathaway, put it, it is only when the tide goes out that you find out who's been swimming naked. Galbraith's analysis was especially apposite to the 1990s, when a large group of top executives were enriching themselves at the expense of unsuspecting shareholders and eventually staff.

In 2005, a former senior director at Schroders, Philip Augar, wrote a damning indictment of financial services in a book called *The Greed Merchants*.[26] He argued that over the previous twenty years, the investment banking industry based in New York and the City of London had effectively creamed off some £100 billion by rigging the capital markets for the benefit of their shareholders and employees, often one and the same. Augar tried, in effect, to put a figure on the scale of the 'bezzle' that was perpetrated in the 1990s. If he is right it has certainly been a monumental redistribution of wealth. It is this that has been behind the lavish and excessive earnings enjoyed by investment bankers, especially those at the top – a position Augar once held himself. The bankers have been involved less in the business of creating value than of transferring existing wealth to themselves. Although Augar stopped short of accusing the banks of operating an explicit cartel, he argued that they were in effect colluding in practices that enable them to maintain supernormal profits at the expense of their customers – mostly savers and pensioners. As Augar put it, 'the investment banks slipped easily into the role of Greed Merchants, trading greed and taking their own turn on the way'.

In *Den of Thieves*, a book on the remarkable excesses of Wall Street during the 1980s, James Stewart headed his first section 'Above the Law', a reference to a kind of condoned corporate delinquency, of how the perpetrators of the criminal fraud of the times believed they could not be caught and could not be prosecuted.[27] Little seemed to have really changed in the subsequent decade. Paul O'Neill, US Treasury Secretary in 2002, recalled a parade of Wall Street professionals coming to see him when he was in corporate management with plans for 'new and exotic' financial ways of reducing company tax or reporting debt in ways 'not clearly prohibited by the tax code or law' but hardly designed to illuminate corporate operations either. The result, he claimed, was 'an ethical vacuum space'. Any moral compass that might have been present in the past in the way business and corporate leaders took their decisions seems to have long been despatched in the new and modern rush for personal enrichment. As Paul Volcker, the former chairman of the Federal Reserve Board, put it, 'corporate greed exploded beyond anything that could have been imagined in 1990. Traditional norms didn't exist. You had this whole culture where the only sign of worth was how much money you made.'[28]

The big US investment banks, which were caught red handed when they were fined more than £1 billion for their role in encouraging the dotcom bubble, may have been at the heart of the malpractices. But their British equivalents can hardly claim innocence. Even though it was US banks that were caught, Hector Sants, a former investment banker who now works for the UK's Financial Services Authority (FSA), is quoted in *The Greed Merchants*: 'Even in the UK there was evidence of systematic bias in analyst recommendations, poor management of conflicts of interest . . . I'm not sure that the UK industry could put hand on heart and say in 2002 there was an inherently better conflict management culture here than in New York.'[29]

The British backwash

Britain has not suffered scandals on the Enron and WorldCom scale, but hardly has an unblemished corporate record. The late 1980s and early 1990s were years of high sleaze. The Conservative Party had been found to be heavily funded by a group of foreign businessmen implicated in criminal tax evasion, insider dealing and fraud. They included the Turkish Cypriot tycoon Asil Nadir and the ex-chairman of Nissan UK, Octav Botnar. In

1990, three senior financiers and businessmen, including Ernest Saunders, the chairman of Guinness, were gaoled for highly complex insider dealing. In the early 1990s, the Mirror Group pensioners faced huge losses as a result of fraud perpetuated by the group's owner, Robert Maxwell. Those who have been caught are likely to be only the tip of the iceberg. According to a report by the Association of Certified Fraud Examiners in 2005, UK companies are estimated to be losing 6 per cent of their annual revenue to fraud and corruption, the equivalent of some £72 billion a year, most of it undetected. Typical examples include overstating profits, setting up complex accounting schemes that involve siphoning money into offshore accounts and a range of elaborate cover-ups.

There is also no shortage of examples of unethical, inappropriate and exploitative corporate behaviour, mostly driven by an obsession with becoming rich, and richer than their peers. The collapse of Marconi, once one of Britain's industrial success stories, is a classic example of the dangers of corporate mismanagement and rashness, of the growing pursuit of 'jam today'. In 1996, a new chief executive, George Simpson, inherited GEC from the industrialist Lord Weinstock, who had built it into a remarkably successful company. In an unnecessary attempt at aggrandisement, Simpson broke up the company by selling off the arms factories to British Aerospace, renaming the company Marconi and reinvesting in American tele-communications companies. It was a fatal error. When the telecom boom collapsed, the new investments had become worthless. The former giant company was ruined, there were mass lay-offs and Simpson, who was one of the first batch of businessmen to be made a peer by Tony Blair, left quickly with the usual controversial pay-off.

It was a failure of the banks, the directors and the institutional investors. The Marconi executives had 'inherited a successful company with a cash pile of over £2 billion and embarked on an extravagant spending spree that left it facing bankruptcy. They left with handsome severance payments. The shareholders have been ruined.'[30] Twenty years ago GEC was Britain's third largest company. In 2005, Marconi was sold to Ericsson of Sweden for £1.2 billion. It was a company effectively destroyed from within by a failed gamble to cash in on the telecommunications boom, while those responsible simply baled out. ICI, another of Britain's leading manufacturing companies at the beginning of the 1990s, has also been wrecked by a failed acquisition-led strategy. Both Marconi and ICI are illustrations of the effect of the dominance of the City, of the new 'deal-driven culture', of the risks of being in hock to fund managers interested in little more than the fast buck. Investment bankers in search of fat fees must take a large share of the blame for their collapses.

For a decade and longer, a large number of major banks and insurance companies have engaged in the over-promotion of financial products from endowment mortgages to private pension funds that have often been totally unsuitable for the clients targeted. The result has been a massive financial bonanza for the companies and some of their over-zealous and commission-driven sales staff at the expense of those often unwittingly buying the products. In the 1980s, the home income plan scandal left thousands of elderly people in financial difficulties after they were persuaded to re-mortgage their homes to invest in bonds that failed. In the same decade, the mighty Prudential sold 870,000 personal pensions. In 1990, the financial regulator found that as many as nine out of ten of them were based on incorrect or misleading advice. Despite this, the company dragged its feet for years in dealing with the compensation required and was later firmly condemned again by the regulator's successor, the FSA. 'The FSA is satisfied that Prudential Assurance's conduct has fallen substantially below the standards the public have a right to expect from a regulated firm.'[31]

The Pru was hardly alone. Most if not all of the giant insurance companies have been involved in some way or another with financial misselling to boost profits and thus their directors' pay. Lord Joffe, former head of Allied Dunbar, once known in the trade as 'Allied Crowbar' for its aggressive selling tactics, is one of the architects of modern insurance industry practice. He later experienced a Damascus-style conversion, exposing many of the life industry's more dubious practices: 'It is the life insurance industry itself which has, by its unprincipled disregard for the interests of the public, earned its present appalling reputation.'[32]

Despite the negative publicity and the critical reports, the financial industry has continued to look for ways in which it can make a killing through unwary customers. Indeed, unscrupulous behaviour continues to be endemic to the industry. In February 2004, Barclays Bank was accused of profiteering from customers who were encouraged to take out greatly over-priced 'add on' insurance on loans and mortgages, products that carried profit margins of as much as 70 per cent. The sales, it was claimed, brought the bank 'excess profits running into billions on this product alone'.[33]

In April 2005, a report from investment bank Credit Suisse First Boston highlighted the way in which a number of banks were profiteering from the promotion of optional, but controversial and often unsuitable, protection insurance for credit card and loan repayments. According to the report, these sales contributed a significant proportion – up to 20 per cent – of some banks' overall profits. A few months later, the charity Citizens Advice called the industry a '£5 billion protection racket'.[34] In 2005, the Office of Fair Trading estimated that British shoppers had been overcharged over £100 million a year because banks were charging excessively high fees on their credit cards, fees that were in effect an unmerited tax on shoppers. Just a year earlier, Matt Barrett, the chief executive of Barclays, had, in an extraordinary gaffe, admitted that he doesn't use a Barclaycard and urged his four children not to either because of the excessive interest rates it charged.

Because of the scale of mis-selling uncovered in the vast financial advice industry, it has become a common practice for some firms offering financial advice to file for bankruptcy largely to avoid paying mis-selling claims. In June 2005, the FSA revealed that eighteen firms had 'potentially' done this only to start up again a few weeks later, shorn of any mis-selling liabilities.

Insurance and banking are not the only industries with appalling records for fair dealing. In 2005, Dave Daley, the head of the National Association of Licensed House Managers, somewhat let the cat out of the bag about the ethics of his industry when he freely admitted, 'How we make our money is to make people binge drink: the more people drink, the more I get as a bonus.'[35] Question marks have long hung over British American Tobacco and whether it has been directly involved in international cigarette smuggling, a charge that it has always denied. In 2003–4, several senior Shell executives were dismissed following the discovery that the Anglo-Dutch company had been deliberately exaggerating its oil reserves for several years in order to maintain its share price. This was serious corporate deception on a grand scale, and in a firm that had developed a reputation for respectability. It is an example of what happens when short-term profits come to dominate all decisions and in which social and environmental concerns begin to count for little.

Blowing away the cobwebs

Throughout the stormy debates on pay, business ethics and performance, the Blair governments have proved largely passive bystanders. In opposition Tony Blair had exploited the growing storm over 'fat cat' pay deals and corporate abuse, but in power Labour has largely tiptoed round the issue, preferring to leave the industry to sort itself out. Eventually the government was forced to respond after the Tory MP and former Asda chairman Archie Norman sponsored a private member's Bill to prevent 'rewards for failure'. In an attempt to toughen up the rules of corporate governance, the government appointed Derek Higgs, a former investment banker, to examine how the role of non-executive directors could be strengthened to prevent accountancy scandals and boardroom abuse.

Company chief executives have mostly preferred non-executive directors to remain powerless. Tiny Rowland once famously described non-executive directors as 'just decorations on a Christmas tree'. Under the new codes introduced in the 1990s, directors' pay was meant to be set by remuneration committees consisting 'entirely of independent non-executive directors'. Yet remuneration committees have typically been packed with non-executives that are anything but independent.

They are typically dominated by former directors or chief executives of the company itself, or by current or retired chief executives or senior directors of other companies, people hardly in a position to rock the boat. The non-executive directors of the top 100 companies consist of around 700 people, a largely closed and self-appointed club, most of them drawn from a small and narrow group of industry insiders with very similar backgrounds, interests and views. Higgs, a semi-detached insider, and a serial non-executive himself, described the system as driven by 'a self-perpetuating tendency'. The result is entirely unsurprising. Executive directors sitting as non-executives on other company boards are hardly likely to bid pay down. In essence, high pay is as much the result of what one insider calls the 'mutual stroking of backs' as of performance.

Higgs reported in January 2003 with proposals that, if fully implemented, would have involved a considerable shake-up in the nature of corporate governance: 'blowing away the last cobwebs' from British boardrooms, as he put it. His proposals – to strengthen corporate accountability and switch the balance of power towards independent directors – went down like a lead balloon. His most radical proposal was to stop chairmen filling the board with old chums by insisting that they should not chair the nomination committee that appoints the non-executives.

Higgs was vilified. A litany of corporate leaders led the counter-attack. Sir Stanley Kalms, the former chairman of Dixons, described Higgs as 'a previously intelligent banker who has obviously been brainwashed'.[36] When

Higgs appeared bruised by the attacks on his proposals, one critic retorted that he deserved to be, that it was 'the price he pays for letting the Treasury write his report'.[37] The storm created by Higgs went on for months. Chief executives rowed with shareholders. The government itself was divided about how to tackle the mounting crisis in British boardrooms. The tabloid and broadsheet press kept the pressure up with one headline after another about fat cats, snouts in the trough and 'rewards for failure'. After six months of acrimony, in June 2003 the Department of Trade and Industry published a consultation document, *Rewards for Failure*, which included suggestions to limit pay-offs to directors of poorly performing firms.

Corporate bosses themselves began to fear that, if they failed to agree to at least some tougher rules, they would risk changes in company law. After more months of bitter wrangling behind the scenes, industry leaders finally agreed to a revised code, a much watered-down version of the original Higgs proposals. The dilution included the outright dropping of the proposal that chairmen should lose the right to appoint non-executive directors. Other proposals were softened, but two key proposals remained. First, to increase the number of non-executive directors from outside business by, as Higgs had put it, widening the 'gene-pool' of independent directors. The second was the 'comply or explain' clause in the new combined code. Under this, executives are now required to publicly disclose their reasons for deviating from the code's best-practice criteria.

Some observers sounded an optimistic note that the new code would temper boardroom excess. But the code is voluntary, business chiefs are proving reluctant to give up their power and rewards easily, there is a limit to how far institutional investors seem prepared to intervene and the government remains a reluctant interventionist. The issue of fat cat pay could be dealt with more effectively if the institutional fund managers themselves flexed their considerable muscles and told companies to cut out the excess. The reason they play it more softly is that, as one critic has put it, 'even the average fund manager is grotesquely overpaid for what he does by any objective standard, while the top people earn telephone number salaries. They do not, and will not make a fuss because they do not want the spotlight turned on them.'[38]

The early signs are that the flak and the reforms, as in the United States, have had little impact on eliminating excess and bringing pay into line with performance. Despite the new requirement to put pay schemes to share-holder votes and despite continuing shareholder rebellions, excessive remuneration and pay-outs for failure remain commonplace. In 2005, for example, bonuses totalling £807,000 were paid to executives of the Jarvis Group despite the company's share price crashing from 566p to 9.5p. A few months earlier, a bruising row had broken out at Sainsbury's over a lavish bonus of £2.4 million to the ousted under-performing chairman, Sir Peter Davis, despite the plunging profits and share price that he had delivered. 'If you want to get a sense of . . . why there is so much cynicism in Britain about fat-cat pay, look no further than the grotesque £2.4 million bonus awarded this week to Davis' is how the Lombard column in the *Financial Times* described it.

In the United States observers of the abuses that had characterised corporate America had started to talk of the lack of a 'shame gene', a phrase that British columnists now started to apply to Britain. As John Plender wrote in the *Financial Times*, 'the honourable course for Sir Peter would be to forgo his right to the shares and to negotiate a severance package that visibly falls short of pushing things to the limit.' He went on, 'I have a funny feeling his shame gene will prove elusive.'[39] Davis, who newspaper cartoonists liked to portray as 'Mr Greedy', apparently 'loved the trappings of wealth too well' to settle for a more modest pay-off.[40]

Ratchet, Ratchet and Ratchet

A few years ago a yawning gap existed between top executive salaries in Britain and the United States, but the gap has been closing in recent years, largely because, although the pace had slowed in the US, it had speeded up in the UK.[41]

Corporate bosses in the UK defend their rates and the closing gap on the grounds that they increasingly work in a global market for top managers, that competitive salaries are required to get and hang on to the best and to prevent the top talent moving abroad. But does such a global market really exist? For the most part, the explosion in executive salaries has been a largely Anglo-Saxon phenomenon.[42]

Despite the narrowing of the transatlantic pay gap, there is hardly a competitive global market. There is no evidence of a brain drain to the US. There is a rising, if still small, flow of executives at junior and middle levels between countries on the continent, but not at the highest level. There remains little demand for UK executives overseas; in fact, the traffic has largely been in the other direction, with a rising number of top chief executives in the UK being foreigners. The fact that top executive pay varies so much between countries is itself evidence that the so-called global market is pretty limited. There may be a market for a handful of exceptional leaders, but it is still common for a chief executive to be someone promoted from within the company.[43]

It may well be true that, in an age of fiercer competition, the job of the chief executive, like that of the Premiership football manager, has got trickier, but by how much is arguable. Senior executives will almost certainly work longer hours but then so will most middle-ranking professionals, from engineers to headteachers. Running a large international company undoubtedly requires rare skills, but the personal financial risks are not especially great. Contracts and rewards are structured in such a way that strategic mistakes are rarely if ever penalised. Most senior executives who lose their jobs as a result of internal restructuring or the arrival of a new chief executive have their contracts honoured in full.

The truth is that the claimed shortage of chief executives 'is something of a myth', as Graef Crystal has put it.[44] Pay will rise if demand rises or supply falls, but the number of large companies is, if anything, falling while the business schools are packed. As one observer has put it, 'it is not the invisible hand of the market that leads to these monumental executive incomes; it's the invisible handshake in the boardroom'.[45] That is, high-level cronyism. An artificial market has been created partly through the increasing use of executive search firms and remuneration consultants to find the right candidate and determine the salary package. The usual argument is that there are only so many good managers around and if you want them you have to outbid the competitors. This has fuelled the upward spiral.

In their recommendations, consultants rarely make comparisons with the 'average', only with the remuneration of a select 'peer group' at the top. This leads to the upward drift of the benchmarks. One American compensation consultant recalls a CEO asking him with a straight face if everyone in his industry was paid the 75th percentile.[46] The use of the upper quartile as a comparator is so commonplace that it is bound to ratchet up salaries irrespective of ability. As Peter Montagnon of the ABI put it, 'for too long now, companies have failed to act on the ratcheting up of pay that has resulted from comparative studies constantly pushing remuneration committees towards taking pay into a range above the average, thereby dragging the average ever upwards'.[47] In the United States,

Warren Buffett has dubbed remuneration consultants 'Ratchet, Ratchet and Ratchet'.

The 'ratchet effect' is fuelled too by the 'politics of envy'. Chief executives like to compare their lot, always unfavourably, with other highly paid groups, including some professionals working in management consultancy, the City or investment banking and, especially galling to some, Premiership footballers and pop stars. Many companies employ senior professionals who earn salaries in excess of £1 million. In 2004, HSBC's most senior bankers earned between £4 million and £13 million a year.[48] Corporate executives also like to point to the sums that can be earned by some fund managers and City professionals. No British chief executives came near the £26 million paid to Tim Shacklock, the former head of investment bank Dresdner Kleinwort Wasserstein, in 2002. Successful hedge fund managers can command salaries upwards of £10 million. In 2004, the private hedge fund firm London Diversified Fund Management paid £55 million to three directors. Evidence about what fund managers earn is not easy to come by, but it is certainly true that many private equity companies and fund management firms, especially those specialising in hedge funds, pay above corporate salaries, though the risks are usually much higher.

Another well-rehearsed defence for escalating rewards is that the right incentives at the top improve company and hence economic performance. Pay the bosses well and we will all benefit. Yet there is no evidence that firms are performing significantly and systematically better than they were in the more egalitarian 1950s and 1960s or in comparison with most of their European and Japanese counterparts. In Britain, the academic research has failed to demonstrate a clear relationship between pay and wider performance. In the early 1990s, several studies showed that the relationship between top directors' pay and shareholder returns was weak.[49] Furthermore, a study in 2000 by the management consultants Kepler Associates found an *inverse* relationship between pay and performance amongst the top 100 British companies. The ten worst-performing companies paid their bosses £175,000 a year more than the top ten performers. In a study of thirty different sectors, David Schwartz, the stock market historian, found that in 2003 the shares of companies run by the highest-paid executives in the sector mostly rose by less than the sector average. He concluded, 'There is no systematic benefit associated with paying executives above the odds.'[50]

One can take the comparison further. Top public sector managers, from the Governor of the Bank of England to the director general of the BBC, are paid much less without seeking to move. There are plenty of 'thin cats' running large companies in the FTSE 100 and 250, from the chief executive of Pizza Express to the head of pipeline manufacturer Rotork, who manage to deliver strong performance on pretty modest salaries compared with other bosses. The lowest paid FTSE 100 chief in 2003 was 77-year-old Antonio Luksic, the outgoing chairman of the family-run mining firm Antofagasta, who paid himself just £127,000. One chief executive said he would work for half his current pay if everybody else did.

The US evidence is also that hiring the most sought-after manager is no guarantee of success. 'We looked at 75 years of company data and never found the slightest correlation between executive compensation and company performance,' said Jim Collins, author of *Good to Great,* the result of a five-year study of 1,500 major American corporations. More than 90 per cent of the successful companies Collins analysed were led by executives promoted from within.[51] The evidence is that, although some highly talented individuals may well be able to make a real difference, more typically, most chief executives seem to have at best only a negligible impact on the performance of their companies. As the US business writer James Surowiecki has put it, 'corporate performance depends far more on what industry a company is in, what proprietary advantages it has and the general quality of its workforce, than it does on who's at the top'.[52] J. K. Galbraith had another explanation: 'The salary of the chief executive of the larger corporation is not a market award for achievement. It is frequently in the nature of a warm personal gesture by the individual to himself.'[53]

In 2000, the average reward of America's ten most highly paid CEOs was $154 million. Yet few of those ten have lasted even a few years. It could be argued that one of them, Jack Welsh of General Electric, had earned his salary if not his highly controversial and disguised retirement deal. Another on the list was Dennis Kozlowski of Tyco. Of the others, three have lasted little longer than they needed to cash in their stock options.[54]

In the United States, the emphasis on stock options created a perverse incentive for senior management to take measures that secured short-term share price gains rather than long-term performance. In Britain, 90 per cent of companies operate share option schemes, and similar doubts exist about their effectiveness as an appropriate incentive to long-term performance. The ABI have certainly raised concerns that generous option schemes awarded when share prices are low are a 'ticking time bomb' which could generate more 'fat cat' slurs in years to come. Sir Nigel Rudd, chairman of Boots, has also warned against share option schemes and so-called long-term incentive plans: 'I've never known a scheme that works. They either make you so rich that you lose all incentive to work or they are so far from making you money that you become demoralised.' His own preference is to pay a proportion of an executive's salary in shares which cannot be touched for years. 'I believe the share part of any reward should be really long-term not just two to three years.'[55]

Most observers, government, public and shareholders alike, would support high pay for real success. The growing flak has been that rewards so often seem to bear little resemblance to performance. Remuneration has been made up of two key elements – basic pay and various performance-related elements including bonuses, long-term incentive plans and share options. In 2004, basic salary accounted for less than a quarter of total remuneration for the average FTSE 100 chief executive.[56] Yet the targets that trigger the performance payments are generally undemanding, enabling schemes to pay out for mediocre or even poor performance. A survey by PricewaterhouseCoopers found that 'seven out of ten directors could be receiving performance related share option payouts, despite their businesses turning in average or below average results'.[57] Arguably, when performance is poor, the pay-out on the performance related elements should be zero.

Bonus rates have also been rising sharply. Like pensions, bonus arrangements are a somewhat opaque area of executive pay, rarely linked openly to clear performance targets. Until the late 1990s, it was the norm to give a maximum of between 40 and 50 per cent of basic salary as a bonus. But increasingly companies are now paying out 100 per cent or more, many of them more or less guaranteed. As Peter Montagnon asked, 'if bonuses have doubled in five years, has performance also doubled?'[58] The rise can hardly be justified by a toughening of the performance targets required to receive a bonus. The truth is that cash bonuses are mostly part of salaries in disguise, yet, as one insider puts it, 'guaranteed bonuses are an oxymoron'.

In general, soaring salaries, first in the United States and then in the United Kingdom, cannot be justified by claims of a tightening global or internal market, exceptional skill or performance. Most chief executives hardly need 'incentivising' to do their jobs. As one fund manager put it,

> it bothers me sometimes when you see the rewards these guys are giving themselves. I suspect they would work just as hard if they were on a tenth of what they earn. People

who want to achieve will achieve, regardless of money. But given a trough and a ladle, we'd all do the same.[59]

Part of the explanation for the continuing surge in rewards lies in a false sense of chief executives' own value. It is all part of the illusion that is being created around the modern boss. They typically believe they are worth what they take home. As the economist John Kay has written, 'chief executives need enormous remuneration packages – which they cannot conceivably find the time to spend – because they are a form of reinforcement of their own sense of self-importance and value to society'.[60]

The central explanation for the contemporary explosion of rewards, however, lies in what the American economist Paul Krugman has called a 'new social norm'.[61] Before 1930, the United States and Britain were highly unequal societies in which a small number of the very rich controlled a large share of wealth. The 1929 crash ushered in a new and more egalitarian political and social culture which lasted for half a century. In both countries, new norms emerged about an acceptable degree of pay differential. Top executives behaved 'more like public-spirited bureaucrats than like captains of industry'.[62] In his 1967 book, *The New Industrial State*, J. K. Galbraith gave a description of typical executive behaviour at the time: 'Management does not go out ruthlessly to reward itself – a sound management is one expected to exercise restraint.' He went on, 'With the power of decision goes opportunity for making money . . . Were everyone to seek to do so . . . the corporation would be a chaos of competitive avarice.' At the time the cultural climate operated to prevent such 'chaos', a kind of hidden and accepted code that was pretty effectively abided by, partly through fear of public outrage of overt excess. It was a code that endured for several decades and was triggered by the profound change in the political and social climate that followed what came to be seen as the costs of the extravagant behaviour and damaging inequality of the pre-1929 era.

The staggering increase in rewards that has occurred in recent years and which would not have been acceptable to public and political opinion even two decades ago has been driven by a dramatic cultural shift. Markets have been deregulated, old social norms eroded, political constraints withdrawn. Exploding rewards might have been easier to defend if they had gone hand in hand with improved corporate performance. But they have not. A small group of business leaders, maybe a few thousand people, aided by professionals from accountants to City analysts, have simply taken advantage of the more liberal climate to seize the opportunity to enrich themselves, often at the expense of their shareholders, their staff and sometimes their customers.

A tighter system of corporate governance might have prevented some of the worst examples of the excesses of the last decade. In the event, chief executives and chairmen have been able to appoint the very people who would determine their pay, compensation and perks. What has been at work is a corporate cartel, an internal and unwritten pact, operating through packed remuneration committees in the United Kingdom and compensation committees in the United States. It is a pact that has been encouraged too by similar rewards enjoyed by the very professional groups in City investment and accountancy firms whose job it is to scrutinise behaviour but who also have a hand in the cartel, and a vested interest in high financial reward.

Of course, the beneficiaries like to defend their rewards by claims that they are part of a new British meritocracy, there by merit rather than privilege. How far this is the case will be examined in the next two chapters. First we look at the extent to which Britain's landowning aristocracy have maintained their longstanding position at the top of the wealth league.

5

A burnt-out class

> I have great confidence in the future of old money, because the current generation are a lot tougher than their forebears. After all, we've had to look after our wealth through some dark days, so the toughness is inbred.
>
> (Alan Clark, 1989)[1]

Supporters of the wealth explosion of recent times have argued that today's wealth tables are much more meritocratic. Today, it is argued, opportunities have spread and most people have much wider choices than in the past if they choose to take them. As a result, modern wealth is said to come more from merit and self-improvement than privilege. According to this view, rising inequality is justified because those making it to the very top reflect a wider range of backgrounds than in the past and ordinary people can rise through the class system if they have the skills and determination to do so.

But is this really true? Are today's rich lists more heavily packed with the 'self-made' than in the past? Are those from ordinary backgrounds more likely to reach the top today, displacing those from more privileged backgrounds? A closer scrutiny of the lists and the backgrounds of today's mega-wealthy suggests the answer is no, that the claim of greater elite mobility is something of an exaggeration.

First, there is the continuing, if declining, presence of the old landowning aristocracy in the wealth leagues. Secondly, there is still plenty of non-aristocratic 'old money' around, wealth inherited from the business and commercial giants of the past. And thirdly, even though there has been a steady increase over the last twenty years in the proportion of the new rich who have not inherited a fortune, a business or land, most, though not all, still come from the relatively privileged background from which the new arrivals have traditionally come. This chapter will look at the role of the old landed aristocracy. Chapter 6 will look at the continuing significance of old commercial wealth and at the backgrounds of the 'self-made' members of the wealth club.

In 2005, the third richest man in Britain was 53-year-old Gerald Cavendish Grosvenor, the sixth Duke of Westminster. The duke has never been lower than seventh in the *Sunday Times* rich list since it started in 1989 and has held first or second place nine times out of sixteen. His wealth derives almost entirely from land passed down through successive generations of the Grosvenor family, which has probably been Britain's wealthiest dynasty for most of the period since the mid-nineteenth century. The Grosvenor estate can trace its origins back three centuries to when Sir Thomas Grosvenor married the twelve-year-old Mary Davies in 1677. She was the heiress to the manor of Ebury, comprising the 'hundred acres' north of Piccadilly, which included most of Mayfair, and the 'Five Fields', now Belgravia and Pimlico. The area was mostly bog and marshland at the time.

Today, the duke, Britain's fifth largest landowner, owns 300 acres in Mayfair and Belgravia, the country's most expensive real estate. The duke's brother-in-law, the late Earl of Lichfield, is said to have once given him a Christmas present of a special Monopoly board in which all the properties were owned by him. As well as the London sites, he has huge landholdings in Ireland, Scotland, Lancashire and Cheshire, where he lives on the 11,000-acre Eaton Park estate. He also owns more foreign real estate than any other property owner in Britain. These holdings include a business park in Vancouver, shopping malls in California and Texas, offices in San Francisco and Sydney, and property in Asia and continental Europe.[2]

The first duke, Hugh Lupus Grosvenor, was the archetypal Victorian gentleman: high minded, morally upright, religious, abstemious. Renowned for his generous philanthropy, he was MP for Chester from 1846 until he inherited in 1869. When he died, it was his grandson, Hugh Richard, who inherited the dukedom. The contrast with his grandfather could hardly be greater. An international sportsman and playboy who could be both charming and autocratic, the second duke married four times and eschewed politics. Rather than posting letters, he would send them by footman with a telegram to announce their arrival. On his death in 1953, he left a fortune so vast that the Inland Revenue set up a separate department to assess and collect the duties of some £11 million.[3] To pay them, the Westminsters had to sell off much of their Pimlico estate. With no surviving son, the

Westminster title passed to three of his cousins, who were able to manage their tax affairs to avoid such hefty duties and handed over their estate to the next generation and the sixth duke largely intact.

The current, chain-smoking duke claims he 'would rather not have been born wealthy' and insists he is not awed by his vast wealth.[4] That may be so, but the duke's fortune has continued to rise since he inherited it. This has much to do with the vagaries of the property market. The value of his extensive land and freehold interests would have soared even if he had chosen to ignore them, purely by virtue of their location.

In fact, he hasn't ignored them, and has been an active and indeed hard-nosed businessman, apparently intent on developing his inheritance and building on his fortune. He is an active property developer with large-scale developments across Britain. His company, the Grosvenor Group, is run by professional property men who regularly find themselves at loggerheads with tenants. As one tenant complained, 'forty years ago, the Grosvenor estate was much more gentlemanly. Now it is run by people who have been to business school.'[5]

The duke is no stranger to controversy. In the mid-1980s, the Department of Health was required to sell part of St George's Hospital, at London's Hyde Park Corner, back to the Grosvenor estate, its original owners. A clause in the lease stipulated that the hospital must be sold back for its original price of £22,700 – a gross under-valuation by then. The *Financial Times* wrote at the time, 'The prospect of an immensely wealthy property owner benefiting at the expense of an impoverished health service has caused a major furore.'[6] More recently, in November 2003, the duke was involved in a fierce dispute with a group of mansion block residents when he tried to impose a new service charge of up to £70,000 each to cover maintenance and repair work. There is of course nothing unusual about rows between landlords and tenants. But this one was a dispute between one of Britain's wealthiest men and the tenants of one of Britain's most prestigious addresses, Eaton Square in Belgravia. Local residents include Sir Sean Connery and Baroness Thatcher and flats in the square cost in the region of £750,000. This was not exactly class war, but wealthy tenants taking on a billionaire duke in full public view was too much for the headline writers, who dubbed it the 'Battle of Belgravia'. The duke was eventually forced to back down and agree to compromise.

For 150 years a single family, a landed dynasty, has held onto one of the top prizes in Britain – to be consistently counted, year in year out, decade after decade, as one of the nation's very richest families, possibly *the* richest for most of the period. The Westminsters have not only managed to survive the extravagant lifestyle of the second duke and the considerable tax bill that he left his successors to pay. They have also survived a century and a half of dramatic economic, cultural and political change. First came the Industrial Revolution, which swept away the dominance of agriculture as the key source of wealth and employment, and then a new technological and service revolution that has displaced manufacturing as Britain's key economic activity. Over the same period Britain moved from a nation where less than 5 per cent of men – and no women – had the vote to one of universal suffrage. The Labour Party, committed to the redistribution of wealth and the narrowing of inequalities, has been in power for a third of the last hundred years. Social and cultural transformation have forced Britain's old ruling elites to adapt to a loss of political power and social deference. Yet a single family, one that typifies old Britain and privilege, has lived, survived and apparently prospered through it all.

Of course, it might be argued that the Grosvenors are an aberration, a single family that for special reasons has been able to ride the storm, to apparently defy the laws of economic, political and social upheaval. In fact, there are three other billionaire aristocrats – Earl Cadogan, Viscount Portman and the Howard de Walden family. All of them are descendants of wealthy landed families of the eighteenth and nineteenth centuries and all are very large central London landlords. The eighth Earl Cadogan owns most of Chelsea – 1,000 acres of it – assets which are estimated to be worth £1.65 billion. His patch includes the department stores Peter Jones in Sloane Square and Harrods in Knightsbridge, and he can walk between them without stepping off his estate. The original estate was formed in the early eighteenth century by the marriage of Charles Cadogan and Elizabeth, daughter of Sir Hans Sloane.

Viscount Portman is worth £1.2 billion and owns Portman Square and much of the prime shopping area in and around Oxford Street. Portman, who lives in Australia, also owns 3,000 acres in Herefordshire, an Antiguan holiday home and a Sydney mansion. Originally covering an area of 270 acres stretching from present-day Oxford Street to the Regent's Canal, the land was acquired by Sir William Portman, Lord Chief Justice, from Henry VIII in 1533.

The Howard de Waldens are another billionaire family by virtue of their ownership of prime central London sites. They own 92 acres between

Regent's Park and Oxford Street. The last Lord Howard de Walden died in 1999, and the estate is now owned and run by his four daughters, the oldest being Mary Czernin.

Of course, the Grosvenors, Cadogans, Portmans and Howard de Waldens are a special case in one sense – their forebears happened to obtain landholdings that were to become the most valuable prime *urban* sites in the nation. It is this that gets them into the premier, billionaire league. None of this is down to super-skill or effort, or great foresight, more to exceptional luck in the location of the original land acquisitions. While the value of agricultural land has fluctuated wildly over the last century, that of urban land has continued to rise.

Nevertheless, although those who have inherited urban land have ended up especially wealthy, many aristocratic families with rural holdings have retained the wealth enjoyed by their forebears. In 2005, the *Sunday Times* top 1,000 contained a total of 124 aristocratic landholders, most of them with large rural holdings. They include the Queen, nine dukes, five marquesses, thirteen earls, five viscounts, twenty-three lords, seven baronets, fifty-four knights, six ladies and two dames.

The last of the squires

It is often claimed that the British aristocracy is a spent force, a burnt-out class. Its members are, it is alleged, shadows of their former selves, a group that has been leapfrogged in the wealth and power stakes by new pretenders, first by the nineteenth-century industrialists and financiers, and then more recently by retail and technological entrepreneurs and media and sports stars.

At the beginning of the last quarter of the nineteenth century, the traditional, titled landowners remained the richest and the most powerful people in Britain. As a group they constituted about 7,000 families – some 0.04 per cent of the population – and owned about four-fifths of land in the British Isles.[7] In contrast, 95 per cent of the population owned no land at all. Despite the rise of commerce and industry, in the 1880s, aristocratic landowners still constituted at least half of the very wealthy while the wealth of the richest landowners greatly exceeded the wealth of the richest businessmen and bankers.

They were not just the wealthy elite, but the governing elite as well. Indeed, while the original Greek meaning of the word 'aristocrat' was 'government by the best', by the nineteenth century the term had been transformed into a status description of the upper classes as the source of the best possible governors of British society. They had packed both Houses of Parliament for centuries and continued to control local government, the law, the judiciary, the army, the church and the top ranks of the civil service. Three-quarters of those with more than 30,000 acres were members of the House of Lords while, until the Reform Act of 1884, the Commons was also a landowners' club, with a large majority of MPs recruited from the British landed establishment.[8]

The landed elite was, however, far from a homogeneous class. About 6,000 families were relatively small landowners, with estates of between 1,000 and 10,000 acres, and they would include the village squire. Within this group, those at the bottom of the hierarchy would still own their own estate and mansion while those at the top end would also own a second mansion and a London town house. The next group of some 750 families, the 'middling' proprietors, owned between 10,000 and 30,000 acres, mostly more than one estate, and all had a London house as well. At the top of the pyramid were 250 landowning magnates, all with several estates totalling more than 30,000 acres, all with more than one mansion and at least one grand London home. The wealth hierarchy closely corresponded to the status and title hierarchy. Those in the top two groups were a mix of dukes, marquesses and baronets. The remaining 6,000 were the untitled aristocracy, the landed gentry, who, though without hereditary titles or legal privileges, remained a pre-eminent social and economic elite, often large employers as well as running local affairs as councillors and magistrates.

The 1870s were to prove the zenith of aristocratic dominance. Today, as a class, the aristocracy retain but a fraction of their former power and status. But, while the last 130 years have undoubtedly seen a steady decline in their previously unrivalled power and influence, it is equally remarkable that the aristocracy, in so many ways a dated and anachronistic institution, and certainly a much smaller and less influential group, have held on to as much wealth as they have after a century and more of sweeping change. They may not dominate the wealth leagues as they did in the nineteenth century, but most of the largest aristocratic families of the time have survived and prospered alongside the new generations of wealth-makers. Indeed, the decline of the aristocracy in terms of wealth is largely, though not exclusively, a story of the fall of the majority group of lesser aristocrats, the landed gentry with smaller estates, rather than the titled classes themselves.

The slow decline of the aristocracy really begins after the 1870s. Up to the First World War, they had to face economic upheaval as a result of stiff foreign competition that brought an influx of cheap foreign goods, and then the agricultural depression. The price of agricultural land fell sharply, as did product prices and rents. The period brought increasing hostility through the birth of new political parties and an increasingly restive landed and industrial workforce. Leading radical politicians took advantage of the aristocracy's waning support to attack them for being an idle, parasitic and profiteering class. David Lloyd George was openly hostile to the landed gentry and was determined to break what he viewed as their unjustifiable monopoly of the soil, their social privileges and their political power. Most of the big landholdings had, after all, been originally acquired through force or favour. He viewed them as a class that enriched themselves while leaving their labourers to live and work in squalid conditions. In his 1906 general election campaign, he promised that he would legislate to emancipate ordinary people from 'the oppression of the antiquated, sterilising and humiliating system of land tenure'.[9]

Such rhetoric found its mark. Attacked for their unearned wealth and leisured lifestyles and for being slum landlords, the old establishment slowly and reluctantly gave way in most of the political and economic spheres in which they had been dominant. The extension of the vote slowly weakened their power in the House of Commons. Although they retained control of the Lords, they could no longer wield the veto in a self-serving and unaccountable way. The landed aristocracy also had to face the emergence of the new wealthy financiers and industrialists who wanted their share of the spoils. The hard times being faced by the landed aristocracy was parodied in the satirical magazine *Truth*: 'The eldest son must live on the estate; the younger sons on the State.'[10]

To deal with the growing financial pressures, an increasing number of aristocratic offspring turned to marrying newly enriched American heiresses, a pretty effective way of protecting their wealth and their class and sometimes of restoring fortunes that had been frittered away on gambling, drink and high living. Between 1874 and 1909, some 500 titled European men married rich American women and $200 million changed hands as a result. Many of the women came from the new American gilded elite – the Whitneys, the Vanderbilts and the Goulds. Many marriages were unhappy, impermanent and costly.

Success in the lucrative American marriage market was only a partial solution. From the 1880s, many landowners were forced to cut back on their indulgent, leisured lifestyles, with fewer expensive country pursuits such as fox-hunting, fewer parties and servants and the shortening of the London season. What was especially galling for the old landed elite was how their former monopoly of high society and genteel living was being broken by the arrival of the new moneyed elite – the industrial and commercial rich.

The levels of new wealth soon started to dwarf all but the very largest landed fortunes. It has been estimated that the proportion of British millionaires who were landowners fell from over 80 per cent at the beginning of the nineteenth century to a third by 1914.[11] It was the new rich who were able to indulge their new-found opulence with their ostentatious weekends and shooting parties. 'Instead of being a patrician preserve, the countryside was becoming a plutocratic playground.'[12]

Retrenchment soon turned to disposal. As soon as the late 1870s, art collections and then estates were being put on the market, and at an accelerating rate. Initially, it was the smaller landowners who were forced into sales, though gradually even the elite landowners had to join in. In the years immediately before and after the First World War, one-quarter of the land held by the gentry was sold. In the House of Commons in 1924, Edward Wood MP spoke of 'a silent revolution . . . We are, unless I mistake it, witnessing in England, the gradual disappearance of the old landed classes.'[13] Some of those buying the land were the new, previously non-landed, wealthy.

In the inter-war years, expensive town houses and country mansions were also put up for auction, most ending up as hotels, flats and occasionally schools. As the market became saturated, many were simply destroyed in order to avoid the costs of upkeep. The decade after the Second World War was to prove the nadir in the fortunes of the aristocracy. As a result of the continuing slump in farm rents and higher death duties imposed in 1948, a further 400 mansions were demolished and 1,000 sold for conversion into orphanages, golf clubs and colleges.

The impact of the changing times was not uniform across the aristocracy. The smaller and less wealthy landholders, the squires and minor gentry with growing debts, were the least likely to survive. Many of the lesser landlords, probably as many as a third, disappeared from the land altogether in the fifty years from the 1880s. By the Second World War, at least some of the surviving aristocracy was more landless than landed.[14] On the other hand, the larger landlords with considerable non-landed sources of wealth were able to weather the storm for much longer. Urban landlords such as Earl Cadogan and the Dukes of Westminster and Portland, in receipt of very large annual ground rents, were much better placed than purely agricultural landlords. Those with a foothold in the industrial and commercial revolution, including those with interests in mining or docks, also had longer rates of survival. Some of the very rich had such extensive landholdings that the sale of one estate or art collection represented only a small part of their portfolio.

Aware of the growing risks of a heavy dependency on the land, many of the super-rich started to diversify their assets. Before the Second World War, the second Duke of Westminster extended his landholdings by buying property in Rhodesia, Canada and Australia. Others turned to the stock market. The richer members of the aristocracy may have been unloading land but they managed to hold on to their wealth. Although it often came from different sources, many were able to continue to live as their forebears in country mansions, with lavish parties and sumptuous lifestyles, as if nothing had changed.

For a period from the Second World War, leading aristocrats took to taking directorships in both industries and banks. Even up to the 1980s, the boards of many of the biggest firms continued to consist of several landed lords and grandees from the top public schools and the Conservative Party. The old boy network was still very much in evidence.

'Thatcherisation'

For the last 100 years, the aristocracy has been written off dozens of times, not least by its own members. In 1919, the ninth Duke of Marlborough sighed, 'The old order is doomed.' In 1943, the third Lord Kinross effectively wrote Britain's dukedom off as 'men who cannot rise, only descend in the social scale . . . men hamstrung by an inherited amateur status, to whom barely a profession is open'.[15] In the early 1950s, the thirteenth Duke of Bedford succinctly summed up the mood of despair and despondency in the drawing rooms of the landed classes: 'There is no future for the aristocracy in England.'[16]

By the end of the Second World War, the aristocracy seemed to be facing inexorable decline. They had sold off land and property, lost their grip on power and were a class out of place in a rapidly modernising world. In the 1865 House of Commons, no less than 31 per cent of MPs were titled aristocrats and a further 45 per cent members of the landed gentry. In 1928, the lower House still contained fifty-eight sons of peers and baronets, but by 1955 this number had reduced to twelve.[17] While old money dominated Cabinets up to the Second World War, its influence has slowly evaporated since then. Sir Alec Douglas-Home had five aristocrats in his Cabinet, Edward Heath had four, both Margaret Thatcher and John Major had several. There have been no aristocrats in Tony Blair's Cabinets and only one, Michael Ancram, an earl, in the Conservative front bench opposition under Michael Howard.

Perhaps one of the most remarkable relics of the past, the hereditary principle, by which hereditary peers could continue to sit and vote in the House of Lords, was only finally abolished, or at least partly so, in 1999, when 600 hundred hereditary peers were expelled with 92 allowed to remain until details of reform of the upper chamber are finally agreed.

Direct political muscle may have gone but not the wealth. When the *Sunday Times* published its first rich list in 1989, nearly a quarter of the 200 on the list were hereditary landowners. They included twelve dukes, six marquesses, twelve earls, five viscounts and six barons. At the time the paper's editor, Andrew Neil, a man not known for his sympathies for the old establishment, was said to have been shocked by the continuing dominance of the landed aristocracy. In 2005, the proportion of aristocrats in the top 1,000 was around 13 per cent, still a not inconsiderable number in view of the earlier foreboding and the wider explosion of wealth of the last decade and a half. Of the twenty-four non-royal dukes, the highest status grouping amongst the titled aristocracy, nine were in the *Sunday Times* top 1,000 in 2005.

A comparison between the very wealthiest aristocratic families today and those that dominated the nineteenth century reveals a considerable overlap. Of the ten landowners in Britain with the highest income from land in 1880, no fewer than eight were in the *Sunday Times* top 1,000 in 2005, with an average wealth of over £900 million.[18] Of the top twenty-nine in 1880, thirteen of them – nearly a half – were in the 2005 list. The old land-owning families remain a pretty powerful economic, if not political, force in modern Britain, more than 150 years after most of them were in their economic supremacy.

This is despite the fact that most of them have much smaller landholdings. The last detailed study of British land-ownership, the 'Second Domesday Survey', was carried out in 1872. It had been commissioned by Parliament under pressure from the Earl of Derby, himself a considerable landowner with 69,000 acres. Derby hoped that the survey would disprove the 'wildest and reckless exaggerations' made by some campaigners that most of the country was owned by a small number of people.[19] In fact, to the peer's embarrassment, the survey proved precisely what the critics were claiming – that four-fifths of Britain was owned by some 7,000 people. The findings were picked up and reproduced by national and local newspapers. So angry were the largest landowners, who had suddenly become exposed, and so sensitive were the findings that the four volumes containing the detailed evidence conveniently disappeared.[20]

No official comprehensive survey of landholdings has been conducted since. As a result, we know less about land-ownership today than we did nearly 150 years ago. While land and house sales have to be registered with the Land Registry, all unsold land has continued to remain unregistered since 1872. In effect, the question of land-ownership and its concentration remains an official secret. The issue has been left to independent scholars who have had to burrow away for years checking individual estates one at a time to make any kind of comparison.

One such burrower, Kevin Cahill, has found that, while large chunks of land have indeed been sold off, land-ownership remains remarkably concentrated. It is today still possible to travel by train through the heartland of rural Britain and pass for mile after mile through land owned by one person. Some of the new plutocracy who didn't feature in 1872 have accumulated large landholdings, such as the Vesteys and the Cowdrays, but private land-ownership remains heavily in the hands of old money. Not that much has changed since 1872. As Cahill concludes, 'the landowners and their descendants hung onto the jewel in the crown, the land, and have kept the rest of the population, as in 1872, corralled in the same relatively small portion of the landscape.'[21]

Part of the reason for the survival of the aristocracy as a potent economic force today, a half-century after they were largely written off, is that only the largest and fittest have survived. Most, though not all, of the non-titled landed gentry have lost their land and properties and, of the wealthiest families at the top of the pyramid, not all have survived. Those that remain wealthy and prosperous have survived by a mixture of adaptability, skill, ruthlessness and good fortune.

The good fortune has come mainly from the steady rise in land, property and art values in the post-war era. This has enabled the landed class to 'increase their wealth massively without any difficulty – simply by sitting on what they already have; for their favourite commodities – land, old houses, old masters, furniture, silver – have all shown spectacular increases in value as their scarcity became greater and the market becomes larger'.[22] The price of farming land, depressed since the agricultural depression of the 1880s, doubled between the mid-1950s and the mid-1960s. From the 1950s, the disposal of land and property came to a halt. Nearly all of the great country houses still in private hands in the mid-1950s remain so today. Those families that had held on to at least some of their land found that their diminished estates were in fact worth more than when they were much larger. At the same time, the market for paintings also soared.

Policies towards land and property from the late 1950s on, while often designed to protect the poor, mostly had the perverse effect of helping large landlords. The great urban property boom of the 1960s had the effect of further enriching large urban property owners such as the Duke of Westminster and Lord Cadogan as well as the new property developers on the scene such as Harry Hyams and Sir Max Rayne. Sometimes the new developers worked hand in hand with the old aristocratic landowners, with, for example, Rayne and Lord Portman combining to redevelop sites around Portman Square. In the 1980s, the property bonanza continued as land was needed for out-of-town shopping, new housing estates and large supermarkets. Many great estates even started to buy back cottages and properties they had sold off in harder times. Following the election of Margaret Thatcher in 1979, the tax regime started to ease significantly and the landed class found more effective ways of avoiding death duties especially through the use of discretionary trusts.[23] Those who turned to equities in earlier years found themselves benefiting from the prolonged stock market boom of the 1990s.

Large landholders have also been receiving substantial state hand-outs through the Common Agricultural Policy (CAP) and European regeneration funds. During the 1990s, the Duke of Westminster received £300,000 a year in subsidies towards his 6,200-acre arable farm on his Eaton estate near Chester. The CAP has long been justified as a way of helping smaller farmers survive, but the lion's share of the subsidy – which accounts for close to half the budget of the European Union – has gone into maintaining the profits of large and wealthy landholders. Despite the large amounts involved, until 2005 there were no publicly available records of the amounts given to individual farmers. In 2001, the Ministry of Agriculture, Fisheries and Food revealed that five farms each received over £1 million in subsidy. An estimated 80 per cent of the total subsidy bill of £3 billion went to the richest 20 per cent of farmers.[24] Finally, in 2005, details of individual subsidies were published but only following a freedom-of-information request by the *Guardian*. These showed that the Royal Family along with large aristocratic landowners were amongst the main beneficiaries. In the two years to 2004, for example, the Duke of Westminster received £800,000 in subsidy, the Duke of Marlborough's Blenheim farm in Oxfordshire received £1 million, while the Duke of Richmond gained £900,000.[25]

The old aristocracy may have been presented a lifeline with these developments, but they have in most cases been forced to adapt their lifestyles as well. It was in 1949 that the abandonment of aristocratic privacy began when the sixth Marquess of Bath opened up Longleat to public viewing. Gradually, many of the old landowners have had to become businessmen, a process one author has described as the 'Thatcherisation of the aristocracy'.[26] Most have not merely opened up their stately homes and gardens to the public, but have turned them into conference centres, museums, hotels and giant family leisure parks. As one earl has put it, 'the most important person in my life apart from my family is my accountant'.[27]

Turning their homes into businesses has, at least for some, brought a new bullishness. As the Earl of Shelbourne put it in 1989,

> right through the 1970s there was an innuendo that we shouldn't be allowed to exist, that people with big houses and estates rolled around with red faces and bottles of claret stuck in their mouths the whole time. Now all that's gone and we've got the confidence to make decisions.[28]

While accepting the need to modernise, or at least be seen to modernise, most keep one foot firmly in the past. Traditional aristocratic pastimes such as grouse-shooting have survived. The titled gentry were at the centre of the vigorous campaigns organised against Labour's ban on fox-hunting, and of those against plans to extend rights of way following the passing of the Countryside and Rights of Way Act in 2001.

But other trappings of the past, as well as the servants, have largely gone. The 'Season' – the period that brought the right families together in a whirl of parties and social and sporting events – has long gone as a purely aristocratic preserve. The highlight of the traditional debutante season, effectively an aristocratic 'marriage market', where eligible girls from the top families were presented to the Queen, ended in 1958 as part of the effort to modernise the monarchy. *Country Life* magazine no longer carries the photographs of debutantes. Many of the events and the parties have continued, even the 'coming out' balls, but today honourables mix with celebrity socialites – pop stars such as Rod Stewart, actors such as Sienna Miller, models such as Kate Moss and 'it' girls such as Tara Palmer-Tomkinson. Much to the disdain of the old elite, who used to have these events largely to themselves, major sporting events – from Ascot to the Henley Regatta – are as likely to heave with secretaries and salesmen as young aristocrats looking for partners. Old money is today forced to brush shoulders with anyone who can afford a ticket.

A spent force?

As little as a hundred years ago, the aristocracy were the establishment. Today they have lost most of their direct political power. Few are involved directly in party politics. Britain is run by a much more complex mix of old and new elites. But the aristocracy is part of that mix. Some members like to portray themselves as a beleaguered class, living on the edge of extinction, whose influence has long gone. As the Duke of Devonshire once put it, the aristocracy is 'an anachronism; it has become irrelevant. They have no power and there is not much point in titles without influence'. Others are more robust. Lord St John of Fawsley, former Conservative leader of the House of Commons, disagrees. 'The great thing about the British aristocracy is not that they have gone into decline, but the way they have hung onto their social and political influence.'[29]

Today the old titled landed class remain a powerful economic force. A handful of families own most of London's most valuable real estate. The old titled aristocracy continue to own and control most of Britain's best and most productive agricultural land. Because of rising share, land and art values, many are even richer than their considerably wealthy ancestors. When the eleventh Duke of Devonshire died in 2004, aged eighty-four, for example, he was much richer than his predecessors and had been able to add many modern works including pieces by Lucian Freud and Elisabeth Frink to his already extensive collection of old masters.[30]

Of course, the aristocracy has had its share of failures too. The eighth and ninth Dukes of Manchester both went bankrupt. Some dukedoms, including Leeds, are now extinct. The Earl of Lucan, of course, disappeared.

The old landed elite has maintained its own, often subtle and hidden but still powerful, influence especially over policy towards agriculture, the heritage industry and land. It is difficult to believe that the hand of the aristocracy is not behind the failure to collect reliable evidence of the ownership and concentration of land in Britain – which has the effect of keeping their true wealth hidden – and of the persistence of planning controls that keep land artificially scarce and valuable. They remain amongst Britain's biggest landlords of small farmers, and in London of leasehold residents. This of itself brings considerable power over the process of property development and rent levels and so over the livelihood of their tenants.

For three years up to 2003, Britain's largest landlord, the Duke of Northumberland, was locked in bitter battle with his long-standing local tenant farmers over the level of their rents. The farmers complained that with the fall in farm incomes, they could not afford the rents they were charged and that the duke had reneged on an agreement to cut rents if livestock prices fell. The dispute was eventually settled, though hardly amicably, after long and expensive arbitration, and typifies the power imbalance between farmers and landlords that results from the continuation of past patterns of land-ownership.

The ownership of land confers huge financial advantages and privileges, often entirely unearned. Land development is a highly lucrative business. Agricultural land sold for housing or other development can bring huge rewards for its owners, mainly because of the artificial scarcity created by a combination of tough planning laws and unequal ownership. In his book, *Taken For a Ride*, the property developer Don Riley showed how surrounding land values along the new Jubilee Tube line corridor rose by £1.3 billion per station, untaxed gains that accrued to local landowners just by virtue of ownership.[31]

Successive governments and opposition parties have flirted with the land question and how to handle the increases in wealth that derive not from personal investment or effort but from wider factors including community decisions and activity. Adam Smith, the free-market economist, was the first to advocate a tax on the income from land in his book *The Wealth of Nations*, published in 1776. A century later, in 1879, the American radical economist Henry George recommended a land value tax of 90 per cent in his book

Progress and Poverty. The first political attempt to introduce such a tax came with David Lloyd George's 1909 taxes on windfall gains – 'the increment value duty' – and undeveloped land. But these taxes were mild, raised little revenue and were repealed in 1920. The comprehensive survey work on land-ownership and valuation that accompanied the taxes was discontinued and what had been compiled lost.[32] A 1942 proposal for some kind of land nationalisation was watered down by the post-war Labour government, though it did attempt to impose a tax levy on the gains from development. A more sophisticated attempt to tax development value was also made by the 1966 Labour government before it was dismantled by the incoming Conservative government in 1970. Today, the gains are simply untaxed, though in July 2005 the government announced it was considering introducing a 'planning gain supplement'. The plan is that such a tax on the gains from property development will help fund infrastructure projects needed to build hundreds of thousands of new houses.

So, do the aristocracy deserve their place at and near the top of the wealth league tables? Have they earned their continuing ability to exercise the influence they do over many important aspects of British land and agricultural policy?

What is not in dispute is that they are where they are by accident of birth. Nicholas Ridley, who held long office in Margaret Thatcher's Cabinets, was pretty scathing about the aristocratic class he came from. When he was environment secretary he was invited to speak at the annual general meeting of the Historic Houses Association, as close to an assembly of the aristocratic ranks as it is possible to get. After some warm words about the importance of country houses, Ridley launched into a stinging rebuke:

> We cannot provide a permanent guarantee to a particular family. Many families who pride themselves on having lived in a house in fact married into it, bought it or stole it at some point in their murky history, when they were robber barons, property speculators, or simply won the pools.

But then he was a younger son and the viscounty went to his elder brother.

Ridley, himself from within the heart of the old political establishment, was merely pointing out, somewhat directly, that the aristocracy's forebears had mostly acquired their land in more or less dubious ways – by theft, bribery, favour or luck. Today's large estates were mostly acquired way back in the past during the three 'great land grabs'. The first was the Norman

Conquest in 1066. Then came the dissolution of the monasteries by Henry VIII in 1533, by which some 10 million acres of land owned by the Catholic Church were redistributed to 1,500 of his loyal barons. Then came the re-allocation of royal land by Oliver Cromwell after the English Civil War in 1649.

The aristocracy would argue that, in return for their heritage, they exercise responsibility through their role as stewards of their estates, though maintaining their land and houses is largely for the purpose of passing them onto the next generation. They have of course been helped in this task of preserving the nation's aristocratic heritage and historic homes by the generous financial help and tax breaks provided by successive governments, a system that some critics have dubbed a 'system of outdoor relief for the old nobility'. While some have accepted, even relished, their new role as hosts to national and foreign tourists, most appear to do so reluctantly, and only to take advantage of the tax benefits and government grants on offer. One anonymous aristocrat rather gave the game away, declaring, 'I treat the public as an untidy and disagreeable great aunt, whom I must humour for the sake of her legacy.'[33]

The thinness of the continuing aristocrat claim to play the role of custodians of the national heritage is illustrated by the way in which some have recently tried to obtain an extra few million for the rare paintings they have inherited. First there was the matter of Raphael's *Madonna of the Pinks*, owned by the Duke of Northumberland. The duke, whose collection includes Canalettos, Van Dykes, Turners and Titians, was offered £35 million for the painting by the Getty Museum in California in 2003. To prevent the painting going abroad, Northumberland agreed to sell the painting to the National Gallery with the help of a £11.5 million lottery grant and a tax saving of £14 million, a deal that divided the art world, the general public and his tenants. Then in the summer of 2005 there was the Earl of Halifax's decision to withdraw his *Portrait of a Young Man* by Titian from the National Gallery – where it had been on loan since 1992 – and sell the painting, which was expected to fetch £50 million from the Getty Museum.

In the past, aristocrats would have justified their role through their wider social responsibilities. Today Mammon would appear to be outweighing patriotism. The old tradition of public duty has been slowly dying out. The sixth Duke of Westminster, despite his immense wealth and his disputes with his tenants, is one who tries to keep up such duties and is renowned for his extensive charitable work and his philanthropy. He and his wife are patrons to hundreds of charities. He once refused to hand over 532 flats on which he owned the freehold to Westminster Council, which wanted to sell them off. In the 1950s, the second duke had made a gift of 6 acres of Pimlico for dwellings for 'working class' people. When the council tried to sell off the properties in the 1980s, the Duke argued successfully in the courts that the lease contained a clause that the flats should be 'used as dwellings for the working classes and no other purposes'. In the early 1990s, the duke also paid the poll tax bills of eighty-seven staff working at his two stately homes.[34]

Rare indeed amongst his class, his children have been educated at the local primary and secondary schools in Chester, and in that sense he is also a very modern aristocrat. He is a professional landlord and property developer on the one hand but an active participant in many social causes on the other. Prince Charles once invited him to head an initiative on rural poverty and he was involved in the prince's Youth Business Trust. He was chancellor of Manchester Metropolitan University and has helped raise money for a multitude of good causes including the Royal London Hospital in London's East End.

Despite their attempts to modernise, the aristocracy remain a highly privileged group who continue to enjoy substantial financial advantages as the result of their controversial heritage. Some put something back but most don't. Public attitudes towards them remain ambiguous. Moreover, they are not the only group that have managed to take a top place in the wealth leagues by virtue of inheritance.

6

To him who hath

Becoming a business leader in Britain is still largely determined by the interconnected characteristics of a wealthy family and a prestige education . . . there has been no democratisation of British business over the last century and a half.

(Tom Nicholas, 'The Myth of Meritocracy')[1]

The rich today are a mix of old and new money, just as they were in the nineteenth century when the aristocracy found their exclusive position at the top being threatened by those making money out of commerce and industry. Today, many aristocrats are still there, as are many descendants of the families who built businesses in the nineteenth and early twentieth centuries. Others in today's rich list include more recent examples of inheritance – from money originally made in the post-war years. The London socialite Lily Safra, who is worth £650 million, inherited money from two of her former husbands. Other rich widows include Lady Hamlyn, the wife of the publishing tycoon, and Elizabeth Tompkins, the wife of Richard Tompkins, who founded the Green Shield trading stamp business and Argos.

Children of wealthy fathers include the offspring of the 'Mayfair set', who together pioneered the hostile takeover activity that had such a dramatic impact on Britain's older companies from the 1960s. Some of the sons of the Mayfair set seem to have inherited the 'Midas touch' more successfully than others. Damian Aspinall has made a personal fortune, independently of his substantial inheritance, through a mix of property and City dealing and more recently Aspinalls Online Casino. Toby Rowland, son of Tiny, set up an internet health and beauty retailer, ClickMango, which collapsed in the 2000 internet bubble, but then took a senior position at a more successful internet company, uDate. Mark Slater has also dabbled, with somewhat mixed results, in internet companies. Lucas White, the only son of the late Lord White, the financier and co-founder of Hanson, inherited £70 million when his father died in 1995. White, then aged twenty, became Britain's youngest tax exile and lives a jet-set lifestyle with homes in London, Bermuda and New York. He is renowned for his polo-playing and international partying and is married to the American model and beauty writer Normandie Keith. He has set up a company, Hanson White Capital, with Robert Hanson, son of the late Lord Hanson.

These offspring of business parents may well be talented at business in their own right but self-made they are not. Members of successive rich elites in Britain have mostly been those who have enjoyed similarly advantaged starts in life. That elite has always contained members who started with little or nothing, but they have always been in a minority. Britain has long been a society in which the chance of attaining wealth and power has been higher, indeed much higher, for those born into the existing elite than those born outside it.

This of course is not a universal law. Some, though not many, of those from a privileged background have ended up slipping down the wealth and class ladder (but not that far). Some who started at the bottom have ended up at or near the top. For example, the Barclay brothers were born to a poorish family in Glasgow in 1934. Brian Souter, who set up the Scottish bus company Stagecoach, now an international transport conglomerate, with his sister Ann Gloag, is a former bus conductor. The two are now worth some £400 million. Alan Sugar, who made his money from Amstrad computers, is a Hackney-bred descendant of a Polish great-grandfather in the clothing trade. He started selling car radio aerials in a north London market before setting up Amstrad in 1968 trading in plastic turntable covers. He was thirty-three when he became a multi-millionaire as a result of launching his company on the stock market. 'I know where my roots are,' he insisted then. 'My family are still working class people.'[2]

Some are more self-made than others. Richard Branson may not have gone to university, leaving school at sixteen, but it was a public school and he had rich and well-connected parents. Few of those who have made it to the top actually start with nothing. Michael Heseltine, who made his money from publishing, left Oxford in the 1950s with a cheque for £1,000 from his maternal grandfather.[3] Philip Green likes to present himself as self-made but in fact was the son of well-to-do Jewish parents. They owned a small property company while his father was also an electrical retailer. Philip was sent to Carmel College, a boarding school that liked to see itself as the 'Jewish Eton'. Although he left school at the age of sixteen with no qualifications, it was not because of his background or ability, but because of his impatience with academia. His background and his mother's contacts within north London's Jewish business community soon enabled him to embark on what turned out to be a remarkably successful business career in clothing.[4]

The cycle of privilege

The rich have always contained a mix of those who inherited wealth and/or privilege, and those who started with little. The balance between the two is an important indicator of how open and opportunistic a society is. So how much has the balance changed over time, if at all? As the economist Joseph Schumpeter once put it, even if the wealth hotel is permanently full, how often do the guests change?

What is clear is that for most of the last hundred years and more, Britain has been a relatively fixed society with a pretty rigid class system where the opportunities for advancement from the bottom of the class structure to the very top have been and continue to be limited. A 'cycle of privilege' has been at work, a process by which the advantaged of one generation have ensured that the family baton is passed onto the next one. In recent years this description has been challenged as out of date. Britain, it is claimed, is now a much more opportunistic society, one in which it is much easier to rise to the top, a society which is increasingly 'classless'.

The evidence about the past is pretty clear cut. In the period up to the Second World War, very few of those who made it into the wealth ranks could be described as strictly self-made. A study by the wealth historian Bill Rubinstein of the backgrounds of all those worth at least a million in the period up to 1939 shows that the great majority 'emerged from backgrounds of affluence or real wealth, while only a small minority were the sons of men without means or from manual or low-clerical occupations'. Over this period, Rubinstein concluded that 'the most important qualification for achieving millionaire status in Britain has been to have had a wealthy father'. He identified a total of 331 millionaires in the period from 1809 to 1939. Of these he found that only fifteen could be described as strictly self-made, that is, born into poverty or the working class – less than 5 per cent of the total.

Widening the original background to include shopkeeping, farming, lower professionals and the 'very smallest businessmen' increased the proportion of self-made to nearly 22 per cent of the total.[5]

The rarity of the self-made in the rich lists of the time is hardly surprising, as Rubinstein explained:

> To leave a fortune of £1 million starting from scratch in the nineteenth century was an astonishing achievement . . . Given the class barriers which undoubtedly existed after the early nineteenth century, for even a single individual to rise from working-class to wealth-holder in the course of one working lifetime is so phenomenal as almost to strain credence, and to rise even from the middle class is a remarkable feat.[6]

Despite the barriers, some from modest backgrounds did build large personal fortunes. In 1857, the banker and warehouseman James Morrison left £4 million, a very substantial sum, enough to get him into the ranks of the top ten most wealthy at the time. The son of a Hampshire innkeeper, he arrived without means in London, worked in a drapery warehouse, married the boss's daughter, became a merchant banker and served as an MP. His eldest son, Charles, continued to run the business and left £10.9 million in 1909. Although Charles was certainly not self-made like his father, he did triple his inherited fortune and may well have been the second wealthiest man in Britain, after the Duke of Westminster, at his death.[7]

John Brunner, who jointly founded the chemical firm that became ICI, was the son of a Unitarian minister and schoolmaster. Brunner's first job, at fifteen, was as an office boy in a Liverpool shipping office.[8] John Sainsbury, who founded the supermarket chain and who died in 1928, was the son of a worker in the frame and ornament trade in Lambeth. Viscount Leverhulme, who founded Lever Brothers, is often claimed to be self-made but in fact inherited £58,000 from his father.

Perhaps the most remarkable story of personal wealth creation in this period was John Ellerman, the shipowner and financier, who left a staggering £36.7 million when he died in 1933 at the bottom of the depression. No less than £9 million of this was cash in the bank. At the age of nine, Ellerman had been left £600 by his father, a small corn merchant, trained as an accountant and developed an empire that eventually extended across shipping, finance, brewing, property and newspapers. His only son, who kept the family business going, left £53 million when he died in 1973.

In contrast with some aristocratic families that still practise primogeniture

– the passing of wealth down the male line – most non-landed wealth-holders have tended to disperse their property evenly amongst their heirs. This has had the effect of creating several relatively wealthy descendants rather than only one very wealthy heir, as has continued to be the more typical pattern amongst the landed elite. This is one of the factors in the reduced concentration of wealth at the very top that took place in Britain from the mid-1930s.

The experience of those who have inherited large sums has been mixed. Many businesses first created in the nineteenth century have continued to prosper with family descendants at the helm, even to this day. A member of the Cadbury family, Sir Dominic Cadbury, was chairman of Cadbury Schweppes until 2000, while Tate and Lyle had a chairman from the Tate family until 1978. The third Viscount Cowdray continued to control Pearson until the 1970s, when he became president. By then Pearson had become a huge conglomerate, spanning the *Financial Times,* the *Economist,* Penguin Books and Longman. One of the clearest examples of longevity is the merchant banking firm Rothschild, which has continued to be run by family members since it was founded at the beginning of the nineteenth century by Nathan Rothschild. He himself was an immigrant from a wealthy eighteenth-century Frankfurt-based banking family. Little of the wealth passed down through the generations has been dissipated. No fewer than twenty-one Rothschilds have left sums over £500,000 since Nathan died in 1836.[9]

While these illustrate the remarkable staying power of many family businesses, in most of today's large firms with histories going back to the nineteenth century, the founding families will have lost control or lost interest. This is not to say that they ended up poor, just mostly less wealthy than their forebears, but still sufficiently wealthy to live, at least in some cases, the life of the idle rich. This appears to be especially true of inheritors in the period from the turn of the century up to the Second World War. As Rubinstein has put it, 'the incentives to continue in the entrepreneurial paths of the founder of the dynasty's fortunes simply disappeared . . . it is more than likely that most of the sons and grandsons simply lived on their interest, invested unimaginatively in blue chip stocks, and in turn left little more than they inherited.'[10]

What was happening is that while a small minority of wealthy families continued to build their fortunes, the majority managed to sustain enough wealth to stay on the fringes of the wealth lists, while the remainder – a small number – gradually dissipated their wealth over subsequent generations, disappearing altogether from the ranks of wealthy society. Some children of industrialists and manufacturers seemed to succumb easily to the pressures to leave the business world and join the landed gentry, the London social scene or, in some cases, the diplomatic service. The descendants of the Arkwrights and Peels, for example, once they gained access to the status that came with great wealth, quickly lost interest in business. The last traceable wealthy heir of Lord Overstone, the Victorian millionaire banker, died in 1944.[11] Nevertheless, the descendants of rich families who ended up back at the bottom were very much a small minority. The process of downward mobility seems to have a pretty firm floor, one that stops towards the higher end of the wealth distribution.

This does not mean that the old rich have had it all their own way. As one set of entrepreneurs have stepped out of the picture, they have typically been replaced by a new group who have built wealth in newer areas of enterprise. Indeed, if the existing rich continued generation after generation to hog all the new economic developments, the baton would rarely get passed on. And passed on it has been, at least to a degree. The combination of wealth dissipation and the arrival of newcomers has meant that 'the nineteenth-century fears of a self-perpetuating, stagnant and even-wealthier caste of great fortune-holders have never come to pass'.[12] In the immediate post-war era, old money continued to maintain a strong presence amongst the very rich, but it was steadily joined by a new generation of entrepreneurs. And while the old rich largely stuck to their old trades, the new entrepreneurs mainly developed the new opportunities – in property, retail, consumer goods and services.

When the *Sunday Times* published its list of the richest 400 in Britain in 1990, it contained many familiar names as well as new ones. As many as 40 per cent were found to have inherited their wealth.[13] As well as aristocratic landowners, heirs of old industrial and trading money on the list included the Pilkingtons, who had started what became the largest glassmakers in the world in St Helens in 1826; Lord Leverhulme of Lever Brothers (later Unilever); the meat and shipping Vestey family; and the Earl of Iveagh, scion of the founders of Guinness. There were also several old banking families, including the Rothschilds, the Schroders and the Kleinworts.

Many of the great Victorian families were not represented. There were no Arkwrights, Brunels, or Dunlops; no steel magnates, textile firms, ship-builders and or shipowners. This was partly, of course, a sign of the steady deindustrialisation of Britain in the previous two decades. Old-style heavy industry and manufacturing had virtually gone as a source of great fortunes. However, some of the family descendants of this group would still have been wealthy but not enough to get them into the top 400.

New entrepreneurs in the 1990 list who had made money in the immediate post-war decades included Garfield Weston, the food retailer, the son of a Toronto banker; property developer Harry Hyams; and the legendary financier Tiny Rowland. Amongst those who had built their fortunes in the period since the late 1960s were the Rausing brothers, Sir James Goldsmith, Robert Maxwell, the Barclay twins and the Saatchi brothers. Amongst the top ten, four were born outside Britain – in Sweden, Canada, the United States and Czechoslovakia.

The list of 400 contained only twenty-three women, including the Queen; Anita Roddick, the founder of the Body Shop; and Vivien Duffield, daughter of Charles Clore. Some of the property developers who made money in the 1960s, such as Lord Samuel of Wych Cross, were of relatively lowly origins. Rowland, who was the son of a German trader, was born in a British internment camp in India in the First World War. Maxwell, as he liked to remind people, had been born penniless in Czechoslovakia. Lord Weinstock, managing director of GEC, was the son of a Jewish tailor who arrived in Britain from Poland in 1906. Some were refugees from Germany before the war. There were a total of twenty-one Asian immigrants, many of whom had fled Idi Amin's Uganda in the 1970s. Others were hardly self-made. Goldsmith's father Frank made millions from hotels and became Conservative MP for Stowmarket. One of those on the list, Gerald Ronson, was serving a one-year gaol sentence at Ford open prison for his part in the Guinness business scandal.

As in 1990, the 2005 list contains many names from the past. As seen in the last chapter, the landed aristocracy is more thinly but still remarkably well represented. Heirs of Victorian financiers and industrialists are also there in force. They include the Sainsburys, the Vesteys, the Guinness family, the Rothermeres, the Rothschilds and the Cowdrays. Some of these are still involved in running the business, others simply own large parts of the former family firm. In many ways, old money has proved more enduring than new. Also strongly represented in the list are a number with second-generation wealth, the children of those who made fortunes in the inter-war years and in the immediate post-war era. As well as the offspring of the Mayfair set, there is Kirsten Rausing, daughter of Gad Rausing, who owned Tetra Laval and whose fortune was shared between his widow and three children when he died in 2000. George Weston of Associated British Foods, which makes Sunblest sliced bread and Wagon Wheel biscuits, is the son of Garfield Weston, who was considered to be Britain's wealthiest man in the 1960s. Many of the wealthy are very well connected. Galen Weston, the Canadian retailing billionaire who now owns Selfridges and is the brother of Garfield Weston, played polo with Prince Charles when he was younger, went to the Queen Mother's 100th birthday party and owns a grand gated community in Florida called Windsor. Lucas White and Normandie Keith are often seen in the company of the London glitterati including the Duke of York, Jemima Khan and supermodel Jodie Kidd.

The list also contains many who have built a fortune without a head start. As well as the Barclay brothers and Alan Sugar, for example, they include John Caudwell, the owner of Phones4U, who left school at sixteen, joined the local Michelin plant as an apprentice engineer, moved onto selling used cars, and sold his second-hand car business in Stoke-on-Trent to go into mobile phones just at the point when the market took off. In 1979, William Adderley was a market stall holder in Leicester. Today Dunelm Mill, his chain of more than seventy-five soft furnishing stores, now run by his son, is one of Britain's most profitable firms. In 1960, Tony Yerolemuo arrived in Britain from Cyprus at the age of eighteen. In 1993 he borrowed £75,000 and started Katsouris Fresh Foods, which he sold for £102 million in 2001.

The apple falls close to the tree

So just how open a society is Britain today? Have the barriers to social mobility that undoubtedly existed in the past been eroded? Those who argue that Britain has moved on from its past and is now a much more opportunistic society often point to the United States as a model of the type of aspirant society they think Britain should be aiming to build.

The United States has long been considered to be a highly socially mobile nation, offering its ordinary citizens every opportunity for advancement. As *Life* magazine put it in 1949, 'this phenomenon of social mobility – the opportunity to move rapidly upward through the levels of society – is the distinguishing characteristic of US democracy and the thing for which it is famous and envied throughout the world'.[14] This is the essence of the American dream, a dream still strongly echoed today. 'So there really is, at our roots, something special about this country that is often not fully appreciated, something that seems to explain why so much of the wealth in America was earned or brought here, and why old money tied to social class and station is just not that important'.[15] In 1996, a CBS poll asked, 'Do you think it's possible to start poor in this country, work hard and become rich?' to which 78 per cent said yes and 18 per cent no.

Just as in Britain, there are many examples of Americans who have risen to the top from humble origins. Andrew Carnegie was a self-made Scottish immigrant whose parents were artisans. Sam Walton of Wal-Mart started with very little and was the first in his family to accumulate significant money. Larry Ellison, the founder of Oracle, was born to a poor single parent. While Britain continues to be obsessed by its class system, Americans routinely deny that they even have one. On the other hand, having a rich and successful parent or grandparent has also proved a pretty good route to success and wealth. Bill Gates's great-grandfather founded Seattle's National City Bank in 1911. There are other prominent examples: George H. W. Bush and George W. Bush; Henry Fonda and Jane Fonda; Estee Lauder and Ronald Lauder; Sam Walton and Jim, John, S. Robson and Alice Walton. The four Walton children, together with their mother, were America's richest family in 2005.

So how much social mobility really exists in America? Studies of long-run social mobility in the United States show that the proportion of nineteenth-century rich businessmen emerging from a lower-class background stood at 10 to 13 per cent across the century, and those from a lower middle-class background stood at 18 to 26 per cent.[16] Another study showed that the proportion of living American millionaires in 1926 from a wealthy background stood at 53 per cent; this compared with 30 per cent for an earlier period and led the study's author, Pitirim Sorokin, to suggest it showed a trend towards 'the wealthy class of the United States . . . becoming less and less open, and more and more closed, and tending. . . to be transformed into a caste-like group'.[17]

A later study published in 1971, entitled *The Egalitarian Myth*, found that only about 2 per cent of the top wealth-holders in four large American cities were born poor, while 6 per cent came from a background of 'middling economic status'. In New York, 95 per cent of the 100 wealthiest persons 'were born into families of wealth or high status or occupation'.[18] The pattern is clear – that, from the Civil War until at least the 1970s, rates of social mobility were low, at best constant and may have declined slightly compared with the nineteenth century.[19] One leading British expert, comparing Britain and America, concluded, 'What emerges . . . is how little the "self-made" components of non-landed millionairedom in Britain differ from that among Americans.'[20] Another American analyst, writing in 1995, has concluded that, over the same time period,

> the concentration of corporate power, the decline of small-scale production, the separation of production from consumption, the growth of the welfare state, the professionalization of knowledge and the erosion of competence, responsibility and citizenship have made the United States into a society in which class divisions run far more deeply than they did in the past.[21]

It is often contended that America has seen considerable downward mobility out of the wealth class. In all affluent societies, there are certainly strong pressures to dissipate wealth once created. Dissolute living, poor business decisions, generosity, tax or sheer bad luck have all contributed to the erosion of once great fortunes. Having a large family can also be added to the list. It was Carnegie who is believed to have coined the phrase 'from shirtsleeves to shirtsleeves in three generations'. Most countries have their own version of the proverb to describe the process of rags to riches and back again – 'clogs to clogs', 'rice paddy to rice paddy', for example.

In the 1980s, Gary S. Becker of the University of Chicago had estimated that the correlation between a father's and son's income was only around 0.15, less than half the correlation between their heights. This means that if a father's income was twice the average, his son's expected income would be 15 per cent above average and his grandson's just 2 per cent above average. This is 'fast regression towards the mean', a concept that the eminent nineteenth-century British statistician Sir Francis Galton used to describe the progression of offspring towards the average height. But in fact, more recent research suggests that this and Carnegie's 'three generations' are a substantial understatement. American economists have marked up their estimate of the impact of parental background on their children's economic position and now argue that it may take five or six generations on average to erase the advantages or disadvantages of one's economic origins. Landmark studies that have reworked Becker's theory using improved data have found the correlation to be much higher at 0.65. The relationship between father's and daughter's earnings was just as strong. This means that a grandson or granddaughter could expect to earn 42 per cent more than average. (In

Britain, the correlation has been estimated to be in the order of 0.4 to 0.6 for sons and 0.45 to 0.7 for daughters.)[22]

This degree of persistence across generations appears to hold for both rich and poor. A child born in the bottom tenth of families ranked by income has a 31 per cent chance of remaining there as an adult and a 51 per cent chance of ending up in the bottom fifth. One born in the top tenth, in contrast, has a 30 per cent chance of staying there and a 43 per cent chance of being in the top fifth. These findings have led one leading American economist, Alan B. Krueger of Princeton University, to argue that 'the data challenge the notion that the United States is an exceptionally mobile society. If the United States stands out in comparison with other countries, it is in having a more static distribution of income across generations with fewer opportunities for advancement.'[23] The international evidence is that only South Africa and Britain have as little mobility across the generations as the United States. As Krueger put it, 'the apple falls close to the tree, even in the land of opportunity'.

It has long been popular in the United States to argue that even the largest of fortunes are mostly short lived, to dismiss the importance of the inheriting rich. Alexis de Tocqueville, for example, a French aristocrat who emigrated to America in the 1830s, once observed that 'in no country in the world are private fortunes more precarious than in the United States. It is not uncommon for the same man in the course of his life to rise and sink again through all the grades that lead from opulence to poverty.'[24] Contemporary writers echo the same view: 'Dynasties based on inherited family wealth don't work anymore, if they ever did.'[25] It is certainly true that fortunes can sink as well as rise.

Since it started in 1982, the *Forbes* 400 list has seen falls and rises, some spectacular, others less so – only fifty-eight names stayed on the list for all twenty years between 1982 and 2002. These include Warren Buffett; William Clay Ford; Roy Disney, the nephew of Walt Disney; Ross Perot; Ted Turner; and three Rockefellers. According to *Forbes*, this movement is due to 'the dynamic nature of American capitalism which never settles into the sort of equilibrium that would give rise to a permanent aristocracy of wealth'.[26] Recent fortunes have certainly been vulnerable to sudden changes in the stock market. Perot was the first person to lose $1 billion in one day when his EDS stock plummeted in 1969. Bill Gates lost $12 billion on 'Black Wednesday' in April 2000. In 2003, four of those on the *Forbes* list of billionaires for 2002 had been wiped out entirely.[27] Since 2000, several very rich Americans have seen their fortunes sink dramatically. The last twenty years have also seen a big shake-up in the country's most profitable industries. In 1982, eight of the top ten were oil moguls – today oil has been replaced by technology fortunes. Not that all the oil barons have disappeared. Philip Anschutz, the oil magnate, who was in the top ten in 1982, came in at thirty-six in 2002, mainly as a result of embracing technology. The oil heir Gordon Getty, who topped the *Forbes* list in 1983 and 1984, was eighty-seventh in 2002.

Nevertheless, despite a good deal of churning at the top, the wealth of many older families has more than survived the economic tribulations of the last century, as have some more recent fortunes.[28] In 1982, one American historian observed:

> Many of the titanic enterprises founded in the heroic age of capitalism are still headed and owned by descendants of the original proprietors: a Rockefeller grandson chairs the board of Chase Manhattan, the nation's third-largest bank and a longtime family-controlled institution; a Ford grandson rules the Ford Motor Company; Hearst's children run his publishing empire; Andrew Mellon's son-in-law and nephew administer that clan's industrial and financial interests.[29]

America's richest forebears may not dominate the very top as they once did, but they are still very much part of America's wealthy elite. In the 1930s, the second-generation Rockefellers, duPonts, Mellons and Phippses were collectively worth between $2 billion and $4 billion. In 2000, they were collectively worth some $38 billion, despite not owning a dominant piece of any emerging industry. (This is roughly a 25 per cent increase, after adjusting for inflation.) A similar pattern is true of other early rich families. Ranked by family wealth, old money in 2000 outweighed first-generation wealth. Some 500 to 1,000 families inherited or amassed between $25 million and $50 million between the Civil War and the 1920s and survived the 1929 crash. By 2000 at least half would have had upwards of $100 million. 'Their various family branches, twigs and tree-grafts, probably some 15,000 to 25,000 heirs, constituted the mainstays of what was quietly becoming an American hereditary aristocracy.'[30] Old robber baron wealth appears to be a good deal more durable than many have claimed. 'Elaborate trusts, well-staffed family offices and professional financial management had combined into the US equivalent of the entail and primogeniture that kept landed wealth intact and concentrated in eighteenth and nineteenth century Britain.'[31] As *Forbes* put it, 'by establishing a family office, you hope to protect heirs yet unborn against economic misfortune long after they are gone'.[32]

Indeed, some of the wealth gains of old families in the 1990s were as large as those of the new technology tycoons. According to one account, the Phipps family, which built its fortune – originally as partners of Andrew Carnegie – through steel, expanded its collective worth from $1 billion in 1982 to $7 billion in 1999, largely through the use of the expertise of the Bessemer Trust, founded by Henry Phipps in 1907 and which specialises in managing the assets of wealthy individuals and families.[33] Bessemer greeted the new millennium with an advert that claimed that its private client investments had annualised returns of 37.9 per cent between 1987 and 1999, mainly because of the pursuit of venture capital and buy-out opportunities not available to the lesser wealthy. This is one of the explanations for the swelling of personal wealth holdings in America in the last decade and a half, a trend that simultaneously entrenched the concentration of wealth at the very top.

In America, there has been much talk of the 'democratisation of wealth', a process by which 'worn-out' inherited wealth would steadily be overtaken, eroded or broken up and replaced by the dynamic and determined newcomers racing up the ladder of opportunity. Eventually ability and drive would come to be more important than birth. In fact, the evidence is that the degree of social mobility actually achieved has been relatively modest and has not proceeded, if at all, at anything like the rate necessary to meet the ideal of Jeffersonian democracy – to replace 'an aristocracy of wealth with an aristocracy of talent'. Kevin Phillips estimates that of the 100,000 richest Americans, all worth $25 million or more, about half are new and the rest represent subsequent generations of earlier families.[34]

The myth of a meritocracy

If the United States is not a model of meritocracy, what about the United Kingdom? Is Britain now a modern, meritocratic society in which economic opportunity is more evenly shared than in the past, or are those with a privileged background still much more likely to make it to the top?

The word 'meritocracy' was first coined in 1958 by the sociologist Michael Young in his book *The Rise of the Meritocracy*. Young's book was a satire that looked at what a futuristic Britain would be like if job recruitment were based not on social origin, but on talent and effort. He was issuing a strong warning about the dangers of the even greater rigidities and unfairness inherent in a society heavily structured by a mix of intelligence and effort alone.

Despite this, the idea of a meritocracy was soon embraced as a desirable goal by liberal opinion. Young's concerns were largely ignored or discounted. Today, it is an aim shared across the political divide. Margaret Thatcher, the daughter of a Grantham grocer, was eager to weaken the power of the old British establishment and replace it with one based on merit, not birth. John Major, himself the son of a circus performer, talked of building a 'classless society'. Tony Blair, minor public school and Oxford, is strongly wedded to an aspirational culture, downgrading Labour's traditional commitment to greater equality of outcome in favour of equality of opportunity.

Nevertheless, while politicians of right and left share the vision, the issue of whether Britain has actually become more meritocratic has proved a much more divisive one. Some commentators on the free-market right have argued that class differences in modern societies are much more closely linked to the genetic inheritance of intelligence and aptitude than to background. The most powerful advocation of this view comes from Richard Herrnstein and Charles Murray, who, in their controversial book *The Bell Curve*, published in 1994, claimed that American society is now close to an IQ meritocracy. A similar view about the UK has been made by Peter Saunders, a right-of-centre British academic. In his tract *Unequal but Fair?*, Saunders argues that Britain is 'much closer to achieving a meritocracy than pundits and public alike seem to suppose'.[35]

The title of the tract is highly significant in itself – it reflects the view that inequality is more acceptable if it is based on merit, a view embraced by free-market neo-conservatives, who claim that today's rising inequalities 'do not in fact reflect any serious social injustice but simply the varying capacities of individuals, whatever their social origins, to take up the opportunities that are available to them'.[36] Today's first-time rich, for example, typically see themselves as part of a new and deserving elite that has earned its place at the top of British society. Entrepreneurs, corporate bosses and professionals alike view their success as the product of merit, hard work and skill and their wealth as a just reward for that. (The issue of whether merit justifies such large rewards is a separate one that will be examined in Chapter 10.)

These views are hotly contested by the majority of academics working in the field of long-term social mobility. Researchers have distinguished between two types of mobility. There has been a substantial increase in *absolute* upward mobility as a result of the swelling of the ranks of the middle classes with rising numbers of working-class children moving to middle-class status. *Relative* mobility, on the other hand, relates to the relative chance of people from different social backgrounds making it to a higher social class.

There are three main conclusions from the evidence about relative mobility. First, it remains low. Second, Britain now has one of the worst international records on social mobility in the developed world. Britain's record is significantly worse than Canada's, Germany's or that of the Nordic countries. Britain and the US, in contrast, exhibit similar levels of mobility. Third, the latest, provisional evidence is that mobility has, if anything, been going into reverse in recent decades – that children born in the 1970s are likely to be socially less mobile than those born in the 1950s, that children's futures are, if anything, becoming even more closely related to their parents' income and class. This is mainly because the increase in educational upgrading of recent times has occurred amongst the offspring of affluent parents, creating a greater divide in life chances between the children of the better off and the poor.[37] It is becoming harder to reverse the advantages of birth because the mechanisms that protect middle-class children from downward mobility through education, contacts and money are becoming more effective. Britain is less a mobile society than a stagnant one.

Of course there are exceptional cases of individual success. Tim Campbell and Saira Khan, who made it to the top on the television reality show *The Apprentice*, are both from humble backgrounds. There are examples of sons and daughters of miners and cleaners making it into the top professions. But, on average, the odds of a working-class child improving his or her relative class position are no higher today than they were fifty years ago, and may actually be worse. According to the Cabinet Office, the chances of a child from a middle-class background making it to the middle class themselves are fifteen times higher than the chances of a child from a working-class background.[38] As two of Britain's leading experts have put it, 'merit in fact plays only a rather limited role in processes of inter-generational class mobility and in no way annuls the effects of individuals' class origins'. They have concluded: 'the prevailing situation is one in which children of less advantaged origins need to show substantially more 'merit' than do children from more advantaged origins in order to enter similarly desirable class positions in the course of their adult lives'.[39]

The studies cited above relate mainly to upward movement from one class or income group to another higher group and therefore compare change across the full class and income range. But there is a third kind of mobility: *elite* mobility, which relates to a more narrow definition involving a move from the bottom or middle to the very top. This book focuses on elite mobility, though the wider studies do throw light on this.

The evidence about trends in the origins of the richest suggests that the proportion of the wealthy who are self-made at any moment in time has rarely exceeded 20 per cent. One work studied the composition of those leaving over £100,000 in 1956, 1965 and 1973, and therefore covering those born from the end of the nineteenth century. Tracing the estates left by their fathers, it found that 'between two-thirds and four-fifths of those who died rich owed their wealth to inheritance and the rest to entrepreneurship or luck'. Inheritance, the authors concluded, is the main determinant of wealth inequality.[40]

In another, later, study, which traced the origins of millionaires who died in 1984 and 1985, three-quarters had inherited over £10,000 – usually a substantial sum at the time they inherited it. Although this study wasn't directly comparable with earlier ones, it also found that the proportion of millionaires who were entirely 'self-made' had doubled from 10 to 20 per cent over the post-war period.[41] But 20 per cent remains a low figure and these studies suggest that, for the period covered, a 'cycle of privilege' undoubtedly continued to exist, with a substantial overlap between the rich of one generation and the next.

Although there has been no systematic study of the period since 1985, there is some evidence on elite mobility for the last fifteen years. One study of successful business leaders – mainly chief executives and chairmen – over time shows that in the 1990s they 'continue[d] to be drawn from economically and educationally elite sections of society'. The study found little change in the relative background of such leaders despite a century and a half of dramatic social and economic change. 'Becoming a business leader in Britain is still largely determined by the interconnected characteristics of a wealthy family and a prestige education . . . Judged against relative mobility measures, there has been no democratisation of British business over the last century and a half.'[42] This confirms earlier studies of the period to the 1970s, which showed that recruitment into elite groups, including directors of leading companies, tended to be highly socially exclusive.[43]

Another study, of the backgrounds of 15,000 company directors, published in 1997, found a similar pattern – that the British business community continued to be a very narrow club, an overwhelmingly male world dominated by Oxbridge and the top public schools. Almost half came from a public school background, with Eton the top choice followed by Rugby, Winchester, Marlborough and Harrow. More than 50 per cent went to Oxford or Cambridge. The directors' ranks also included more than 400 with aristocratic titles. Some prominent business leaders did have more modest starts. Granada's Sir Gerry Robinson was educated at St Mary's Seminary in Lancashire and began his career as a clerk in a toy factory, Tesco's Sir Terry Leahy was brought up on a Liverpool council estate and went to the local grammar school, while Dame Anita Roddick went to Littlehampton Secondary Modern; but on the whole, the breeding grounds for the business elite seem to have moved very little in more than a hundred years.[44]

More recent studies show a slight increase in the proportion of top business leaders who went to grammar schools. A comparison of the backgrounds of a much narrower group – those heading FTSE 100 companies, for example – suggests that the influence of Oxbridge and the top public schools is less amongst this group. In 2003, the proportion from grammar schools was on a par with those from fee-paying schools, while less than a fifth came from secondary moderns.[45] The presence of those from grammar schools, of course, is not in itself a sign of a significant improvement in mobility. It simply means that opportunities have passed slightly down the chain. Indeed, the fifth of all pupils who enjoyed a grammar school education in the 1960s would have come disproportionately from affluent middle-class backgrounds.

The *Sunday Times* claims that the proportion of those in their list who have inherited their wealth has steadily fallen from some 40 per cent in 1990 to closer to a quarter in 2005, while the proportion who are self-made has risen to 75 per cent over the period. The paper has used this trend to claim that the top 1,000 are 'becoming more meritocratic'. But the paper defines the 'self-made' in a very specific way – as all those without an inheritance. This is a very wide definition which says only a little about background. Many of the 750 defined as self-made in the *Sunday Times* list for 2005 will not be so by the definition used in academic studies, which have typically examined parental background and wealth. While many of the 750 do come from humble beginnings, as we have seen, many also come from relatively wealthy and privileged backgrounds, even if they did not inherit, or have not yet inherited, a business or a large financial sum. James Dyson was born to middle-class academic parents and was educated at Gresham's School. Lord

Lloyd Webber, the son of a composer who was awarded the CBE, went to Westminster School. Sir Martin Sorrell, the head of WPP, and Michael Green, the former chairman of Carlton Communications, both went to Haberdashers' Aske's independent school at Elstree. These men may be self-made in the sense that they did not inherit a business, but they still come from relatively privileged backgrounds compared with most of the population. A head start they have certainly had. The likelihood is that most of the 750 will have been born to families towards the top end of the income distribution. The 75 per cent is thus an overstatement of the proportion who are self-made in the sense of rising from the bottom of the pile.

There is another factor at work in the apparent rise in the number of 'self-made' in the *Sunday Times* list. Over the last fifteen years, the proportion of rich celebrities, rock musicians and television stars in the list has been rising – the direct result of the staggering increases in fees and in some cases lucrative sponsorship deals they have been able to command in this time. Celebrities, sports stars and rock musicians typically, though not always, come from more modest backgrounds. If the list of the rich was confined to business (that is, excluding celebrities, musicians and sports stars), the proportion of the 'self-made', as defined by the *Sunday Times*, would be lower.

In addition, if there had been a noticeable increase in the rate at which new wealth was emerging and replacing past wealth, one would expect a considerable degree of churning across the lists. In fact, the movement in and out of the *Sunday Times* list over the last fifteen years has been somewhat limited. Indeed, there is a substantial overlap between the 1990 and 2005 lists. Of the top fifty in 1990, forty-three of them or their families were still in the top 1,000 in 2005. Of the seven who had dropped out, one had given his money away, and two had died, including Robert Maxwell. Of the top 100 in 1990, no fewer than eighty-one of them or their offspring were still in the top 1,000 fifteen years later.[46] This suggests a considerable degree of short-term stability.

There is certainly no strong reason to believe that the wealthy are a significantly more meritocratic group than in the past. The strengthening competition for the top prizes in business and the growth of more demanding entry requirements may mean that the top posts have increasingly become open to only the best and the brightest. There may therefore be fewer 'duds' who make it to the top just because of their background. Nevertheless, this in itself is not an indicator of a significant improvement in elite mobility. Many of those who might be capable of making it to the top may be missing out because of the continuing political and social constraints laid in their way. Applications for the top jobs in business and the City have been escalating sharply, which means that firms can be increasingly choosy. Often the first criterion for getting onto the short-list is school and university. 'Playing safe' is commonplace. The selection process is thus still likely to favour those from the elite educational institutions and a privileged background, with the brightest of those making it.

The best evidence is that although there is undoubtedly fluidity, with some people from poor backgrounds making it to the top as they have always done, and some descendants of the rich dissipating their inheritance, birth remains the most powerful indicator of where you are likely to end up in the wealth stakes. Wealth buys a high and secure living standard. But it also buys life chances, just as it has always done. The wealthy, unsurprisingly, pass on their own advantages to their children.

Just as in the United States, there has only been a somewhat limited 'democratisation of wealth' at best. In the UK, a century and more of economic and social upheaval has had at best a marginal impact on the chances of those from lower income groups making it to the top. The wealth tables tell us a lot about social and economic change in Britain over the last century and longer, but what they do not show is the advent of a meritocracy and a sharply improved elite mobility.

But what do they tell us about wealth and power? It is generally argued that power in modern Britain is much more diffused than it once was. But has the rise in personal enrichment of the last two decades changed the power balance as well?

7

The new super-class

The rise of the Super Class . . . is a seminal development in modern Britain, as critical as the rise of the gentry before the English Civil War and the rise of organized labour a century ago, and rivalled in contemporary significance only by the disintegration of the manual working class.

(Andrew Adonis and Stephen Pollard, A Class Act)[1]

At first glance, it might seem that today's business elite is not a class apart in the way that the old upper class could be seen as a single, monolithic and powerful entity. The members of that class – a mix of the old aristocracy and the new industrial and commercial barons – were unified by the enormous power and social status they enjoyed. Today's wealthy elite, in contrast, have a different, more modern feel. They mostly have a very strong work ethic. Few if any could be described as 'idle'. Today's entrepreneurs, executives and bankers are in many ways more diverse. The old rich groups would have contained few if any Asians, like the Hinduja brothers or the hotelier Jasminder Singh, and few if any women, like Penny Streeter and Emma Harrison, who have built up successful businesses from scratch.

Some of the modern rich have tried to infiltrate the networks of the old rich. In the 1990s, some members of the Garrick Club – an organisation that once epitomised the old establishment and still counts amongst its members many who had been the most powerful in the land – started to complain that it was now full of businessmen. But one sign of the changing times has been the emergence of new networks formed by younger rich arrivals who prefer to shun the clubs frequented by old money.

In 1998, the deal-making multi-millionaire Luke Johnson formed the Mandrake Club, a private, networking group for young or youngish, wealthy and often maverick entrepreneurs. Today it is jointly run with the Carphone Warehouse tycoon, David Ross, and meets once a month in Mayfair. Membership is exclusive and by invitation only. New entrepreneurs have typically eschewed the traditional gentleman's clubs favoured by the old establishment that are based around Pall Mall in London. Nor do they choose to drink champagne ostentatiously at the haunts preferred by highly paid City brokers. As Johnson put it, 'we needed to find somewhere to hang out that was not full of blokes from Unilever or Coopers & Lybrand'.[2] It is doubtful if the Mandrake Club numbers any dukes or viscounts amongst its members.

The new entrepreneurial style is also distinctive and often much more informal. The modern tycoon tends to be laid back, casually dressed, preferring the t-shirt to the pin stripe, the black BMW or Mercedes to the Rolls-Royce, Notting Hill or Canonbury to Chelsea or Surrey, a Gucci leather jacket to a black mink coat. The casually dressed traveller in the airport check-in queue next to you might be a travel agent or a hedge fund millionaire. Financial deals that would have been dreamt up over a lunch at the Savoy a decade and a half ago are as likely today to be agreed in informal conversation at more discreet gatherings such as those at the Mandrake and other exclusive rich clubs and dining circles.

Nevertheless, despite their diversity and their sometimes casual appearance, the rich today have a number of important characteristics in common that also make them a pretty unified group. First, they are an almost entirely private-sector club. Although a small proportion work in the public sector, a public-sector salary alone won't get you close to today's wealth-leaguers. The highest-paid public servant in Britain – Adam Crozier, chief executive of the Post Office, earns around £500,000 a year and received a £2.2 million bonus in 2005, but this was exceptional. The highest-paid civil servant, the director of information technology at the NHS, earned a meagre, at least by comparison, £250,000 in 2004, not enough to get him to the starting point. The Governor of the Bank of England earned £263,000. Mark Thompson, director general of the BBC, earned £450,000 in 2005. In contrast, the chief executive of ITV, Charles Allen, had a deal worth £21 million over four years.

Second, as we have seen, the new rich may contain some from modest backgrounds, but they remain a largely privileged group by upbringing. Although the proportion from Eton or Harrow, the traditional training grounds of the British upper class, has been declining, and the proportion from grammar schools rising, the composition of the wealth league is not yet a sign of a fundamentally more opportunistic Britain. Most members of the Mandrake Club, for example, are well connected, with public school and Oxbridge backgrounds. Johnson himself is the product of a grammar not a public school, the result of his father's early flirtation with the Labour Party, but went on to the distinctly posh Magdalen College, Oxford. David Ross went to Uppingham. Although today's business elite move in very different circles from their predecessors, they have formed their own powerful, interlocking and exclusive networks that make them members of the very kinds of elite business group that distinguished their entrepreneurial forebears. This is a new establishment in the making, joining and sometimes displacing those who once held the strings of financial power. It was perhaps no accident that Johnson, rather than the expected grandee, was controversially appointed the chairman of Channel 4 in 2004.

Third, if the old elite was obsessed with their social status, what binds the new rich is an obsession with money. 'Nobody is scared anymore to make money,' as one insider put it. On Johnson's appointment, one businessman who knows him well described it as an extraordinary decision: 'Luke is completely money-mad.'[3] This is a group that pursues wealth for wealth's sake and in general feels much less guilty about it and responsible for it. Fourth, the new rich remain a largely male club, just as they have always been. Few women have risen to the top of the entrepreneurial and City banking and corporate trees. As the *Sunday Times* described the proportion of women in its own rich list – 8 per cent in 2005 compared with 6 per cent in 1990 – 'it's nothing to shout about'.

And finally, today's rich are mostly driven by a strong sense of self-belief and determination, a desire to be noticed, to make their mark. As a group they may not want to rule the country directly as their plutocratic predecessors once did when political power and wealth went hand in hand. But, although they might deny it, power is very much at the heart of the ambitions of the new business elite. That power is exercised in different ways. Some have concentrated on building their businesses, enjoying their celebrity status, or on lavish living. Others have chosen to exercise their undoubted financial muscle to influence the political process and shape economic and tax policy. Some are happy to accept the social responsibilities that have traditionally been associated with wealth, but most are not. As Anthony Sampson has put it, they feel much less need than their predecessors to account for their wealth, whether to society, to governments or to God . . . The respect now shown for wealth and money-making, rather than for professional conduct and moral values, has been the most fundamental change in Britain over four decades.[4]

It might be argued that today's wealth elite is a group relatively well integrated into wider society, perhaps closer to the professional middle classes than the old upper classes they are slowly displacing. But, though they dress differently, mostly join different clubs and live in mansions that are more modern in style, their aspirations are identical to those of the old upper class – power and wealth and respectability and the symbols and trappings of status that go with it.

Wealth and power

For most of the eighteenth and nineteenth century, wealth and political power in Britain were inextricably interlinked. The rich, who were then dominated by the aristocracy, effectively ruled Britain. Today the link between wealth and Parliament has largely gone. The aristocracy is barely represented in the lower House. Since Sir Alec Douglas-Home, no Prime Minister has been synonymous with great wealth, most coming from middle- or lower middle-class backgrounds. There are several millionaires in Parliament but only a handful of very wealthy MPs. They include the controversial Geoffrey Robinson, who made his money through business, was a Treasury minister in Blair's first government and became notorious as the man who lent Peter Mandelson £370,000 to buy a house in Notting Hill. The richest MP is Shaun Woodward, worth over £30 million, and who left the Conservatives to join Labour in 1999. Although Woodward comes from a modest background, he married the wealthy supermarket heiress Camilla Sainsbury.

Old and even new money may be a largely spent force in Parliament, but whether wealth is synonymous with power remains a hot issue. On the morning of 6 October 1996, listeners to the BBC's *Today* programme were treated to an ill-tempered spat between two leading public figures, Andrew Neil, former editor of the *Sunday Times*, and Peregrine Worsthorne, former editor of the *Sunday Telegraph*, over the question of whether Britain was still run by a small and narrow elite. According to Neil, 'the establishment does exist. It's not as omnipresent as when you and I were wee lads but it's still around, it still controls a lot of levers of power.' Worsthorne retorted, 'That's a nonsensical theory. Andrew Neil and Rupert Murdoch have a conspiracy theory that members of what we call the establishment are running the country which is not wholly different . . . than the one Hitler had that the Jews were running Germany.'

Together with Margaret Thatcher, Neil and Murdoch believed that behind the scenes there was a group of people who had powerful connections with old money – Royalty, the landed aristocracy and parts of the established business community and press – who were still able to pull strings at the highest level. They included some senior journalists such as Worsthorne. In his autobiography, *Full Disclosure*, Neil called Worsthorne and his journalistic colleagues, Paul Johnson and Charles Moore, 'the Establishment bovver boys of the Tory press'. He reports Murdoch as warning him 'to beware the wrath of the Establishment: they will try to destroy you'.[5] The warning came because the *Sunday Times* serialised Andrew Morton's explosive book *Diana: Her True Story* in 1992. The book, sympathetic to Diana, unveiled the stormy marriage of the Prince and Princess of Wales.

The two former editors perhaps symbolise the changing face of the power stakes that has occurred in recent decades. The confrontation between the two men was in many ways a clash of the classes, a struggle between old and new Britain, the ex-public schoolboy from Stowe and Peterhouse against the ex-grammar schoolboy who went to Glasgow University: as Neil put it himself, somewhat ironically, 'the stuffy, snobbish, established, pseudo-aristocratic, High Tory versus . . . the brash, upwardly mobile, meritocratic Thatcherite'.[6] In the Radio 4 spat, both claims had elements of truth. An establishment still existed but it contained two different and sometimes warring camps: the old establishment, including Worsthorne, but in decline, and a newish establishment, including Neil himself and his proprietor, Murdoch, and very much in the ascendancy.

So to what extent is Britain today characterised by a small coterie of powerful elites and set of networks which wield power if not directly, then behind the scenes? And if such elites exist, how closely linked are they to personal wealth and just how different are they from those that held sway in the past? The issue of elites is an important one because the more powerful they become, the greater the danger that they undermine the democratic processes by usurping that power for their own benefit, destabilising society in the process.

No single group in modern Britain holds such a grip on power as the aristocracy once did. But that does not mean that elites have disappeared, or that power is now fully democratised or diffused. What has happened is that power has slowly shifted from the old single 'establishment' once dominated by the landed and industrial magnates. Today's 'power lists' are dominated by two main, and for the most part separate, groups – top politicians and their advisers on the one hand, and business leaders and their acolytes on the other. Of course, others who do not belong to either of these groups do play a role in shaping lives and influencing opinions and values. They might include newspaper editors, the director general of the BBC, celebrities such as David and Victoria Beckham, directors of leading charities and pressure groups, and senior civil servants. But their influence is secondary in comparison with that of the first two groups. In one power list drawn up by the *Observer* and Channel 4 in 2000, no fewer than thirty-eight of the top 100 represented business.

The term 'the establishment' was first coined by A. J. P. Taylor, the historian and broadcaster, in an article for the *New Statesman* in August 1953. It was then popularised by the journalist Henry Fairlie, writing in the *Spectator* in September 1955:

> By the Establishment I mean the whole matrix of official and social relations within which power is exercised . . . Anyone who has at any point been close to the exercise of power will know what I mean when I say that the Establishment can be seen at work in the activities of, not only the prime minister, the Archbishop of Canterbury and the Earl Marshal, but of such lesser mortals as the chairman of the Arts Council, the director-general of the BBC and even editor of the Times Literary Supplement, not to mention divinities like Lady Violet Bonham-Carter.

What Fairlie was referring to was a group of people in different walks of life that were linked by an interlocking network of background, schools, colleges and often clubs that gave them a privileged influence over key national decisions. In 1955, of course, the Prime Minister was Sir Anthony Eden, son of a baronet, married first to the daughter of another baronet, then to Sir Winston Churchill's niece. Eden attended Eton, served as an army officer in the First World War and then studied oriental studies at Oxford. Those were the days when the establishment could be spotted over lunch at the Savoy Grill, talking in hushed tones at the Garrick Club or drinking champagne at the first day of the Henley Regatta.

When Anthony Sampson published his first *Anatomy of Britain* in 1962, he was able to identify an establishment, a group of individuals and professions still able to pull the strings in many areas of British public and private life, from business and the City to the civil service and the military. In his later editions, published in 1992 and 2004, he found it more difficult to pin one down. Perhaps what distinguished the establishment of the past was its tradition and exclusivity. It was above all a social caste, drawn from narrow roots. It had its own hierarchy, with the law higher than medicine, medicine higher than the military, the army above the air force and the navy, and the diplomatic service the cream of the civil service. Right up to the 1960s, each continued to be drawn from privileged and narrow groups, using their own tight entry criteria and inbuilt resistance to change.[7] Today most of these groups, including the civil service and the medical profession, have become much more meritocratic and professionalised.

During the course of the 1980s, Margaret Thatcher declared war on this old establishment, which she believed was paralysing Britain. She had a deep distrust of most of the major institutions, from the civil service and the law to the church and academia, for she thought that they continued to be run by an old guard. She set out to replace them with a new guard, a wealth-creating elite. To some extent, the real agenda of the Thatcher era, reflected in the deregulation of markets and the cuts in taxation, was a return to the commitment to the rights of wealth and property that she felt had been undermined by four decades of egalitarianism. Thatcher's attempted revolution via political diktat has been at least partially successful, though it is also one aided by a powerful process of organic change.[8]

In a book published in 1996, *A Class Act*, Andrew Adonis and Stephen Pollard claimed the rise of a 'Super Class', 'a new elite of top professionals and managers, at once meritocratic but exclusive, very highly paid, some extraordinarily so, yet powerfully convinced of the justice of its rewards, and increasingly divorced from the rest of society by wealth, education, values, residence and lifestyle'.[9] The authors – one of whom, Andrew Adonis, has been made a peer to enable him to become a government minister – estimated the 'Super Class' to number some 8,500 people, somewhat larger than the aristocracy at the height of its power in the mid-nineteenth century. Membership is drawn from a handful of professions – lawyers, accountants, stockbrokers, company directors, bankers and financiers.

Such a power group undoubtedly exists and it is one with intricate links to wealth. Its members are distinguished by lucrative pay and comfortable lifestyles and, unlike the industrial barons of the late nineteenth century, are heavily London based and part of a relatively small and closed circle. As Sampson describes it, 'visiting Americans are surprised that most people they want to see can be found at a few clubs, dinner-parties or gatherings, without ever leaving a handful of postal districts in central London'.[10]

Members of this business elite believe strongly that they are there by merit, by personal effort and ability, and it is certainly true that background alone would not be enough – it would be difficult to survive for long with the right parents but the wrong aptitude and indeed attitudes. Nevertheless, although much of their wealth is new money, most do come from privileged educational backgrounds. Unlike the old landed aristocracy, they do not have land or titles to pass on. They have, however, found alternative ways of perpetuating themselves. As Pollard put it, 'it is an elite that is remarkably self-selecting and self-replicating'.[11]

The power brokers

There is certainly a powerful business elite in Britain today, just as there always has been. Those with real power – to change the course of events, to influence and alter government policy, to control important institutions – probably constitute maybe less than half the full membership of the 'super-class' – a 'hyper-class', an elite within an elite. But how much real power and influence do they wield?

Power is certainly a key motive for acquiring wealth. Back in 1929, when Henry Luce set up the American business magazine *Fortune*, he nearly called it 'Power'. In the nineteenth century, great fortunes brought public prominence, the opportunity for lavish living and for some the chance to do good. But, as one historian has put it, 'the ultimate gift of colossal wealth, at least for the founders of the richest families, was power. Money begat authority – and authority power.'[12] James Stillman, along with J. P. Morgan one of the great financiers of the Gilded Age, declared, ''Twasn't the money we were after, 'twas the power. We were all playing for power. It was a great game.'[13] Cornelius Vanderbilt once justified his lack of interest in charity by claiming that 'if you give away the surplus (Money), you give away the control'.[14] A century later, Howard Hughes, whose fortune fluctuated between $100 million and $1 billion, and who enjoyed both great wealth and great power, said, 'Money is the measuring rod of power . . . the effective use of money can bring power. The effective use of power can bring money.'[15]

It is often claimed that modern individual power is much less than it was. Bill Gates may be the richest person in the world but his nineteenth-century predecessors such as Morgan and J. D. Rockefeller wielded more direct power over the American economy, which was much less well developed at the time. Indeed, Morgan was arguably the most powerful American businessman who has ever lived. He controlled assets equivalent to some two-thirds of the nation's output. In 1901, he purchased Andrew Carnegie's empire to create the world's first billion-dollar corporation, US Steel. Morgan had a stranglehold over American business. Few corporations could borrow large sums other than through Morgan & Co. and a few other smaller investment banks. The flow of investment thus took place only in areas that he and a handful of his peers approved of. At one point, Morgan had sufficient liquid capital to finance all the capital needs in the United States for four months. While Morgan's economic power exceeded his wealth, Gates, in contrast, could finance the current American economy for only part of a day.[16] Nevertheless, although compared with their nineteenth-century predecessors the economic muscle of today's business mega-rich may have been diluted, it is still pretty potent.

In more recent times, the rich have preferred to play down the wider significance of their wealth. As one observer has put it, the rich seem to be 'in a kind of collective denial about their dominance. The rich claim never to exercise power in any sense more forceful than "responsibility" or "leadership".'[17] Sir James Goldsmith claimed that the power of an individual fortune today is very limited: 'It will never be as powerful as in the nineteenth century, nor should it be. It will always be a marginal personal thing compared to the major power of the state.'[18] That may be so, but as we have seen, Goldsmith and fellow conspirators in the Mayfair set collectively had a dramatic impact on the course of the British economy in the 1960s and 1970s. They may have been less powerful than the state, but their actions were still fundamental and irreversible in their repercussions.

Throughout the 1950s, British industry was run by a small group of elite businessmen, the 'captains of industry', men who played by the rules and liked to work in partnership with government. They may not all have been patricians, but they often had patrician attitudes and were a powerful part of the British establishment. They included Sir Charles Hambro, the banker; Sir John Hambury-Williams, the chairman of Courtaulds; and Lord

Kindersley, a City grandee, senior partner at Lazards and chairman of Rolls-Royce. They mostly liked to keep a low profile, and, unlike at least some modern businessmen, were not public figures. Many of them were members of the Court of the Bank of England. The 1950s was a decade, too, when the pursuit of shareholder value was not a primary objective of industry.

The takeover tycoons of the 1960s were to change all that. The predatory financial raids of the time steadily supplanted the old industry bosses. When Edward Heath became Prime Minister in 1970, the Slater Walker partnership found itself at the heart of the political establishment. Peter Walker became a Cabinet minister and his business partner, Jim Slater, an informal government adviser. They had achieved not just great wealth, but power as well.

Part of their objective was to tear up the old industrial model and displace the old establishment who ran it. For them an added bonus was to humiliate the old captains of industry. During the 1960s, Tiny Rowland built a huge industrial empire in Africa. As the British Empire disintegrated and one African nation after another became independent, Rowland started to buy up companies that were pulling out of the area. Sweeping through the continent in his private jet, he did deals with African leaders to secure companies, deals that he rarely honoured. Millions of pounds were also used to bribe top African politicians. Rowland liked to recruit old establishment figures from each of the companies he had bought as non-executive directors on his board. Sir Colin Mackenzie, ex-Eton and Sandhurst, a distinguished soldier and businessman, was on the Lonrho board from 1970 to 1973. As he put it, 'it was partly to beat the likes of us, he didn't like us very much, by us I mean the old establishment, he liked Etonians and put dozens on his board, he wanted to beat us at our own game'.[19]

To support his share price during the turbulent stock market conditions of the early 1970s, Rowland had resorted to a number of irregular accountancy devices to give the impression that the company was more profitable than it was. Although he resented the British establishment, to give the company prestige he had persuaded two well-connected former ministers, including Duncan Sandys, an old Etonian and former Commonwealth Secretary, to join the board. Sandys had agreed provided he was paid in part through an offshore account in the Cayman Islands. It was these controversial methods that led to Heath's direct attack in the House of Commons. When the old board members found out about the unorthodox accounting and the offshore payments, they revolted. The 'straight eight', as they became known, waited until Rowland was out of the country and then ousted him as chief executive. As well as Mackenzie, the rebels included Sir Edward Spears, a former chairman of the Ashanti gold mine in Ghana, and Sir Basil Smallpiece, the former chairman of Cunard.

The Lonrho scandal had much wider political significance. It came to symbolise the hidden fakery and sleaze that characterised much of the new tycoon activity. It was far from the end of Rowland, however. He summoned the company's many small shareholders – whom he had effectively enriched – to an emergency general meeting at Westminster Hall in May 1973, where the 'straight eight' were jeered as they were voted off the board. The battle for power between the old and new business establishment had been firmly won by the new. Despite his record, Rowland was later allowed to take over two national newspapers, *Today* and the *Observer.*

Just as business muscle was changing hands from the 1950s, today it is consolidated in a number of small, if different, centres of power, which together make up the super-class. One of those groups consists of the new, private equity tycoons, entrepreneurs such as Richard Branson, Rupert Murdoch and Philip Green, all of whom continue to play a central role in the companies they own.

Another group at the centre of the business power class is made up of the corporate managers of Britain's biggest companies, a group that has steadily risen up both the power and wealth ladders in Britain. These managers belong to a small and exclusive circle as a result of the remarkable overlap of directors across companies. Chairmen and chief executives of one company often sit as non-executive directors of another, giving them enormous business clout. In 2003, for example, Sir Robert Wilson was chairman of Rio Tinto and a director of Diageo, the drinks giant, and gas group BG. He is a former director of Boots and BP. At the end of the year, he stepped down from Rio Tinto and Diageo and took up a non-executive post with GlaxoSmithKline (GSK). By shuffling his portfolio of directorships he has close ties with a large number of directors and companies across British industry. The *Times* named him top of their Power 100 list in 2003. He is far from unique. Others on the list with multiple directorships and links included Sir Mark Moody-Stuart (Anglo-American, Shell, HSBC), Rob Margetts (Legal and General, BOC, Anglo American) and Sir Ian Prosser (InterContinental Hotels, BP, GSK).[20] Yet most of them and others in the *Times* Power 100 are barely known outside a small business world.

This reveals just how concentrated and narrowly drawn power is at the top of British business. Just six women make it into the top 100 companies and there are none in the top thirty-five. As a *Times* editorial put it, the country's top companies are still run by people who are part of 'extensive personal networks of influence . . . Two directors could easily have sat on the same CBI committee, be members of the same club, or contemporaries at university, and these links have not been catalogued. In other words, the old boy network (for there are few "girls") is still remarkably strong.'[21] A year later, in Power 100 for 2004, the *Times* commented, 'The incestuousness upon which we remarked last year is, if anything, even greater today.'[22]

The third group at the centre of the new power elite consists of several hundred City and international money brokers, traders and fund managers, a group that has also been rising up the power stakes in the post-war era. The international capital markets exercise a real grip over national economic policies. The ebb and flow of capital has become a prime determinant of interest and exchange rates. The number, size and speed of capital movements has escalated as new technology has helped create an increasingly global market, open twenty-four hours a day. The volume of money crossing the currency exchanges in pursuit of short-term speculative profit is more than fifty times greater than needed to finance the whole of world trade. At the end of 2000, the three biggest investment banks – Merrill Lynch, Morgan Stanley and Goldman Sachs, all American – were together managing $2.7 trillion of other people's money round the world, more than twice the combined value of the stock markets of Hong Kong, Taiwan, Singapore, South Korea, China, Malaysia, Thailand, Indonesia and India.[23] Investment bankers switch between markets relentlessly, 'in flight from assets which are falling, in pursuit of assets whose price is rising. They switch time zones, firms and businesses with disarming ease.'[24] In the process, the top managers at these giant banks – which make their money through arranging and financing takeovers, lending currency and buying and selling shares – wield enormous power over the future course of companies. They are also, as we have seen, central to key decisions affecting investment and corporate expansion, takeovers and mergers.

National governments can be brutally punished if they take economic decisions that international speculators and investors judge are unrealistic. Such doubts led to the devaluation of sterling by the Wilson government in 1967, the collapse of fixed exchange rates in the early 1970s and the reversal of Labour's economic policies in the mid-1970s. Denis Healey, Labour's Chancellor of the Exchequer from 1974 to 1979, described the financial markets as 'behaving like hysterical schoolgirls'.[25] He knew he could do little to 'buck the markets' and spent a good deal of time trying to reassure the small coterie of international dealers that held the fate of the public finances in their hands. A series of mini-Budgets and interest rate hikes was the result of what became known as the 'gilts strike' – the refusal of fund managers to buy government gilts because of their growing concerns about the scale of government debt and the unsustainability of fiscal policy. The effect of that refusal was higher taxes and interest rates and lower public spending. Shortly after the 'strike', the chief executive of the Prudential, one of the big market players, was invited to join the Court of the Bank of England, the first institutional investor to do so, and an acknowledgement of their growing economic strength. The City and Wall Street traders behind the action would argue that such interference was justified by the need to correct undisciplined economic policies. But the markets are just as vulnerable to economic misjudgement as governments.

The memory of the power of the markets stayed in the minds of the next generation of Labour leaders. In the early 1990s, members of the shadow Cabinet, led by the shadow Chancellor, John Smith, toured the dining rooms of the City of London to assure their hosts that Labour would not pursue 'reckless' economic policies. It became known as the 'prawn cocktail offensive'.

In the 1990s, one of the world's most powerful fund managers was George Soros, the man most responsible for breaking the power of the Bank of England and forcing the government out of the Exchange Rate Mechanism in September 1992. Soros, through his Quantum hedge fund, borrowed short term some £10 billion and switched it immediately into dollars, thereby causing an unstoppable surge against sterling. In the process, he made close to $1 billion in a day. Soros is also believed to have taken the most aggressive position against a number of south-east Asian currencies in the 1997–8 turbulence. Dr Mahathir bin Mohamad, the Malaysian Prime Minister, called him a 'rogue speculator' for helping to precipitate the crisis. Mahathir questioned whether countries should allow investment capital to flow unimpeded across their borders and imposed capital controls on the Malaysian currency, the ringgit. Other countries, including Hong Kong, took evasive action to try and deter speculation. But such attempts are usually futile.

Soros apart, only a few members of the international financial power class have become household names. Nick Leeson became famous as the young rogue trader who single-handedly brought down Barings, one of Britain's oldest banks. In 1997, Nicola Horlick, a publicly unknown 35-year-old fund manager on £1.15 million a year, hit the headlines when she was dismissed from Morgan Grenfell for planning to move her team to a rival bank. In 2003, star manager Anthony Bolton of Fidelity also hit the press after attempting to change remuneration and appointments policy at BSkyB, Carlton, the new ITV and other high-profile companies. In the City, Bolton is known as the 'quiet assassin'. For a while, the renowned and glamorous City deal-maker Robin Saunders was both the most powerful woman in the City and also a regular in the gossip columns before she fell under a cloud at WestLB.

Managers of the big institutional pension and insurance funds also hold the destiny of individual public companies very much in their hands, merely through the power to switch in and out of their shares. Moreover, this power is highly concentrated in relatively few hands. The top fifty fund managers control up to three-quarters of the London stock market.[26] Much of the power is exercised overseas: the top half-dozen American fund managers control 5.5 per cent of the London stock market.[27]

> An astonishing power over the corporate economy and the state is now concentrated in the hands of a few dozen people. Between them, [the institutional investors] have effective control of every major public company in Britain, and a right of veto over the ability of the government to tax and spend.[28]

The fate of Marks and Spencer in Philip Green's failed takeover bid in the summer of 2004 was effectively decided by a handful of big opportunistic fund managers, most of them American.[29]

In more recent years, those running the international private equity companies and hedge funds – maybe a few hundred people – have joined the ranks of those wielding enormous business power. It was a group of hedge funds that provided Malcolm Glazer with the extra money he needed to buy Manchester United. In 2005, the deputy Governor of the Bank of England warned that the growth of hedge funds, which are subject to relatively minimal regulations, had added to the 'risk of instability arising through leverage, volatility and opacity', a warning that recalled the 'irrational exuberance' augured by Alan Greenspan before the millennial crash.[30] Similar concern was being expressed about the risk of a bubble attached to the borrowing activities of private equity firms.

'Government of the corporations by the corporations for the corporations'

In the United Kingdom the link between wealth and political power has become increasingly indirect. Gone are the days when the country's political leaders were heavily drawn from the ranks of the very rich. In the United States, however, as in Italy, where the country's richest and most powerful man, Silvio Berlusconi, is also Prime Minister, the link between politics and wealth is much more direct. For most of its history, America has been ruled by an elite drawn from a small pool of very wealthy families.

Averell Harriman and Nelson Rockefeller, who were successive governors of New York, both gained office by virtue of their enormous wealth. John F. Kennedy owed his presidency to a wealthy father, Joseph P. Kennedy, a *nouveau riche* financier who built his wealth in the aftermath of the 1929 crash. If anything this is becoming more the case. Michael Bloomberg, the owner of Bloomberg TV, the business equivalent of CNN, and mayor of New York, is one of the richest men in America. In his campaign to become mayor in 2001, he spent $69 million, a tiny fraction of his estimated wealth of $5 billion but still the equivalent of $92 per vote. The Presidents Bush, senior and junior, are wealthy oil magnates from Texas. As the historian Linda Colley has put it, 'just as great aristocratic families . . . once dominated British politics, so now great plutocratic families stalk the jungle of modern American political life'.[31] One recent study has shown that almost all the nation's governors and presidents have been from the very wealthiest segments of society.[32]

Although nineteenth-century America was more democratic than Britain, wealthy elites were able to exercise an enormous grip on the political system. Collusion included the granting of bank charters, railway rights, tariff protection and the acceptance of monopolies. Corrupt dealing was widespread. As the power of the corporation, sometimes wealthier than the local state, spread in the late nineteenth century from rail to oil, lead, sugar and leather, public indignation mounted against the economic and political stranglehold that the giant corporations were able to wield. It was this that galvanised Theodore Roosevelt to launch his rhetoric on the giant monopolies in the early 1900s, which led to the modest anti-trust legislation that eventually followed.

The power of money hardly abated. While Secretary of the Treasury from 1921 to 1930, Andrew Mellon reduced profits, income and estate taxes sharply. One historian described it as a 'notorious example of self and class interest . . . saving millions for himself and his companies, and hundreds of millions for his peers in the highest circles of wealth and commerce'.[33] Following the 1929 crash, Franklin D. Roosevelt railed against the economic elites he labelled 'the money-changers'. Looking back from the 1930s, the historian Arthur Schlesinger Sr noted that 'America, in an ironical perversion of Lincoln's words at Gettysburg, had become a government of the corporations, by the corporations and for the corporations'.[34] In 1936, the President told a political audience, 'I should like to have it said of my first administration that in it the forces of selfishness and lust for power met their match. I should like to have it said of my second administration that in it these forces met their master.'[35] For the first time, the wealthy business elite was heavily split between those who sided with Roosevelt and those who opposed him.

To some degree, much of the history of America can be seen as a power struggle between elected Presidents, especially though not always Democratic ones, on the one hand and powerful economic elites on the other. In the nineteenth century, big fortunes were acquired partly because economic muscle outweighed state power. In the first decade of the twentieth century, the political pendulum swung a little against the mega-rich and the corporate barons, swinging back in their favour in the 1920s. The forty-year period ushered in by the New Deal Democrats led by Roosevelt was one in which the rich were forced to take more of a back seat.

The last two decades have seen the return of individual and corporate might and a new fusion of politics and money. Winning political office in America depends either on having access to personal wealth yourself or getting backing from the extremely wealthy. The electoral outlay per successful Senate candidate rose from $610,000 in 1976 to $7.3 million in 2000, much of it targeted at members of congressional tax-writing committees. Money also works. The evidence from the 1996 congressional races is that the candidates who raised the most money won 92 per cent of the time in the House of Representatives and 88 per cent of the time in the Senate.[36] Molly Ivins, a biographer of George W. Bush, has described campaign financing in America as 'legalised bribery'.[37]

Money from conservative multi-millionaires and foundations has also been pouring into a complex network of journals, academic positions and think-tanks. Originally designed to counter what was seen as a liberal bias, this network has been highly influential in peddling new policy ideas in tax, monetary policy and business regulation. Paul Krugman, the academic and *New York Times* columnist, has described 1990s America as a period of the comprehensive takeover by the radical right. He has likened that movement to a 'revolutionary power' that now 'controls the White House, Congress, much of the judiciary and a good slice of the media'.[38] This movement has a very radical agenda, from the dismantling of the New Deal and New Society programmes to the elimination of capital taxation. It is a movement that would like to minimise the responsibilities of the rich and corporate America towards the common good and is vehemently opposed to the very ideas of income redistribution and progressive taxation.

Democratic commentators have likened the last two decades to a return to the last decades of the nineteenth century, when money power was at its height. As Richard N. Goodwin, former speechwriter to John F. Kennedy, put it,

> the principal power in Washington is no longer the government or the people it represents. It is the Money Power. Under the deceptive cloak of campaign contributions, access and influence, votes and amendments are bought and sold. Money establishes priorities of action, holds down federal revenues, revises federal legislation, shifts income from the middle class to the very rich.[39]

Asked if the wealthy have more political power now than they did in the gilded age and the 1920s, the political scientist Kevin Phillips replied, 'It is a pretty close run thing between now and then. That, in itself, is damning because the conclusion . . . was that the rich had way too much power by the first decade of the twentieth century.'[40]

In April 1998, Travelers Insurance, owners of the investment bank Salomon Smith Barney, merged with the commercial bank Citicorp to form Citigroup, in defiance of the rules introduced under the Glass-Steagall Act in 1934. Citicorp had donated $4 million in campaign contributions during the 1996 and 1998 electoral cycles. The then Treasury Secretary, Robert Rubin, sanctioned the merger to form a new mega-bank. Five months after resigning that post, he was appointed chairman of the executive committee of the company, by then the country's largest financial institution.

Today, the great majority of American senators are millionaires and both Houses of Congress are increasingly unrepresentative of society as a whole. President George W. Bush's administration is packed with former chief executives and business leaders, more than any American government in recent history. Bush's first Cabinet had a combined wealth more than ten times that of Bill Clinton's.[41] His administration has been dubbed a 'junta of major corporate interests'.[42] Bush was himself on the board of Harken Energy, largely through family connections. The Vice-President, Dick Cheney, was chief executive of Halliburton, another oil company. Thomas White, the former head of energy trading at Enron, was appointed Secretary of the Army. Most of the former chief executives in Bush's administration became wealthy because of the connections they had acquired in Washington in earlier times.

The effect of the resurgence of money power has been that for the last decade, American policies have been especially favourable to the rich and to corporate America. The Nobel prize-winning economist Joseph Stiglitz, who was also a senior adviser to the Clinton administration, claimed that under Clinton 'finance reigned supreme' and the President 'buckled to pressure from big financial interests' time and again.[43] Clinton may well have wanted to check the plutocratic power wielded by US businessmen but the key influences in the framing of his economic policy came not from within the Democratic Party but from Wall Street.[44]

Bush has introduced generous tax cuts to the wealthy and business alike. Nearly half the benefit of Bush's $1.35 trillion tax cut in 2001 went to the richest 1 per cent, while 60 per cent of the 2003 tax cuts went to those with incomes of more then $100,000. The energy industry – 'Bush's finishing school' – has been one of the powerful interest groups to benefit from what Krugman has dubbed 'crony capitalism'. Energy companies retain a strong interest in Washington, the White House and the administration. Cheney has met repeatedly with energy company officials, who seem to have played a strong role in government energy policy. The obvious conflicts of interest involved have been mostly ignored. One commentator has described the government's energy plan as little more than 'a sop to big oil'.[45] There is also good reason to believe that the big winners have been those that gave the largest donations to the Republican Party, 'not corporations in general, but a small group of companies with a quite specific set of business interests'.[46]

Labour: 'the natural party of business'

Britain is nothing like as plutocratic as America, but, although the direct link between political power and wealth has gone, the indirect links remain.

Tycoons and business leaders alike have long made generous financial contributions to political parties. Such business support used to be confined mainly to the Conservative Party, with Labour depending on the trade unions. Today the two parties enjoy similar levels of business funding. In the crucial quarter leading up to the 2001 general election, three rich men, led by Labour minister Lord Sainsbury, donated £6.1 million between them to Labour's election fund. That just topped the £6 million given by the affiliated unions.[47] In the last three months of 2003, Labour received £4.1 million. About 40 per cent came from trade unions – of the rest, some £1.8 million came from three individuals – Sir Christopher Ondaatje, Lord Hamlyn and William Haughey.[48]

The link between business donation and personal reward is much weaker in the UK than in the United States. Donations do not always overtly have strings attached. Nevertheless, Tony Blair has courted business in a way that previous Labour Prime Ministers courted union leaders. Indeed, Blair now sees Labour as 'the natural party of business'. He is not the first to try and work closely with business, but he has made the overall relationship between business and Labour closer than before. The top business super-rich have flitted in and out of 10 Downing Street and are on first-name terms with Blair, or know those who are. Visitors to No. 10 have included not just press barons such as Rupert Murdoch and Richard Desmond but also high-profile donors such as Bernie Ecclestone, the Hinduja brothers and Lakshmi Mittal. Some, though not all, would appear to have benefited personally from their generosity. Ecclestone, the owner of Formula One motor racing, donated £1 million to the Labour Party in the run-up to the 1997 general election. When the Labour government subsequently banned tobacco advertising, Formula One was made exempt until 2006. When news of the donation broke, uproar forced Labour to return the money, but the policy still worked in Ecclestone's favour.

The last few decades have seen a steady rise in the political muscle of the modern business elite, even if it still stops well short of the power exhibited by America's top business leaders. Harold Wilson's honours list looked like the pay-off for financial contributions. During their eighteen years in power between 1979 and 1997, the Conservatives were rocked by one scandal after another about attempts by leading businessmen to buy parliamentary influence through Tory MPs.

The political influence of the modern business elite has, if anything, risen under New Labour. That wealth can still buy power today, indeed immense power and influence, is perhaps best illustrated by the case of Murdoch, owner of the *Times*, the *Sunday Times*, the *Sun* and the *News of the World* as well as the country's most watched satellite television channel, Sky. Blair and his advisers have always believed that the press, and the *Sun* in particular, have proved highly influential in the way electors think and vote. As opposition leader, Blair met Murdoch on several occasions and controversially flew halfway round the world to address a meeting of top executives of News International in Australia, in order, as Blair later explained, to reassure the company that New Labour would not 'strangle business'.

The wooing worked for Blair. During the 1997 election campaign, 'The Sun backs Blair' was splashed across the tabloid's front page. The courtship has continued into government and Murdoch – and his 'emissaries' – have had 'tea at No. 10' on many occasions. There is no suggestion that Blair has done an explicit deal with Murdoch in return for his continuing support, though Andrew Neil, a former editor of the *Sunday Times*, has claimed that there was 'an implicit understanding' between the two men. What this means, according to Neil, is that Blair 'was clear that if they beat up on Blair in the way they attacked Neil Kinnock in the 1992 election then who knew what a Labour Government would have in store'.[49] Certainly in government, Blair has left Murdoch's business interests pretty much alone. He has not legislated on press ownership or to regulate satellite TV in a way that would harm Murdoch.

Journalists on Murdoch's papers have certainly been favoured when it comes to leaks and tips from inside No. 10. For several years, Murdoch waged a damaging price war that deliberately targeted rival newspapers such as the *Independent*. In 1998, a Competition Bill was being debated and some backbenchers wanted an amendment to prevent such predatory pricing. Blair announced that he would not support such an amendment. In the same year, Murdoch was trying to buy the Italian Mediaset television station from Silvio Berlusconi, the former and future Italian Prime Minister, and himself a giant media baron. Murdoch is said to have been worried that the Italian government would intervene to prevent the country's leading television network falling into foreign hands. It is then claimed that Murdoch lobbied Blair, and that in a conversation with the then Prime Minister, Romano Prodi, Blair intervened on Murdoch's behalf.[50]

Murdoch's international commercial empire is prodigious, and stretches from Adelaide to Hollywood, London to Seoul. His destruction of the print unions was one of the most symbolic events of the Thatcher decade. He continues to operate direct editorial control over the *Sun* and the *News of the World*. It was Murdoch's decision to back Blair in 1997, against the opposition of Trevor Kavanagh, the paper's respected political editor. The effect of Sky on British broadcasting has been huge. It is arguable too that he has used his newspapers cynically in an attempt to gain commercial advantage in Britain. He has long waged a journalistic war against his main commercial television rivals – ITV and the BBC. Whatever his protestations, he ensured that his son James was made chief executive of BSkyB at the age of thirty-one, against the majority wishes of the institutional shareholders.

How much actual political muscle he has exercised over Blair is unclear. Murdoch is a fanatical anti-European, and Blair has almost certainly taken a softer line on the European Union for fear of upsetting Murdoch and turning his papers against Labour. According to the diaries of Lance Price, a former aide at No. 10, Blair is said to have promised News International that he wouldn't change the UK's position on Europe without consulting them. What initially tipped the balance for Murdoch backing Blair in 1997 was an article Blair wrote for the *Sun* at the start of the 1997 election campaign, which was distinctly Eurosceptic in tone. There has been much well-informed speculation that Blair's 2004 U-turn on the referendum over the new European constitution was down to a warning that Murdoch might switch support from the *Sun* without one. Irwin Stelzer, the ferociously Eurosceptic American economist and one of Murdoch's leading aides and columnists, was known to be closeted with Blair for a full two hours at No. 10 a few days before the announcement of the spectacular U-turn.[51]

To Murdoch, his readers are essentially pawns in his wider commercial and political ambitions, and so in a way are Blair, George W. Bush and John Howard. He in effect treats his UK papers and their eight million readers as a kind of block vote, and one exercised by a foreign citizen. Like all powerful people, Murdoch denies his influence. 'We're minnows,' he once said. As the American commentator Michael Wolff has put it, 'moguls want power, but they want it with a certain order of ritual deniability'.[52]

The government at times seems driven by a fear of offending corporate interests. It was representatives of the American gaming industry that persuaded Blair that casinos would revive the inner city. According to internal papers published by the *Guardian,* it was at a breakfast meeting that the directors of British American Tobacco (BAT) persuaded the Prime Minister that a proposed public inquiry into allegations that BAT was colluding with cigarette smugglers – which could have been highly damaging to the firm – should be replaced with a much weaker non-public investigation.[53]

Blair has ennobled dozens of business leaders, many of them high-value donors such as David Sainsbury and the late publisher Paul Hamlyn. Six weeks after Paul Drayson, a biotechnology entrepreneur, was made a life peer, he gave Labour a donation of £500,000. Another high-profile donor, Sir Gerry Robinson, chairman of Granada, was made head of the Arts Council. Several business leaders have been made ministers, including David Simon, the chairman of BP, first made a peer and then elevated to a trade minister, and Sainsbury, who became minister of science.

Before he lost his job as chief executive of British Airways, Bob Ayling, a particular favourite of Blair's, had been asked if he would head the Policy Unit at 10 Downing Street and, having refused, later took a leading role in the Millennium Dome. Malcolm Bates, chairman of the insurer Pearl Group, was awarded a knighthood in 1998 and then became chairman of London Regional Transport. Scores of top businesspeople have been given key jobs on review groups and task forces. Within weeks of the election, Martin Taylor, the chief executive of Barclays Bank, was asked to undertake a review of the tax and benefits system, while Adair Turner, the former director general of the CBI, was made chairman of a special government commission to look at the growing crisis in pension provision. Top businessmen have effectively been given open access to the Prime Minister. 'I came to learn that the Chairman of British Aerospace appeared to have the key to the garden door to Number Ten,' wrote the former Foreign Secretary Robin Cook.[54] Of course there is nothing wrong about business lobbying government, but it has now grown to a level where businessmen appear to have a special access denied to other legitimate groups. Roy Hattersley is one critic of the closeness of the relationship: 'The Prime Minister only gives audiences to the rich and powerful . . . the lobbying of government has grown to levels that raise fundamental questions about standards in public life.'[55]

The Indian-born Hinduja brothers, with an international empire embracing oil, transport and media, who tried to buy the *Express* newspapers before Richard Desmond, sponsored the Millennium Dome's Faith Zone to the tune of £1 million in 1998. They are extremely well connected and have also made donations to the Conservatives. It is claimed they sought to use Peter Mandelson's influence in support of one of their applications for a British passport, an application that was granted in record time. When the news broke that Mandelson had made enquiries on their behalf when he was a Cabinet minister, enquiries that he has always claimed he couldn't recall, he was forced to quit the government for a second time. In 2005, the Hindujas were embroiled in another, less public, controversy. The BBC's *Newsnight* was about to transmit an investigation into alleged sales of military equipment to Sudan by a company owned by the brothers, when it was suddenly pulled from the screens following intervention by a team of lawyers operating for the company. This was despite the programme having already being approved by the BBC's own lawyers.[56] Such is the power of the international super-rich.

Lakshmi Mittal, the Indian-born steel entrepreneur, gave a donation to Labour before the 1997 election, a further £125,000 to Labour in May 2001 and then £2 million in 2005, making him Labour's biggest donor alongside Lord Sainsbury. Within four weeks of Mittal signing the 2001 cheque, Blair sent a letter to the Romanian Prime Minister in support of Mittal's bid to acquire a state-owned Romanian steel concern. Much of the subsequent controversy surrounded the description of Mittal's company as British, despite its somewhat tenuous British links. It was, for example, registered in the Netherlands Antilles, not the UK.[57] Desmond made a donation to Labour of £100,000 and some commentators have linked this to the decision by Stephen Byers, the then industry secretary, to allow Desmond's takeover of Express Newspapers without an enquiry by the Monopolies Commission into his suitability. In 2004 Desmond warned that he would switch funding to the Conservatives if Gordon Brown became Prime Minister. He had previously told Blair that he didn't like Brown and feared that he would raise taxes and redistribute wealth.[58]

Of course, some try to buy political influence more directly, though rarely successfully. Along with fellow millionaire John Aspinall, James Goldsmith helped form the Referendum Party in opposition to European economic and political integration. The party fielded 580 candidates at the 1997 election, with Goldsmith standing in Putney. It proved an expensive political gesture – nearly all the candidates lost their deposit.

It might be expected that, as well as indulging their hobbies and lobbying governments, the rich would also take up the higher ground of philanthropy. As shown in the next chapter, they do, but with much less generosity or zeal.

8

Nothing to spare

He who dies rich dies disgraced.
(Andrew Carnegie, The Gospel of Wealth, 1890)

In the autumn of 2000, hundreds of guests gathered for a service of thanksgiving at Chester Cathedral. They were there to celebrate the life of the third Viscount Leverhulme, KG, former Lord-Lieutenant of the City and County of Chester and senior steward of the Jockey Club, who had died at the age of eighty-five. This was no ordinary thanksgiving service. The Queen and the Duke of Edinburgh were represented by Lord Carrington, KG, CH, and Queen Elizabeth the Queen Mother by Sir William Gladstone, KG. The Princess Royal was represented by the Countess of Lichfield, Princess Margaret by Viscount Ullswater and the Duke of Kent by Viscount Ashbrook. The cathedral was packed with guests whose names were a roll-call of the old British establishment, dukes, earls, countesses and knights of the Garter by the dozen, a group joined by representatives of local and national charities funded by the Leverhulme Trust.

Philip Lever, who went to Eton and Trinity College, Cambridge, died a rich man, with wealth estimated at around £30 million. The wealth had been created not by him but by his grandfather, William Lever, who in 1885 had had the inspiration to start producing the world's first branded soap – Sunlight. Lever, who had learnt an early lesson about dealing with competitors, decimated his rivals by breaking a taboo against advertising. He went on to become Baron Leverhulme in 1917 and Viscount Leverhulme in 1922. By the time he died in 1925, Lever Brothers had become one of Britain's most profitable companies. Four years later, it merged with a Dutch rival, Margarine Unie, to become Unilever. Leverhulme is much admired for what he achieved. As the biscuit baron Sir Hector Laing has put it, 'if you look at what people like Lord Leverhulme did, or the other City fathers did, their achievement was enormous'.[1]

William Lever was not just a great entrepreneur, he was also one of the early business philanthropists, the nineteenth-century industrialists who believed that privilege came with responsibility, in his case for the welfare of his workers, mostly former farm labourers who had moved from their previous dependency on the land. Lever not only created an international business empire, he built one of the first model villages, Port Sunlight, for staff in his Liverpool factory. He also established the Leverhulme Trust, which is invested in Unilever shares and is one of Britain's largest sources of grants for educational, scientific and medical projects. The third Lord Leverhulme had no son and his title died with him. One former employee described him as 'a gentleman in every sense of the word'.[2] That gentlemanly, paternalistic tradition represents one strand of British wealth-making history, albeit a small one and one that has more or less died out.

Most British entrepreneurs of the nineteenth century were ruthless and competitive businessmen who felt little wider responsibility. A minority, on the other hand, men such as George Cadbury and Joseph Rowntree as well as William Lever, believed that they had some social responsibility to the former agricultural labourers now working in their factories. Early pioneers of the philanthropic tradition such as William Wilberforce and the Earl of Shaftesbury, with their ethical crusades against slavery and child labour, were motivated by a non-conformist conscience. These paternalistic industrialists were mostly rich campaigning social reformers, driven by religious or political evangelism to change society or to improve the lot of ordinary people.

As well as Lever, other entrepreneurs who built similar 'model villages' to improve the housing conditions of their factory workers included the Quaker Cadbury family, who built the Bournville suburb outside Birmingham. Although they had been motivated by philanthropy, they still ran things on pretty authoritarian lines. Cadbury campaigned hard for old age pensions and against sweated labour. Rowntree, the chocolate tycoon based in York and also a Quaker, started the Rowntree Foundation, which continues to award grants for research into contemporary poverty, housing and social policy issues. Lever Brothers and Rowntree were amongst the earliest companies to set up their own occupational pension schemes.

One of Rowntree's sons, Seebohm Rowntree, one of the directors of the family factory, pioneered modern poverty research with the first major survey of poverty in 1901, brought in an eight-hour day, and introduced a works' doctor at the beginning of the twentieth century. Other industrialists of the time were more conventional in their donations. The sugar refiner Sir Henry Tate gave £80,000 and sixty-seven paintings to build and endow the Tate Gallery. He also funded public libraries. The textile heir Samuel Courtauld spent £300,000 assembling the collection of impressionist paintings at Somerset House. The period also saw the birth of a number of charitable foundations, including the Nuffield, Wolfson and Wellcome trusts, which have survived to this day.

Today, that philanthropic tradition pioneered by Britain's early industrialists has largely petered out. Wealthy Britons are less active philanthropists than their early predecessors and mostly much less generous. They are also much less inclined to give than their American counterparts. Giving in Britain accounts for less than 1 per cent of gross domestic product, compared with 2 per cent in America.[3]

In 1994, the charity Directory of Social Change put together a list of the country's top millionaire givers. It did not go down well with those making it onto the list. Letters from solicitors claimed privacy had been invaded and a follow-up has never been published. Ten years later, the *Sunday Times* published its own list. The most generous donor was Sir Tom Hunter, the self-made Scottish sportswear entrepreneur and the man who helped to popularise the trainer. He has committed £100 million to his charitable foundation established six years ago. This is one of the largest ever charitable donations in Britain. The other most generous donations listed were from the Sainsbury family, from George Weston to his father's W. Garfield Weston Foundation and from the Rausing family.

Donors of more than a million pounds ranged from celebrities such as Sir Elton John, who gave £19 million, to businessmen such as conservatory maker John Lancaster (£5 million) and car dealer Sir Peter Vardy (£4.7 million). John, who devotes a fifth of his time to charity, supports Aids work in Britain and Africa, Lancaster has funded community, social and religious projects and Vardy has given £2 million towards the new South Middlesborough City Academy. In 2005, the same names dominated the list. John topped the list, followed by Weston, Hunter, Vardy and Lord Sainsbury. By then Hunter's foundation had grown in value to £120 million through aggressive investment. Commitments included education projects, the Kelvingrove Art Gallery and Museum in Glasgow, the Make Poverty

History campaign and the tsunami appeal. A feature of all Hunter's gifts is what he calls 'venture philanthropy', with the sums committed being dependent on key objectives and targets being met.[4]

Levels of corporate giving typically tend to lag behind those of individuals. Public companies have to publish donations in their annual returns and since 2001 the *Guardian* newspaper has published an annual Giving List, a kind of regular naming-and-shaming ceremony. This confirms Britain's relative lack of generosity. In 2001, the top 100 companies gave an average 0.4 per cent of their pre-tax profits to charity and community projects, rising to 0.95 per cent in 2002 and then falling slightly to 0.8 per cent in 2003. In 2003, only twenty-seven top 100 companies made it into the PerCent Club, set up by the charity Business in the Community, membership of which requires giving at least 1 per cent of pre-tax profits.

In recent years, the term 'corporate social responsibility' has evolved out of pressure from global activists and environmentalists to encourage business to accept greater community responsibility for their actions, including towards the societies in which they manufacture and trade. Most companies now pay lip service to the idea, with the publication of social reports highlighting their activities. Despite such initiatives, corporate generosity is not much greater today than it was a decade ago. Business contributed less than 5 per cent of charitable income in 2002 – £760 million compared to £5.41 billion from the general public.[5]

The evidence is also that the level of giving at the top has actually been falling despite the growth in personal levels of wealth in recent times. Despite the Tom Hunter, Elton John and Garfield Weston foundations and other new ones of recent years, today there are fewer foundations than in the past. This may be because of the decline in rates of direct taxation, which has made charitable giving relatively more expensive. Indeed, since the 1990s, charities have been talking about the 'British philanthropic deficit'. The rich are actually relatively mean – they give less proportionately than those on lower incomes. The richest 20 per cent of British households give only 0.7 per cent of their incomes to charities compared with the poorest 10 per cent who give 3 per cent. More recent research even suggests a larger discrepancy. Giving is certainly not common amongst the rich or affluent.[6]

The more liberal tradition of some wealthy nineteenth-century reformers seems to have been steadily eroded. The rich today seem to be increasingly detached from society in general. They often lead separate lives geographically, socially and culturally, with only a small proportion accepting a role in civil society. There is a continuing, if weakening, commitment to civic duty in Britain, but it appears to be stronger amongst ordinary people than the rich. Annual awards ceremonies for individual generosity identify people who have given a lifetime to helping others, usually, though not always, with time rather than money. The Beacon Awards in 2003 named the City professional who gave up his job to set up a diagnostic charity after his daughter died of a medical error involving a rare disease; the quadriplegic who designs low-cost wheelchairs for the disabled in developing countries; the Liverpool single parent who singlehandedly organised fellow residents to take an active role in local regeneration.

Of course, there are many generous sponsors in Britain. The Sainsbury dynasty have continued to make a family business out of giving money away, with a total of twenty trusts disbursing large sums to charities for the environment, medicine and the arts. High-profile donations have included the Sainsbury wing of the National Gallery and the Sainsbury Centre for the Visual Arts at the University of East Anglia as well as donations to the Tate, the Dulwich Picture Gallery and the Royal Opera House. Lakshmi Mittal is expected to donate millions to rebuilding Long Beach in Mississippi following its devastation by Hurricane Katrina.

Besides these examples, Lord Rothschild has contributed to the cost of renovating Somerset House. Sir Peter Moores, son of the founder of Littlewoods stores, has given away nearly £100 million over the last forty years. The multi-millionaire property dealer Peter de Savary, who bought Andrew Carnegie's Scottish castle, Skibo, is a regular giver and organises big events to raise charitable funds. His own trusts include the Carnegie Youth Trust. 'I don't mean that I am leaving my five children absolutely nothing,' he says. 'I wouldn't have anyone to Sunday lunch if I said that. But I do think a modest provision is appropriate.'[7] Dame Anita Roddick, former owner of the Body Shop, has promised to give all her money eventually to the Body Shop Foundation. Garry Weston handed over £20 million to the British Museum in 1999 with no strings attached.

More recent members of the giving club include J. K. Rowling, who has given £500,000 to the National Council for One Parent Families. She has also donated the full proceeds of the sale of a book specially written for Comic Relief. The Stagecoach boss, Ann Gloag, has given millions to hospitals in Malawi, Kenya and India, while David Gilmour of Pink Floyd handed over £4.5 million from the sale of a house to Crisis, the homeless charity. In 2002, 37-year-old Niall Quinn, the former Irish international and

Sunderland footballer, raised £1 million at his testimonial match and announced that he was giving the proceeds away to children's hospitals. Quinn, who has two children, said, 'There are far more important things to give my children than money.'[8] But high-level contributions to public life such as those by Hunter, Elton John and more recently Mittal are relatively rare.

Super-rich hedge fund managers have been among the more conspicuous givers of recent times. Influenced by the most famous hedge funder of all, George Soros, several funds donate a proportion of their profits to charity. In 2003, the children's charity Ark (Absolute Return for Kids, which helps children in eastern Europe and Africa) collected £4 million from a dinner and charity auction for the hedge fund industry. The prizes included Hugh Grant and Elle Macpherson as golf partners for a day. In 2005, the Ark Ball raised £12 million. During the auction, one hedge fund executive paid £230,000 for a ticket on the first space flight of Richard Branson's Virgin Galactic, due to launch in 2008.

The American tradition

Philanthropy appears to be one area where the cultural gap with the United States is not closing. The attitudes towards charity amongst Britain's growing number of multi-millionaires could hardly be more different from their American counterparts, where giving appears to be much more part of the fabric of life. This is not to say that all wealthy Americans are generous.

Larry Ellison and Bill Gates, the billionaire owners of Oracle and Microsoft respectively, are close rivals in the international world of computers. Both are extraordinarily successful entrepreneurs. Both have become rich by creating a near-monopoly product – Gates in the PC desktop market and Ellison in data-processing. Otherwise, the two men could hardly be more different. Gates is into golf and hard work and has been content with only one wife. Ellison is into fast cars, fast boats, fast planes. A renowned playboy who once briefly dated the actress Sharon Stone, he married for the fourth time in 2003. Ellison is flamboyant, risk-taking and doesn't like being second best, something Gates rarely has to worry about. Ellison is said to have once quoted Genghis Khan: 'It is not sufficient that I succeed; everyone else must fail.'

Unlike Gates, Ellison prefers high living to charity. He has his own private air force, which includes a Gulfstream V jet, complete with two marble bathrooms, a Marchetti fighter plane from Italy and a handful of other aircraft. He tried to buy a Russian MiG-29 fighter in order, he jokes, to zap Gates's home near Seattle, but was refused an import licence. His fleet of cars is modest by comparison – a Porsche Boxster, two customised Mercedes, a convertible Bentley, and a $900,000 silver McLaren.

He owns a house in San Francisco's Pacific Heights, one of the most expensive stretches of real estate in the western United States. When the key to the house is inserted, the opaque glass front door turns transparent to reveal a Japanese rock garden in the middle of the house, which also contains an indoor swimming pool and an eight-foot plasma screen television overlooking the Golden Gate Bridge. He also owns a $100 million Japanese-style palace with 44 acres near Why Not Lane in Woodside – one of the most desirable addresses in America, and effectively a billionaire's village above Silicon Valley. According to a local saying, 'there's rich, there's filthy rich, and then there's Woodside'. And then there are his yachts, one of them amongst the longest in the world, and his love of ocean racing.

Ellison's desire for such extravagant, and sometimes death-defying, living may well be down to his modest upbringing. He was born to an unmarried teenage mother in a poor neighbourhood in South Chicago, does not know who his father is and was adopted by his Russian uncle and aunt, who told him he would never amount to anything. Today, Oracle employs some 40,000 people and has designed data-processing systems for clients including MI5 and the CIA. His desire to unseat Gates has long been a personal passion. Both their companies floated on the stock market in 1986, and it is Microsoft that has been ahead since the beginning. Ellison has attacked Gates for issuing overpriced and bug-filled 'vapourware' and has compared him to the Wizard of Oz, a small man hiding behind a big machine.

Ellison is outraged at Gates's hero-like appearance on the front covers of international business magazines in sloppy sweaters and believes that he, not Gates, should be being courted by popular TV chat shows. As he put it, 'IBM is the past, Microsoft is the present, Oracle is the future'. Gates, in contrast, is less well known for his humour or daring, and describes Ellison as 'a pain in the ass'. He does, however, enjoy recounting a story that still circulates around Silicon Valley: 'What's the difference between Larry Ellison and God? Answer: God doesn't think he's Larry Ellison.'[9]

Ellison is largely scornful of charity. His third wife used to throw big charitable parties and Ellison is pouring money into research into the hormone DHEA, which some scientists think can slow ageing. But that is because Ellison would rather not grow old. Gates, in contrast, is now the world's most generous giver – indeed, the most generous giver of all time. He has donated a total of $25 billion to the Bill and Melinda Gates Foundation, which he runs with his wife. The foundation has spent some $3.2 billion on health projects – including anti-Aids programmes in Africa -- since the late 1990s. The foundation is some ten times the size of the Rockefeller Foundation and three times that of the Ford Foundation.

Today Gates vows that he will give away his total fortune, bar a few million dollars for his three children, aged nine, six and three, before he dies. When asked about their generosity, Melinda Gates said that it is down to family tradition. Bill had been raised by upper-class parents who volunteered for civic committees and raised money for charities in Seattle. His father is still involved in high-profile campaigning, and was one of the leaders of the campaign to stop the Bush proposal to end estate duties. Melinda too comes from a background that was predisposed towards *servium*, her Catholic school motto, which means 'to serve'.

Inevitably, the couple have invited criticism. Before he set up the foundation, Gates was criticised for being mean. Now he's giving on a huge scale, some have questioned the motives and timing. In September 1997, Ted Turner, who had built a personal fortune through creating the cable world news channel CNN, announced, entirely out of the blue, that he was giving away $1 billion, in annual $100 million chunks, to the United Nations to combat epidemic disease and help with population control. It was reportedly a spontaneous decision cooked up in a taxi on the way to make a speech at the UN. Gates was, at the time, one of Turner's rivals for the accolade of most successful American business tycoon, as was Rupert Murdoch.

According to one account, Turner had 'nurtured his megalomania with more than one hundred viewings of the movie *Citizen Kane*'.[10] Richard Conniff, a natural-history expert whose book *The Natural History of the Rich* draws parallels between the behaviour of the rich and of the animal kingdom, argues that Turner's decision was a deliberate strategy to outwit his business rivals:

> Any damned fool can compete at the standard Darwinian game of gathering market share and piling up resources. But by giving away $1 billion to the United Nations, Turner could lay claim to the largest single act of charity by a living person in history.

It was, of course, also an act of prosocial dominance, a bid for status, as plain as the chest-thumping of rival silverback gorillas or the philanthropic trilling of the Arabian babbler.[11]

Indeed, in case anyone should 'mistake this for mere philanthropy', Conniff continued, Turner announced the gift with a series of gibes against the stinginess of his fellow billionaires: 'There's a lot of people who are awash in money they don't know what to do with. It doesn't do any good if you don't know what to do with it.'[12] Turner mentioned Gates by name but not Murdoch. Both had made very limited gifts at that point. Turner was not the first to criticise the richest man in the world for his previous charitable efforts – in the range of $100 million to $200 million – but this seemed to get at Gates. *Slate*, Microsoft's online magazine, responded by establishing its own list of the country's biggest givers, called Slate 60. Although Gates and his co-founder, Paul Allen, appeared on the 1997 list, they hardly stood out against the likes of Turner and others such as George Soros. Gates soon put that right. Exactly one year less two days after Turner's announcement, Gates declared a $1 billion donation to fund scholarships for minority students. Today it tops $25 billion.

It is difficult to overstate the scale of money involved. Andrew Carnegie, perhaps the principal architect of the art of philanthropy, gave $350 million before his death in 1919 – the equivalent of about $3 billion now. The $540 million that John D. Rockefeller dispensed would amount to some $6 billion today. Moreover, $25 billion is similar to the value of some of America's largest companies. The Ford Foundation, America's second largest, has an endowment of $14 billion, but its growth, like that of most philanthropic institutions, has come from asset appreciation over time.

Next to these Olympian sums, the recent charitable gifts of mere mortal billionaires – like the $150 million given to Stanford University by Jim Clark, the co-founder of Netscape, in 1999, or the $134 million that Warren Buffett and his wife, Susan, divided among four organisations – begins to look like pocket change.[13]

Gates has also been accused of giving as a way of trying to buy back the public support lost because of Microsoft's high-profile legal problems. From the late 1990s, Microsoft had to fight a series of anti-trust actions, which dented its founder's popularity. Much of his wealth derives from Microsoft's near-monopoly in PC operating systems, largely because ruthless business tactics had been used to eliminate the direct competition. In April 2000, Judge Thomas Penfold Jackson, who described Gates as having a 'Napoleonic concept of himself', ruled that Microsoft had repeatedly exhibited anti-competitive behaviour and that the Seattle-based software giant should be split into two. The ruling knocked billions off Microsoft's value and Gates's own fortune. He moved from being portrayed as a geek-hero in newspaper cartoons to a bullying, Rockefeller-esque monopolist.

Over a year later, this decision was overturned in the US Appeals Court. Microsoft was far from fully exonerated, however, and since then the company has had to be much more careful to avoid actions that could be construed as an abuse of power. In June 2002, Microsoft's chief executive, Steven Ballmer, sent a new mission statement to the company's 50,000 employees: 'to enable people and businesses throughout the world to realise their full potential'. This was in sharp contrast to the company's previously aggressive, uncompromising and ruthless culture. At one stage, Ballmer had addressed a mass staff meeting about how Microsoft should destroy the upstart internet browser company Netscape. Ballmer 'simply yelled into the microphone that Netscape must be defeated at all costs'.[14] There is little doubt that this change in tack was heavily political. As one tech industry watcher with close ties to the company put it, 'this was a company that never stopped for self-reflection until the world forced it to stop for self-reflection'.[15]

Whether or not his public spat with Turner or the attacks on his business methods influenced Gates's personal mission to fund health projects in Africa is impossible to know. These are the sorts of argument that have raged throughout the history of giving by the rich.

The birth of serious philanthropy dates back to Carnegie and Rockefeller, two of the richest industrialists in American history. In 1889, Carnegie, the Scottish-born steel magnate, wrote his famous tract, *The Gospel of Wealth*, which has become the bible of organised giving. In it he warned that 'he who dies rich dies disgraced'. Carnegie, the son of a hand weaver, rose from a bobbin boy in a local cotton mill in 1840s Pittsburgh to become one of America's most successful tycoons. He waited until his fortune and his business empire were secure, and then began giving in the 1890s. In 1901 he sold his steel empire to the banker J. P. Morgan. His reason: 'I resolved to stop accumulating and begin the infinitely more serious and difficult task of wise distribution.'[16] Carnegie, whose antagonism towards inherited privilege came from his radical roots, was also an early advocate of death duties. Before he died, in 1919, he had given away 90 per cent of his fortune. The money paid for 2,500 free public libraries and an array of educational initiatives, including funding pensions for teachers, support for universities and scientific research. Carnegie once summed up his philosophy in this way:

> This, then, is held the duty of the man of wealth: First, to set an example of modest, unostentatious living, shunning display or extravagance; to provide moderately for the legitimate wants of those dependent upon him; and after doing so to consider all surplus revenues as trust funds, which he is called on to administer, and strictly bound as a matter of duty to administer in the manner which, in his judgement, is best calculated to produce the most beneficial result for the community – the man of wealth thus becoming the mere agent and trustee for his poorer brethren.[17]

Nevertheless, Carnegie was just as ruthless in the way he accumulated his wealth as he was determined in his later philanthropy. In Pittsburgh, where he built his steel empire, even today he is not remembered with generosity. This is mainly because of the crippling Homestead strike that occurred in his local steel plant in 1892. The strike had been called because of cuts in wages imposed when the price of steel fell. Carnegie was in Europe when the strike occurred and it was left to his partner, Henry Clay Frick, to deal with. Frick brought in 300 armed guards from a local detective agency to secure the works and allow in strike-breaking labour. In the ensuing confrontation, some twenty people died. It was one of the bloodiest episodes in the already somewhat violent history of American labour relations in the nineteenth century. There was also a wider agenda. Carnegie knew he had to break the union in order to mechanise the plant, simultaneously laying off workers, introducing longer shifts and cutting wages. One chronicler of the strike said that 'it was common knowledge that the monumental profits earned by Carnegie steel in the 1890s grew directly from the defeat of unionism'.[18]

Rockefeller, equally ruthless in business, also espoused the 'stewardship of wealth' and like Carnegie came from a family with an active social conscience. Rockefeller gave away half his fortune before his death. It didn't appear to make him popular. Indeed, newspapers had dubbed him 'the most hated man in America'. One leading union leader declared, 'The one thing that the world could gracefully accept from Mr Rockefeller would be the establishment of a great endowment for research and education to help other people see in time how they can keep from being like him.'[19] Rockefeller's charitable instincts have subsequently been continued by his descendants, who have maintained the family foundations.

Nevertheless, like Gates today, Carnegie and Rockefeller were exceptions in the scale of their philanthropy. While they pioneered modern upper-class philanthropy, most of their fellow rich at the time were much more niggardly. As Cornelius Vanderbilt put it, 'if I was to begin that business [alms-giving], a deluge of supplicants would engulf me', a viewpoint embraced by subsequent generations of the family.[20] When Vanderbilt, 'the Commodore', died in 1877, he left nearly all his $100 million fortune to his son William. Before his death, he claimed that he wanted to keep the fortune intact as a 'monument to his name'.

Despite the mixed views, later American industrialists have continued the tradition started by Carnegie and Rockefeller. Before 1910, thirty-six foundations were created with a minimum of $100,000 worth of assets. Between 1910 and 1929, a further 163 were founded. During the 1930s, the numbers grew by 288. By 1962, there were more than 14,000 and by 1976, 26,000.

Even the rich with humanitarian instincts have had to choose between what one author has described as 'conspicuous consumption and inconspicuous charity – many donations are an aspect of Conspicuous Consumption anyway'.[21] A generation ago, the Houston oil magnate and multi-millionaire Hugh Roy Cullen showed how to resolve the dilemma: 'I have taught my children that if they feel like buying some jewellery, they should find out how much it costs and give that amount to a school or hospital.'[22]

Today some rich people continue to eschew excessive materialism. Sam Walton, founder of Wal-Mart, the world's largest retailer, used to drive himself around in a pick-up truck. 'I have concentrated all along on building the finest retailing company that we possibly could. Period. Creating a huge personal fortune was never particularly a goal of mine.'[23] Warren Buffett, the international investor, still lives in the Omaha bungalow he bought almost fifty years ago and, apart from his jet, has a generally modest lifestyle. 'It's not that I want money. It's the fun of making money and watching it grow.'[24] Nevertheless, Buffett has been criticised for his decision to leave his wealth, which is likely to be the biggest single bequest in history, to his foundation *after* he dies, as opposed to giving it now. His response is that he will continue to do what he does best – make money – and then leave a big pile behind him. He has also decided to take the advice of the 1877 *New York*

Daily Tribune, which declared that 'inherited money has done so little for its possessors', to largely disinherit his children, who he believes will be happier to pursue their own lives by their own efforts.[25]

The peacock's tail

It might be asked why the rich give at all. Are they driven by guilt, by religion, to avoid taxation? Is it to impress? Or are they driven by a deep sense of responsibility or altruism? J. P. Morgan supposedly once said that a man always has two reasons for the things he does: a good reason and the real reason. It has been widely assumed that the 'robber barons' of the Gilded Age tried 'to buy their way through the eye of the needle with large gifts to libraries, medical research, educational and cultural institutions and the arts'.[26] Nevertheless, it is doubtful if Rockefeller, Carnegie and Morgan believed that they had built their fortunes in sinister ways. They saw themselves as building great industrial or financial empires that helped to make America rich, without needing to atone for commercial wrongs by giving money away.

In his diatribe against fellow billionaires in 1996, Ted Turner blamed the *Forbes* 400 list for making the mega-rich stingy. 'That list is destroying our country!' he complained to the *New York Times*. 'These new superrich won't loosen up their wads because they're afraid they'll reduce their net worth and go down the list. That's their Super Bowl.'[27] Most philanthropy probably has a strong element of self-interest. Commentating on his own donation, Turner said, 'I have learned that the more good I do, the more money has come in.'[28]

Some of the early manufacturers, such as George Eastman of Kodak, the Mellons of banking and oil and the du Ponts, funded schools, hospitals, parks and social welfare projects because they believed that improving the social environment also served their business interests. Eastman and the du Ponts also funded the Massachusetts Institute of Technology, a university attended by several du Ponts and many Kodak and DuPont employees. Another example of 'enlightened self-interest' is the Mellon Institute, an industrial research centre whose patents and discoveries swelled profits in the family enterprises. Such giving was also highly egocentric, a way of ensuring that your name was there for posterity. It meant that major public institutions, from universities and libraries to art galleries and parks, carried the name of their benefactors: Stanford University, the J. Paul Getty Museum, Carnegie Hall, the Guggenheim Museum. The names have thus been remembered not for the sometimes questionable ways in which they made their money, but for their generosity.

Many of these industrialists may also have carried a strong sense of social responsibility, of noblesse oblige, a British-born puritan belief that under-pinned feudalism and was transported to America with the early settlers. Carnegie argued that it was the responsibility of the rich to further 'the common good' by reducing economic inequality, thereby reconciling the tension between the rich and the poor. Nevertheless, there was also a strong sense of defensiveness, even fear, underlying these views; generosity was seen as one way of preventing social unrest. In 1930, Henry Ford echoed this by arguing that the rich had a responsibility as 'servants of the people' whose 'tenure would be very short' unless they ensured their 'activities were beneficial to the people as a whole'.[29] In 1945, Marshall Field III, a multi-millionaire with liberal views looked on wealth as

> a privilege Western society has traditionally granted to its stronger or more fortunate members, and like every privilege, it carries with it certain obligations as a kind of payment for the privilege. Those who neglect the obligations, I am convinced, speed the day when this privilege will be curtailed or perhaps denied.[30]

In nineteenth-century America, the public had a schizophrenic attitude towards the corporate barons – they disliked the power but admired those like Rockefeller and Carnegie who had risen from modest beginnings. Gradually business realised that such contradictions needed to be tackled if the public mood was not to become too hostile and dangerous, a realisation that led to a similar outbreak of early 'corporate social responsibility' as was occurring in some quarters in Britain. As in Britain, in the decade before the First World War several companies started to set up pension funds for workers and company towns spread across America to provide better housing and education. While the enormous wealth created by the expanding companies continued to finance the lavish social lives of the barons and their families, it also went to build museums and art galleries, to support universities and to finance generous endowment funds.

Charity also undoubtedly offers pleasure to the endowers. George Peabody, the Anglo-American banker who founded the Peabody housing estates, said, 'For the first time, I felt a higher pleasure and a greater happiness than making money – that of giving it away for good purposes.'[31] As Carnegie pointed out, acts of charity also bring the approval and admiration of others. They thus double as a form of personal advertising, of making the donor appear more attractive, what one observer has called the 'rich person's equivalent of a peacock's tail'.[32]

Most big-league gifts in American giving have been concentrated amongst high-profile universities, museums and arts projects that are already richly endowed. In contrast, social projects such as homeless shelters rarely benefit. One critic, the wealthy American columnist and television commentator Arianna Huffington, has pointed out that most large donations have gone to 'already-flush universities and museums, often to fund buildings bearing their names' rather than to helping the needy.[33] Huffington recalculated the *Slate* list of the top sixty givers to create a 'compassion index' or, as *Slate* dubbed it, 'the *Slate* 60 Huffington Virtue Remix'. The revised index awarded minus points for 'self-aggrandising gifts', such as investing in buildings named after yourself or projects directly connected to the donor's business, and awarded plus points for gifts that tackle poverty, alleviate suffering and turn lives around. Extra points were awarded for giving while young and for giving time as well as money. The effect of the index was that forty-three donors out of the sixty had more points taken away than added, with only four gaining points. A few donors dropped more than twenty places and one moved up thirteen.

In 1998, a number of leading philanthropists and charities gathered at a conference held at the striking Getty Centre in Los Angeles, where participants talked of a 'tradition in jeopardy'.[34] In the 1980s, one effect of the cuts in higher rates of tax introduced by Ronald Reagan seemed to be a fall in the overall level of giving by the very rich since they now had less incentive to make donations. This appeared to underline the more cynical explanations offered for giving by the rich.

A study of the history of American private foundations published in 2001 was similarly scathing. It concluded, 'The sad fact is that a majority of America's 50,000 or so private foundations are mindless, lawyer-ridden tax dodges that accomplish little beyond the transfer of riches to already wealthy institutions.' The author, Mark Dowie, went on, 'The exceptions, of course, deserve public acclaim.' He singled out Irene Diamond, who 'spent out' the Diamond Foundation in ten years on ground-breaking and effective Aids research. But such examples that were not merely an adornment of the donor, he concluded, were the exception rather than the rule.[35]

Giving something back

There are no real British equivalents of Carnegie, Rockefeller or Gates. The British have always been less generous than Americans, and have a very different tradition of philanthropy. It is telling that one of the most generous British givers of contemporary times was Paul Getty, an expatriate American who took British citizenship and died in 2003. Getty had listed his occupation in *Who's Who* as 'philanthropist', at least until 2000, when he dropped it and listed no occupation. He once said of his gifts, 'I think that since I've lived here and been happy here for such a long time, I think it's my duty here.'[36] Getty had inherited his wealth from his father, who made it through oil, and was himself a generous benefactor. When Paul Getty, the son, died he was reputedly worth over £1.5 billion. Recipients of his gifts over several decades included the National Gallery, Lord's cricket ground, St Paul's Cathedral, the British Film Institute, the Conservative Party and, less well known, the families of striking miners. Nevertheless, even he was by no means a 'five-star deluxe' giver by American standards. His total donation of some £120 million over two decades was small in comparison with his own wealth and the levels of the most generous American contemporaries, and amounted to no more than 10 per cent of his annual income.

One member of the British billionaire club who is renowned for his conspicuous giving is Philip Green. Green likes to see himself as a generous man. In December 2003, he made a donation of some £4 million to help fund care homes provided by Jewish Care, a large health and social care charity. In the aftermath of the tsunami disaster that hit south-east Asia on Boxing Day 2004, killing 300,000 people, Green was one of the first off the mark with a donation of £100,000 in cash and £1 million in clothes. He is a regular at high-profile charity auctions, where he usually leads the bidding, and likes nothing more than to force prices up often to the point 'where it becomes embarrassing', according to one observer. He often competes with his friends Richard Caring and Tom Hunter at such events for spending the most. At the Retail Trust's annual charity ball in 2004, Green and Hunter between them spent £270,000 on a £20,000 MG. Hunter first bought it for £120,000 and then redonated it for Green to bid a further £150,000.

Although the sums he gives are large in absolute terms, to Green they are little more than pocket money. In 2004 and 2005, he paid himself close to £1.7 billion in dividends from his companies. And judged by the standards of some of the super-rich, he is not especially generous. He does not come close to people such as Hunter, whose own philanthropy makes Green look comparatively mean. His critics also claim that Bhs and Arcadia also have a somewhat mixed record when it comes to corporate social responsibility. In 2004, at the height of Green's battle to take over Marks and Spencer, Julia Cleverdon, the director of Business in the Community, suggested that if Green was successful, the values of social responsibility embraced by M&S would go. Although Cleverdon was forced to apologise for her remarks, a similar view was expressed in a letter to the *Financial Times* by the environmental campaigner Jonathon Porritt:

> Where is the evidence of his [Green's] personal leadership on these issues in Bhs or Arcadia? What evidence is there that he really understands that critical nexus . . . between brand, trust and performance on social responsibility – hard-edged, world-beating performance on issues that consumers really care about, as well as world-beating performance on financial returns?[37]

Green would argue that his companies are putting something back through charity sponsorship and investing in education. He has put £50 million into secondary schools specialising in enterprise, and has also taken the lead on sponsoring a government initiative to establish an entrepreneurial retail academy aimed at sixteen- to eighteen-year-olds, with the government and Green each putting in £10 million.

Not all givers are motivated by the status or prestige it brings. A number of 'stealth givers', secret givers who apparently shun public recognition, have been unveiled in recent years. One of the most generous is Chuck Feeney, the Irish-American who founded Duty Free Shoppers (DFS) with his business partner, Robert Miller, in the early 1960s. The hundreds of outlets at airports around the world have earned both men billions of dollars. In the 1980s, Miller moved to Hong Kong to avoid American taxes, and, unknown to him, Feeney set up a charitable trust and put almost his entire fortune into it. Atlantic Philanthropies was registered in Bermuda, thus avoiding the media gaze, and spent $1 billion over the next fifteen years mainly on universities and youth projects, much of it in Ireland, where he retained citizenship.

In 1997, Feeney and another major shareholder tried to sell their shares in DFS (they owned nearly 60 per cent between them) to the French luxury goods company LVMH Moet Hennessey Louis Vuitton. Feeney needed a more conservative form of investment that offered a steadier income flow to finance his charitable commitments. But Miller was opposed and took his former partner to court to try and stop the sale. It was as a result of the court action that the extraordinary giveaway was revealed. The American media later labelled the two men 'the billionaire prince and the billionaire pauper'. On the rare occasions when Feeney has agreed to be interviewed about his apparent altruism, he said he 'had enough money. I believe that people of substantial wealth potentially create problems for future generations unless they accept responsibility to use their wealth during their lifetime to help worthwhile causes.' He once told the *New York Times*, 'You can only wear one pair of shoes at a time.'

Feeney is seen as somewhat eccentric as well as reclusive. He does not own a house or a car, flies economy class and travels on the metro.[38] On visits to Dublin, he takes the bus into the city centre. *Forbes* estimates his personal fortune to be in the region of $5 million, and he has set up trusts for his five children 'with enough money for what they should and will need for life'. Cynics would question even such stealth giving. Charles Lamb, the nineteenth-century society satirist and essayist, once wrote, 'The greatest pleasure I know is to do a good action by stealth and to have it found out by accident.'

One reason for Britain's lower commitment to giving is that buying into elites is an accepted part of the American culture, but is less accepted in Britain. In general, the British are also less persuaded by the duty argument. Wealth here is not associated with bringing equivalent social obligations. There is little sense of the importance of 'giving something back'. This is as true of the modern aristocracy as it is of the new self-made rich. One recent survey of the attitudes of the rich (defined as those earning over £80,000 a year, roughly the top 2 per cent of earners) to giving found that 'it's not my responsibility' was central to the lower donation rate in Britain.[39] Non-givers tended to define their responsibilities in terms of their family but not more widely. There was a strong sense of 'not on my doorstep'. As one respondent put it, 'people who are poorer, they come into contact with people that need help more and therefore they relate to it better. They might know someone who's homeless or someone who's got no-one to look after them . . . whereas people who are rich don't talk to people like that.'[40]

Even those who did give saw it as a matter of personal choice, not a social obligation or duty. Some argued they already 'gave' in taxes. 'I paid £27,000 in tax last year, which is sort of giving to charity in my view . . . I'm paying more than other people. The Welfare State is a safety net for people who can't support themselves . . . I've never had anything out of it.' Another common explanation was that they couldn't afford to give because they were not rich enough to be able to. One respondent who didn't contribute to charity explained, 'Wealthy? It's £50 million and upwards. That is the point at which you don't have to panic anymore.'[41]

Another reason is that the Americans give heavily to what the British largely regard as the state's responsibility – hospitals, colleges, museums and scientific research. As Simon Jenkins remarked,

> having paid taxes to sustain a welfare state, they are reluctant to pay to plug its gaps. They give to cancer research and Comic Relief, and they back the arts. Old money maintains country houses and ancestral collections, braving taxman and burglar alike. New money goes to museums, galleries and opera houses. It builds Clore and Sainsbury wings . . . Where Tate, Guinness and Leverhulme went before, Rothschild, Hamlyn and Lloyd-Webber follow.[42]

Rich Britons also tend to have other ways of spending their money. When it comes to funding their own 'hobbies', the rich have tended to show much less reticence. Robert Maxwell gambled much of his wealth away. A popular hobby for the rich has been to buy up newspapers. These are rarely ways of increasing your fortune, though they are all ways of gaining influence. Maxwell not only lost money at roulette, he also backed a number of failed newspapers, including the *London Daily News*. When Conrad Black was ousted as chairman of Hollinger after eighteen years' ownership of the *Telegraph* newspapers and they were put up for sale, those who led the battle for acquisition included many existing press barons, from Richard Desmond to the secretive multi-millionaires the Barclay Brothers, who eventually bought it.

Buying a football club is another increasingly popular way of spending a personal fortune, one followed by Alan Sugar when he owned Tottenham Hotspur, Mohamed al-Fayed, who owns Fulham, and Roman Abramovich, who bought not only Chelsea, but some of the most expensive players in the world as well. Abramovich's wealth now casts a deep shadow over the world's top clubs as he eyes up the potential of their stars. Chelsea has enjoyed a transfer budget worth almost as much as that of the rest of the professional football clubs together, and enough to take them to the top of the British premiership in 2005 and to persuade the bookies to close the books on Chelsea winning the 2006 championship. Sepp Blatter, Fifa's president, described the impact thus: 'Unlimited cash has given a handful of club owners the wherewithal to control the global game by splashing unimaginable sums on a tiny group of elite players.'[43]

Others like to buy art collections. Maurice Saatchi's promotion of the 'Brit Artists' such as Damian Hirst, Gary Hume and the Chapman brothers has brought him as much influence over the course of British art as other poorer grandees such as Nicholas Serota, chairman of the Tate, and Jay Jopling of the White Cube gallery. The daughter of Hans Rausing, the Tetra Pak tycoon, bought Granta, the upmarket literary magazine and publisher. The takeover of football clubs, media outlets and art collections by the super-rich means that much of our cultural and sporting output and political opinion is expressed and determined by a small number of largely unaccountable individuals and their whims and personal views. Bernie Ecclestone is not only a member of the billionaire's club; his wealth has the power to determine the fate of the British Grand Prix, despite its fifty-year tradition. In 2004 he threatened to pull the race from Silverstone merely by refusing to moderate what most commentators thought were Formula One's inflated demands.

The relative British meanness in giving by the rich might be more understandable if they were heavily taxed. In Britain, the state has assumed a more interventionist role, taking most of the responsibility for implementing social welfare and redistributive programmes. In the post-war era, progressive taxation meant that the rich paid a larger contribution towards the cost of such programmes. In general the rich resented such a requirement and never accepted that it was a part of a formalised 'social bargain'. Tax has been seen as a 'burden', official 'confiscation', and the rich have consistently used their political muscle to try and reduce the bit that falls on them, with notable success. Steadily, taxation on the rich, both income and wealth, has been pared back to a point where Britain's tax system is now regressive: the rich pay proportionately less of their income in tax than the poor.

Indeed, as we will see in the next chapter, the evidence is that many members of the mega-rich club pay little tax at all. Increasingly, it appears, the rich are being treated as a special case in Britain, not in the sense of being required to pay more, but being legally allowed to pay much less.

9

Only little people pay taxes

The tax burden avoided by the few falls on the many. A government committed to the proper funding of public services will not tolerate the avoidance of taxation and will be relentless in its war against tax avoidance.

(Gordon Brown, July 1997)

Social responsibility is not just a matter of putting something back via charity. It is also about paying one's fair share of national taxation. Far from taking such an obligation seriously, many of the richest people in Britain have enhanced their personal fortunes substantially by exploiting Britain's relatively lax tax rules on the wealthy. Indeed, contemporary entrepreneurship and tax avoidance seem to go hand in hand. It's all perfectly legal if you can afford the usually massive accountancy fees involved.

Some of these special tax advantages have been allowed with the agreement of HM Revenue and Customs (HMRC). Indeed, in many ways, the British tax authorities allow the mega-rich to be treated as a special case. One of the 'rules' that is widely used by the rich is that of 'non-domiciliary status'. Under this rule, residents in Britain who were born abroad can register as 'non-domiciles', declaring in effect another country as their real home or, in tax jargon, domicile. They then only pay tax on that part of their income that is 'remitted' back to Britain or otherwise derived in the UK.

An estimated 60,000 rich residents benefit from such a non-domiciliary arrangement. They include Greek shipping magnates, Saudi princes and American corporate heirs. Individual beneficiaries include the Indian steel magnate and Labour Party donor Lakshmi Mittal, the publisher and financier Christopher Ondaatje, also a Labour donor, and a number of foreign business executives. In the past, the German-born Tiny Rowland, the

Czechoslovakian-born Robert Maxwell and the Cypriot Polly Peck chairman, Asil Nadir, were all substantial beneficiaries of this deal. The ever-expanding galaxy of highly paid foreign football stars playing for British clubs also benefit. Nearly all of these will also not pay tax in the country in which they claim to be domiciled because those countries collect tax only on residents. Those wishing to take such status merely have to fill in a straightforward form called DOM 1, and few applications are rejected. Apart from the Irish Republic, no country in the world allows residents to claim that their real home lies elsewhere.

One of those who enjoyed such an arrangement was Mohamed al-Fayed, the billionaire owner of Harrods, the Paris Ritz and Fulham football club. In 1985, the Egyptian businessman struck a secret tax deal with the Inland Revenue that he would pay a fixed annual level of tax amounting to £240,000 a year, without having to declare his real income and gains like other UK residents. The justification for the 'forward tax' arrangement, as it was called, was that it would save the Revenue from a complicated investigation of the businessman's financial affairs. The annual sum paid was a tiny proportion of the actual tax he should have paid, with the shortfall later estimated at up to £6 million a year. The contract had never been mentioned in any Inland Revenue report, and the Treasury had done its best to conceal the truth about it.

Al-Fayed's special tax status arose partly because, although he had been resident in Britain for thirty years, he was born abroad and was treated as a 'non-domicile'. The deal struck was based on an assumption that he was domiciled in Egypt and could plan his affairs such that only capital was brought into the UK, but that he still had some tax obligation. First agreed in 1985, the deal was revised twice, in 1990 and then 1997.

The deal eventually unravelled as a result of the high-profile libel case brought by the Conservative MP and former minister Neil Hamilton against al-Fayed in 1999. The case arose because al-Fayed had alleged that he had made secret payments to four Conservative MPs, including Hamilton, in return for 'parliamentary advocacy'. Al-Fayed won the 'cash for questions' libel case but, in testimony during the trial, he made an extraordinary claim: 'Always in my briefcase I carry £10,000, £15,000 cash in my briefcase or in my private office in Park Lane.' Al-Fayed's personal assistant put the sums at up to £50,000. The money was drawn from an account at his local bank in Park Lane on a regular basis. Hamilton and the other MPs had been paid in sums of up to £2,000 at a time, in £50 notes stuffed in brown envelopes.

Unfortunately for al-Fayed, his claim of access to large cash deposits – up to £50,000 a week – had been spotted by the Inland Revenue, which, unsurprisingly, wanted to know where the money was coming from. Following the disclosure in the trial, the Revenue cancelled the deal they had struck with al-Fayed and began an investigation into his finances. Al-Fayed drew no salary from Harrods but tens of millions of pounds were paid in dividends to an offshore trust based in Bermuda, a perfectly legal arrangement. Harrods' accounts showed that such dividends amounted to £100 million between 1995 and 1998 alone. The disclosure at the trial seemed to reveal that some of this money, indeed quite a lot of it, was seeping back to Britain untaxed.

Al-Fayed challenged the Inland Revenue's decision to withdraw the 'forward contract' in court, but the presiding judge ruled that such deals put individuals, mainly rich foreigners, 'outside the tax system' and were unfair to other taxpayers. 'The al-Fayeds became a privileged group who are not so much taxed by law as untaxed by agreement.' After losing, al-Fayed went into tax exile in Switzerland in 2003. Following the judgment, the Revenue finally revealed that it had struck around twenty similar 'forward contracts', but would not reveal with whom. However, the judgment does mean that no further deals will now be agreed.

Al-Fayed is not alone amongst the rich to pay so little. Entrepreneurs, businessmen, City dealers, footballers, pop stars and television presenters are known to use a variety of schemes dreamt up by highly paid accountants to minimise their tax bills. When Bianca Jagger divorced Mick Jagger, she revealed how the wealthy pop star was obsessed with avoiding paying taxes, not just in Britain but in any country he feared might seek to claim them. 'Throughout our married life, he and I literally lived out of a suitcase in a nomadic journey from one place to another in his quest to avoid income taxes.'[1] Some top British footballers use a perfectly legal offshore scheme devised by the accountants Deloitte & Touche that funnels performance-related bonuses into special accounts to minimise their tax bills. Many England international players protect the fees they earn from advertising through other tax avoidance devices. One former international player and coach, Jack Charlton, said, 'I cannot understand why the tax people are not involved. Like everyone else looking in from the outside at football today, I find some of the financial figures staggering.'[2]

An increasingly popular route is to live in a tax haven. The French have started calling Monaco *le rocher anglais* – the English rock – because of the estimated 5,000 Britons who have chosen to live there and thus escape HMRC. Although they include a number of famous names such as Ringo Starr, Roger Moore and David Coulthard, most are British businessmen who simply fly in for half a week every week to run their companies and then fly back. This is sufficient to avoid tax on investment income. They include John Hargreaves, chairman of Matalan, and Philip Green and his wife Tina.

Philip Green moved to Monaco with his family in 1998. While Tina has taken Monaco residency, Philip retains British residency and is thus liable to pay UK taxes as a result. This is because the tax rules make it clear that you are liable to UK taxes if you are in the country for ninety or more days a year. Green – the ultimate hands-on proprietor – could not run his companies if he spent less than ninety days a year in Britain.

But, with the aid of highly paid tax accountants and lawyers, Green has set up his companies, which are registered offshore in Jersey, in such a way that his dividends accrue not to him but to his wife. It is no wonder that he sometimes likes to joke of Tina that 'he cannot afford' a divorce. Arcadia, for example, is in effect owned by her rather than Philip. So, while his companies will pay British corporation tax, it is Tina rather than Philip who received the £1.2 billion Arcadia dividend paid at the end of 2005, and because Tina is based in Monaco, which has no income tax, the dividend would have come tax free. Without such an arrangement – which is perfectly legal – Green would have had to pay tax at 25 per cent on the dividend payments. The Exchequer is short of tax revenue of the order of some £300 million as a result. This is despite the fact that the dividend arose from business activity conducted in Britain, using, for example, staff mostly educated and trained in the British educational system.

Green argues that he invests in Britain and has always denied that placing his companies in Tina's name is about tax planning, though it is difficult to see what other purpose it could serve. It is he who works long hours to improve Bhs's and Arcadia's profitability, and rings in every day when on holiday. He is the brains and the inspiration. He takes the stage at the very public events he likes to hold for Bhs and Arcadia while Tina sits in the audience.

You don't have to live in a tax haven to benefit. An increasingly widely used tax avoidance device is the offshore account. Offshore havens charge an annual fee for the right to register, in return for a range of privileges from secrecy to artificially low taxes. Shell companies can be formed and bank accounts opened for a modest fee, often through e-mail and with minimal checks. Such accounts can be used to move money around the world. Wealthy individuals such as Hans Rausing, Mohamed al-Fayed and numerous footballers and pop and film stars are known to use offshore accounts – 'closets with computers' as they have been dubbed by the *Financial Times*.[3] Although Rausing is a multi-billionaire, he has used the offshore device to hide his true wealth and income in a way that saves him probably millions of pounds a year in tax.[4]

Since the 1970s, the number of offshore tax havens has doubled to around seventy. The capital of the Cayman Islands, George Town, is the world's fifth largest banking centre, with nearly 600 banks and trust companies, though only fifty actually have a physical presence there and just thirty-one are authorised to trade with the local residents.[5] The country has a population of 35,000 but it is home to some 48,000 corporations and trusts. Most exist as nameplates on a local accountant's door. Offshore companies are being formed at the rate of about 150,000 a year and are now numbered in the millions.[6] Most large accountancy firms have set up branches, or what they like to call 'networks', in the havens. Britain itself is widely seen as a semi-tax haven, a country where large corporations and rich individuals can legally treat tax as a largely optional obligation. It is indeed a location apparently favoured by Russian oligarchs, Greek shipping magnates and Swedish entrepreneurs. One study has estimated that the world's richest individuals have placed $11.5 trillion in offshore tax havens.[7] This growth, made possible by the same process of globalisation of money flows that is changing the nature of entrepreneurship, is a huge headache for the tax-raising ability of governments, not just in the UK.

The extraordinary rise in the role of the offshore haven has been aided by the liberalisation of global capital markets, the telecommunications revolution and the rise of the multi-national company, all of which have facilitated the freer flow of money around the world. The City of London has itself played a central role in the development of the offshore economy. In addition, competition to attract foreign investment has led many developing countries to offer tax inducements. Estonia, for example, which joined the European Union in 2004, levies no corporation tax at all.

Incorporating a company in these countries offers a number of financial advantages – most charge no tax on profits provided you don't trade with anyone on the island, few if any questions are asked, secrecy is guaranteed and there are usually no requirements for public disclosure of meaningful financial information. In 2004, after a hunt spanning three continents and two years, legal investigators found that Dame Shirley Porter and her family had hidden up to £30 million in obscure offshore accounts. Porter had been heavily surcharged for selling council houses in Westminster when she was council leader in the 1980s in order to boost the Conservative vote. She had always claimed she could not afford to pay the surcharge. Those alleged to have used offshore accounts have included Conrad Black, Geoffrey Robinson, once Labour's Paymaster General, and even the Conservative Party itself.[8]

Tax havens are also increasingly used by some of the world's largest corporations, which book their revenue and profits there, even if the actual economic activity takes place in London or New York. Multi-national companies that use offshore tax havens include Virgin, Microsoft, General Motors, Kodak, News Corporation, Boeing and Chevron. Almost one-third of the world's gross domestic product passes through offshore havens such as Belize, Guernsey, Bermuda, the Isle of Man, the Bahamas and the Cayman Islands. The flow has been increasing by up to 15 per cent a year.[9]

Offshore accounts facilitate the widely used but complex system of 'transfer pricing' or 'profit laundering', which involves the shuffling of costs and revenues around the globe to anonymous subsidiaries in tax-free jurisdictions as a way of disguising the real level of profits. Losses are transferred to companies in high-tax areas and profits shifted to areas with low-tax regimes. A report by the US Senate in 2001 claimed that multi-nationals evaded up to $45 billion in American taxes in 2000 through transfer pricing. One firm, for example, sold toothbrushes between subsidiaries for $5,655 each.[10]

The use of offshore accounts also allows the levying of 'management charges', another favoured way of moving money around to avoid tax. One arm of the company network simply charges another for services like consultancy or technical advice that do not have to be identified in detail. Experts refer to these devices as 'fictitious spaces'. Although firms are required to identify their subsidiaries held in offshore havens in their annual returns, no company is obliged to justify such skeletal locations. Yet, according to one tax expert, 'I have never come across any reason for people to set up an offshore trust other than to avoid UK taxes.'[11]

Sir Richard Branson's Virgin Group is one company that specialises in the use of offshore accounts. The network of nearly 300 separate companies that makes up his group are nearly all registered in offshore accounts, mainly the British Virgin Islands. Belize is best known as the home of the former Conservative Party treasurer, Lord Ashcroft. Belize granted a thirty-year lucrative tax concession to his company, Carlisle Holdings, which provides staffing, cleaning and security services. Carlisle's tax-free status in Belize has saved the company an estimated £13.7 million in tax since 1997.[12] Before it was vetoed by the Treasury, top City banks even set up offshore trusts to pay their staff bonuses, not in sterling, euros or dollars but in a weak currency such as the Turkish lira or Argentinian peso. If the currency weakened, the recipient would make a gain when converting to sterling, but one that was free of tax.[13]

To take another example, Rupert Murdoch's media empire has paid hardly anything in tax in the UK since the late 1980s. When a task force from Australia, the UK, Canada and the United States was formed to investigate why News Corp pays virtually no taxes, fear of a backlash by Murdoch led to the investigation being dropped.[14] News Corp consists of a web of 800 subsidiaries, many of them registered offshore. A study of the 101 subsidiaries of the UK holding company for an eleven-year period revealed profits of some £1.4 billion, but minimal corporation tax.[15]

The loss of revenue in the UK from tax avoidance and evasion is huge, variously estimated at between £25 and £85 billion a year.[16] When it comes to corporation tax, the actual tax paid by most large British companies, from the Prudential to Dixons, is less, often considerably less, than the full 30 per cent rate. The owners of the *Daily Express* paid tax at the rate of just 3.6 per cent from 1992 to 1999.[17] One study found a shortfall of some £5 billion in taxes by sixteen randomly picked companies, all quoted on the stock exchange.[18] A former tax compliance officer has said that, routinely, the largest UK corporations now pay their tax 'by agreement', adding, 'We have no way of telling whether [their accounts] are accurate or not.'[19]

In the United States, corporate and individual tax avoidance is also endemic. In 2003, a report by the US Senate's Joint Committee on Taxation found that the disgraced company Enron had been able to eliminate most of its tax liabilities of more than $1.3 billion in the five years before it went bankrupt by operating through 881 offshore companies. Many multi-national companies, including Nike, Morgan Stanley, Hewlett-Packard and Halliburton, use similar schemes. It has been estimated that such legal corporate tax avoidance costs the US taxpayer more than $170 billion a year, on top of the $85 billion lost from tax avoidance by wealthy individuals.[20]

The Senate committee also severely criticised a number of the nation's largest and most prestigious accounting and law firms and investment houses as the 'real engine' of the tax shelter industry. Especially criticised was the ethics of the accountancy giant KPMG, which was found to have put together no fewer than 400 off-the-shelf tax avoidance 'products' for use by firms. Some members of the committee accused the company of a 'culture of deception'. The investigation turned up internal e-mails exhorting partners and colleagues in the firm to 'SELL SELL SELL' the shelters to clients. According to the investigation, between 1997 and 2001, the accountancy firm had collected $124 million in fees for devising tax shelters that had cost the American government $1.4 billion in lost revenue.[21] Following the allegations and widespread criticism of the company, KPMG announced that its deputy chairman was stepping down and that its top tax shelter partner had been put on administrative leave.

In his annual letter to investors for 2004, Warren Buffett explained that his investment company, Berkshire Hathaway, paid $3.3 billion in 2003, 2.5 per cent of the tax paid by all American companies, even though its market worth was only 1 per cent of corporate America. Buffett went on to imply that American companies were not pulling their weight on tax, adding, 'If class war is being waged in America, my class is clearly winning.' As the *Daily Telegraph* described his suggestion, 'it's the sort of accusation that gets you called a communist on Wall Street'.[22] Sure enough, the *Wall Street Journal,* the voice of corporate America, swung back with an icy editorial on Buffett's remarks.

The billionaire backlash

Luke Johnson lists his pet hate as 'paying taxes'. He is hardly alone, but for the rich, taxes appear to be a special anathema. As Leona Helmsley, the widow of a New York property tycoon and multi-billionaire, once put it, 'only the little people pay taxes.'[23] She was later convicted and gaoled for evading taxes by claiming a mountain of personal expenses against her business.

The history of taxation can be seen, at least in part, as something of an ongoing war between government and the wealthy. Today the wealthy are winning the war, but it was perhaps less so in the past. At the beginning of the twentieth century, successive attempts to impose higher rates of income and inheritance tax in Britain were bitterly opposed by the wealthy establishment. When estate duty was introduced in Britain in 1894, it was described by its opponents as 'perfectly monstrous' and the maximum rate of

8 per cent was described by one MP in the House of Commons as ' throwing into the shade everything that had ever been done in the way of highway robbery'.[24] Leading aristocrats protested strongly. A famous cartoon in *Punch* of 1894 shows two of the richest men in Britain at the time, a disconsolate Duke of Devonshire saying to a worried-looking Duke of Westminster, 'We may consider ourselves lucky if we can keep a tomb over our heads.'[25] A prolonged political battle also ensued over David Lloyd George's controversial 1909 proposals for a 'surtax', an income tax surcharge on higher incomes.

As the rich lost some of their power and esteem, the tax system in Britain became increasingly progressive. From the 1930s onwards, rates of income tax on top incomes rose sharply, as did estate duty. Until the 1980s, Britain used to have a modestly progressive tax system in which the rich generally paid a higher share of their income in tax. Gradually, the progressive elements of income tax have been stripped away while the burden of tax has been switched gradually to more regressive indirect taxes including VAT and excise duties on alcohol and cigarettes. As a result, the tax system passed from being broadly progressive to broadly regressive in the mid- to late 1980s (see Figure 9.1). This is despite the fact that the progressive principle, that tax fairness requires the rich to pay proportionally more than the poor, has been endorsed by successive Tax Commissions and has been enshrined in tax practice for over a century. In 2002 (see Figure 9.1), the top fifth of taxpayers paid some 35 per cent of their income in tax compared with 37.9 per cent for the poorest fifth. As in the United States, the shift to a more regressive tax regime has been inspired by a belief in supply side economics, that the rich would respond positively to tax incentives. As J. K. Galbraith once pointed out, there is something strange about a doctrine which holds that the rich work harder if they have more money and the poor if they have less.

A similar war over taxes has ensued in the United States. The early attempts to introduce income and capital taxes were as heavily fought there as they were here. In 1894 the US Supreme Court struck down an 1893 law establishing a minimal federal income tax of 2 per cent by calling it a 'stepping stone to other, larger and more sweeping, political contests . . . a war of the poor against the rich'.[26] The opening years of the twentieth century brought the near elimination of federal estate and gifts taxes, thus enabling the great fortunes of the time to be passed largely untaxed to the next generation. But the accumulation of such vast personal fortunes produced an angry backlash. Theodore Roosevelt declared that 'each

Figure 9.1 How Britain's tax system has increasingly favoured the rich
Total taxes paid as a proportion of gross income by the richest and poorest fifth of the population.

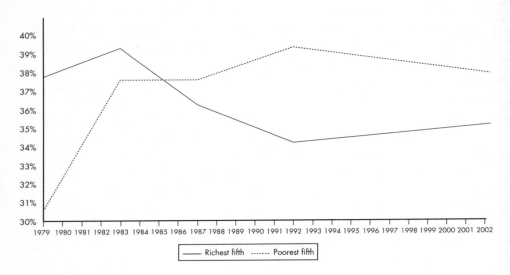

Source: C. Larkin, 'The Effects of Taxes and Benefits on Household Income 2002–3, *Economic Trends* (2004), no. 607, 39–84, Table 3; earlier figures are from earlier versions of the same series. The figures show all direct and indirect taxes on households (adjusted for size) as a proportion of gross income.

generation should have to start anew with equal opportunities' and, despite a decade of opposition, a full federal income tax system was finally introduced in 1913.

President Roosevelt first proposed an estate tax in 1904 in response to the growing outrage about the excesses of the Gilded Age. Progressive reformers were concerned that if wealth concentration continued unchecked and untaxed it would evolve into a permanent and dangerous wealth aristocracy. Yet it was not until 1916 that Congress finally introduced an estate tax, aimed at restraining the concentration of wealth and power. It raised the rates a year later, with the highest set at 25 per cent on estates of more than $10 million, while, between 1921 and 1928, the Republican administration substantially reduced the tax burden on the rich, saving wealthy individuals and corporations over $4 billion a year.[27]

In the 1930s Franklin Roosevelt raised the top income tax rate and tightened inheritance tax, higher tax burdens that contributed to the process of income and wealth 'levelling' that occurred from the mid-1930s until the early 1970s, when conservative thinkers found a novel way of justifying tax cuts on the wealthy. In 1974, the University of Chicago economist Arthur Laffer was having lunch with a Wall Street writer. He drew a graph on a napkin that purported to show that above a certain income level, higher taxes lead to lower tax revenue because the incentive to work falls and that to evade tax rises. The 'relationship' became known as the 'Laffer curve'. Although it was never statistically proven, it was pounced on by ideologically conservative think-tanks and low-tax-supporting politicians and used first by Ronald Reagan and then by both Presidents Bush to justify their subsequent waves of tax cuts on the rich. This is despite the fact that George H. W. Bush, the father, had once dismissed the idea as 'voodoo economics'.

In 1981, President Reagan began the rush to reduce taxes, which were certainly high at the time, with an unprecedented package of cuts on both income and corporate taxation. By the end of the 1980s, the effect of the changes was that, as in Britain, the very rich – those with incomes over $170,000 – actually paid a lower tax rate than those with less, leading the *Economist* to argue that 'America has one of the world's least progressive tax structures'.[28] Moreover, the evidence is that the magic predicted by Laffer failed to work. Far from the predicted rise, income tax revenue fell sharply from 1980 to 1984. The cuts further enriched the already wealthy but at the price of a yawning budget deficit that has long haunted American economic policy. In 1993, in an attempt to tackle the deficit, President Clinton raised the top rate to 39.6 per cent. This was a move that the anti-tax school believed would end in disaster, cutting incentives and economic growth and aggravating the deficit. The predicted gloom never materialised, however. In fact, growth accelerated and the budget deficit turned into a surplus, though this was aided by broader economic trends.[29]

In 2001 and 2003, President Bush, the son, introduced two highly contentious tax cut packages, both presented as a patriotic economic stimulus that only traitors could disagree with. Under the plans, estate duty is being slowly phased out over ten years, with a combination of a declining rate and a steadily rising exemption level, while marginal rates on top incomes, capital gains and dividends are being cut to a top rate of 15 per cent.

Despite claims that the cuts will benefit the middle classes, most of these 'giveaways' are of greatest benefit to the rich and especially the very rich, who have had their taxes cut to levels last seen in the 1920s. According to one independent estimate, 42 per cent of the benefit of the 2001 cuts, once phased in, will go to the top 1 per cent – those earning more than $330,000 a year. The very rich have also gained disproportionately from the 2003 cuts.[30] The evidence is also that when the American rich enjoy tax cuts, the effect is to swell the country's massive overseas deficit as any extra spending goes on imported rather than domestic goods. The giveaway goes on Mercedes rather than Buicks, Armani rather than Brooks Brothers.

Ironically, it was a small contingent of the super-rich themselves who led the campaign against the Bush tax bonanza. On 18 February 2001, an advertisement in the *New York Times* called on President Bush to drop his proposal to abolish estate duty. It was signed by 120 of America's wealthiest people. *Newsweek* called it 'the billionaire backlash'. It was an intriguing alliance of some of those who stood to gain most from the tax's abolition. Signatories included William H. Gates Sr, the father of the richest man in America, the billionaire investors Warren Buffett and George Soros, David and Steven Rockefeller, Ted Turner and Ben Cohen, a founder of Ben and Jerry's. Supporters of the campaign included Robert Redford and Paul Newman.

Those opposed to repeal made a number of arguments: that it would reduce the incentive for the rich to set up foundations funding good causes; that it would shift the tax burden from the rich to the poor and the middle class; that the effect of capital taxes is to make America more meritocratic, not less; that the effect would be to create an 'aristocracy of wealth' as Theodore Roosevelt had feared a century before. This was a taxpayers' revolt like none other. Most of those backing the group were characterised first by their generous philanthropy, and second by their public commitments to limit their bequests to their own children. As Buffett has put it, it is wisest to leave children 'enough money so that they could feel they could do anything, but not so much that they could do nothing'.[31] Buffett likened the repeal of estate duty to 'choosing the 2020 Olympic team by picking the eldest sons of the gold-medal winners in the 2000 Olympics', thereby encouraging a society based on inheritance rather than merit.[32]

Buffett was also opposed to the proposals to cut taxes on dividends, which, as he pointed out, would mean he would pay less tax than his secretary. President Bush's tax proposals were not just opposed by some of the country's richest citizens. Even the President's own treasury secretary, Paul O'Neill, sacked after two years, did not believe that tax cuts on the rich were the best way to revive the American economy. Economists feared they would return the country to another prolonged deficit and to the need for substantial cuts in public spending to close the gap.

Those backing Bush argued that the wealth gap doesn't matter. As Grover Norquist of the National Taxpayers Union puts it, 'if there was no Bill Gates, there'd be less of a wealth gap, but it wouldn't help anyone down below . . . Some people with extra time go out and drink beer. Some people with extra time invent Microsoft. But that's no reason for government to take their hard-earned money away.'[33] Others dismissed billionaires opposed to tax cuts as indulging in a 'new guilt culture'. There was also a return to old arguments that tax stifles wealth creation and inhibits creative entrepreneurs and, echoing Laffer and others, that its elimination would increase revenue and benefit the poor through a 'trickle-down' effect. It is an argument that has polarised America around issues of the wealth gap, progressive taxation, the budget deficit and even the nature of democracy. It is a debate that has raged for more than a hundred years, since the estate tax was first mooted, and one that has finally been won by the tax's opponents.

The pin-stripe mafia

Today, the tax war has largely been won by the super-rich, not just in the US but also in Britain. In 1993, Gordon Brown, the then shadow Chancellor, had promised a crusade to minimise avoidance. 'Is Britain's tax system in need of being cleaned up? The answer is yes.'

In power, after winning the 1997 election with such a sweeping mandate, Labour has found the going somewhat tougher. They have introduced dozens of anti-tax-dodging measures, especially in more recent Budgets. In 2004, Brown unveiled plans to crack down on the more outrageous avoidance schemes by imposing new disclosure obligations on companies and their tax advisers, similar to those in force in the United States. The Treasury will then close schemes deemed to be 'abusive'. The government backed away from introducing the more draconian anti-avoidance devices imposed in Australia and Canada, however, and few experts think the proposals will prove very effective at recovering unpaid tax from corporations and individuals. In 2005, further proposals were announced and the Treasury now has new powers, under a new EU directive, to be given access to foreign bank accounts.

Despite the predictable howls of protest from individuals, companies and lobbyists at the new proposals, critics say that they will barely scratch the surface of tax avoidance, which has become a massive and lucrative industry.

They claim that HMRC is under-resourced and losing the war. Indeed, the level of tax recovered from companies and individuals by revenue investigators fell from £5.5 billion in 2000 to £3.8 billion in 2002. Although it recovered partially to reach £4.6 billion in 2004, it is still not back to 2000 levels.[34] Part of the Revenue's problem lies in the technical difficulty of closing every loophole. Every time HMRC identifies and shuts down a tax-dodging scheme, the avoidance accountants get paid a lot of money to dream up another. It's a constant game of 'cat and mouse', as one former Revenue official put it. Some years ago, many City firms paid their staff bonuses in the form of gold bars and fine wine. When the government closed this loophole, accountancy firms devised a new scheme to pay directors through 'employee benefit trusts' based offshore.

But this is not the only obstacle. In 2002, Brown announced a review of the domiciliary scheme. Following the announcement, the representatives of those likely to be affected – lawyers and tax and business advisers – moved into action in what one Whitehall source described as a 'fantastic lobbying campaign'.[35] John Christensen, a former tax and economic adviser to Jersey, the British tax haven, calls the anti-tax lobby the 'pin-stripe mafia'. One group of specialist tax advisers even circulated a memo to their clients detailing ways of avoiding tax if Brown implemented his threat. Defenders of the rule claim that scrapping it would lead to a mass exodus of the rich, despite the fact that there is limited incentive to do so as no other country operates such a rule. The traditional defence of the rule is the appeal to the 'trickle-down effect'. But how does the wealth of the Russian oligarchs, for example, many of whom have chosen to settle in Britain, benefit ordinary citizens? Roman Abramovich's single most important contribution has been to turn the Premiership into a one-horse race. As the historian Tristram Hunt has put it, 'where are the businesses, cultural patronage or charitable institutions from this new Russian community?'[36]

The Treasury has often considered abolishing the domiciliary rule only to be thwarted by a lobby of the rich and powerful. Margaret Thatcher vetoed reform being considered by Chancellor Norman Lamont because she was persuaded there was a real economic risk. When he was Prime Minister, John Major held a dinner at Downing Street for a group of Greek shipping magnates, who warned him that they would move their business elsewhere if their tax status was tightened. It proved an effective threat. The idea was dropped. Labour's review has also achieved little more than some new restrictions at the margins.

At the heart of the 'mafia' is the all-powerful accountancy industry, which enjoys huge financial fees from constructing tax avoidance devices, though it prefers to use terms such as 'tax efficiency', 'tax planning' or 'tax management'. Governments are increasingly dependent on the big accountancy firms such as KPMG and Ernst & Young for the implementation of their policies. A senior accountant from Arthur Andersen seconded to the Treasury during the non-domicile review was one of those issuing internal warnings of a mass exodus of international businessmen.[37] Thatcher's programme of privatisation depended on the accountancy profession and the big corporate accountancy firms. Labour's programme of expanding public investment through the private finance initiative has been similarly dependent. This has given the firms a unique form of access and power. Many leading Labour figures, including Patricia Hewitt and Peter Mandelson, have worked for or acted as consultants to major accountancy firms.

Different arms of government also work against each other. HMRC has found that, while it was pursuing some wealthy individuals for tax, the Foreign Office had been advising the same individuals how to avoid it, for fear of losing inward investment. Many of the tax havens are UK Crown dependencies, yet successive British governments have done little to impose reform. Because of growing international pressure, the British government did order a review of Jersey's system of financial regulation in 1998. In the event the terms of reference were very narrow, no hearings were heard in public, the evidence has not been published and the report largely endorsed the status quo with few significant reform proposals. More recently, international pressure has been growing from the European Union and the Organisation for Economic Co-operation and Development, the world's rich-nation club, to persuade tax havens to co-operate to minimise tax evasion and to be more transparent. Unsurprisingly, given the financial benefits to the islands concerned, little progress is being made.

The failure to act is not down to a lack of political power. Half the world's tax havens are British territories or Commonwealth members. After the 11 September attacks on New York, the US government sought information on the financial links of Osama bin Laden that had been traced to the Bahamas. When a Bahamas bank refused to open its records, the US had it cut off from the world's wire transfer systems; the bank co-operated within hours. According to one account, 'the same political will is absent when Western governments deal with tax avoidance/evasion, banking secrecy and regulation hopping. One possible reason is that too many major corporations are using tax havens to slash their tax bills. The same corporations are also funding political parties and institutions.'[38] For example, during the 1990s, Enron gave away $5.9 billion in political contributions, including donations to the presidential campaign of George W. Bush and £38,000 to the 1998 Labour Party conference.[39]

The principal explanation is politics. The British government makes the right noises about tackling avoidance, but it is hardly one of their top priorities. The rich have no greater champion behind them than the Prime Minister. Tony Blair is personally opposed to higher taxes on the rich. Partly this is a product of Labour's growing support amongst the business elite, support which dates from Labour's 'prawn cocktail' offensive to woo businesses and obtain their funding while in opposition. Partly it is philosophical. Blair believes that while poverty matters, wealth does not, and has, for example, long been opposed to the introduction of a higher rate of tax on very high earners, a policy favoured by many in the Labour Party.

In June 2003, the newly appointed leader of the House of Commons, Peter Hain, was preparing the text for a lecture in honour of Aneurin Bevan, when a leak was obtained by the *Daily Mirror*. The draft floated a proposal for the reform of higher rate taxation. Hain wanted the higher rate tax band of 40 per cent to start at a higher level of income because the threshold had fallen over the years and now caught an increasing number of middle income groups including teachers and police officers. His suggestion was that the cost would be met by those with higher incomes bearing more of the burden. When No. 10 heard of the speech, Hain was forced to retract. He was effectively frogmarched onto BBC Radio 4's *Today* programme to deny it all. When he delivered his speech in the evening, it said precisely the opposite of the original draft: 'We will not raise the top rate of tax and there is no going back to the old days of punitive tax rates to fund reckless spending.' The re-draft is believed to have been overseen by Blair's then press secretary, Alastair Campbell. This was re-education, New Labour style. Honest and open political debate about an important subject had lasted barely a morning.

Blair favours a cap on tax rates on the rich because he does not want to discourage an aspirational culture. Before the 1997 general election, he blocked a proposal for a higher rate in the manifesto. 'If you cap someone's income with the international market what it is, that would drive them abroad,' is how he put it on *Newsnight* in 2001. He would also seem to have been a convert to Laffer's theory, arguing that higher taxes on the rich would not lead to increased revenue because, as he put it in an interview in the *Guardian,* 'large numbers of those taxpayers, probably the wealthiest, would simply hire a whole lot of new accountants to do this and that. And actually your whole tax take would be a lot less.'[40] When he gave his first speech on economics for years, in 2004, Blair chose an audience of city financiers and a venue at Goldman Sachs, and bragged about how little tax they pay under a Labour government, 'lower than in most of Mrs Thatcher's years'. Imposing higher tax rates on the rich is one thing. Turning a semi-blind eye to wholesale tax avoidance is another.

The effect of recent tax policies is that today the tax burden continues to be inversely related to the ability to pay, a pattern that breaches one of the fundamental principles of a fair tax system. Avoidance has greatly exacerbated this trend. One tax expert, Professor Prem Sikka of the University of Essex, has described our tax system as a form of 'reverse socialism'.[41] The great majority of individuals pay their dues, while very rich individuals and also large corporations increasingly choose and have the power to opt out of their tax obligations. By hiring the best legal and accountancy brains, it is possible to exploit tax loopholes in a way that makes tax a largely voluntary act.

Today the debate about tax is much less about tackling avoidance and more about reducing taxes still further. For many years, business has lobbied, with some success, for cuts in corporate tax rates across the globe. The headline rate of corporation tax has been falling and the *Economist* magazine has argued it should be abolished altogether.[42] Others favour the phasing out of inheritance tax, despite its inherent fairness. Neo-conservatives believe that tax is a kind of theft and have been behind a new idea that is becoming increasingly widely advocated – the flat tax, a concept that has already been adopted by a number of nations in eastern Europe including Russia and Ukraine. Under a flat tax system, all exemptions and allowances would go and be replaced with a single rate, much lower than at present. The effect would be a tax system even more favourable to the rich. Indeed the doctrine of the flat tax stems in part from a belief that current inequalities are acceptable and desirable.

Behind the legitimacy of the British welfare culture is the ability to persuade all citizens – rich and poor alike – to pay taxes as a symbol of a common culture and interest. If the rich choose to opt out of taxation, why shouldn't the middle classes and the poor? Here is the danger: that the whole edifice could come crumbling down. Yet, increasingly, the super-rich are choosing to become free riders, opting out of the social contract to which ordinary citizens sign up. They are typically not paying a fair contribution for the essential public goods such as health, education, security and the rule of law that benefit them as well as everybody else and without which societies could not function.

These are issues that are central to the debate about the virtues or otherwise of the recent wealth revolution. How much is deserved, how much is undeserved? Has the wealth revolution benefited us all or just the few? It is to this issue that we now turn in the final two chapters.

10

The good, the bad and the ugly

> We can and should take action if the earnings of the rich, and how they are achieved, set them apart from the rest of society. We should tackle social exclusion at the top as well as at the bottom.
> (Lord Giddens, former director of the London School of Economics)[1]

The debate about the role and merits of the rich is nothing new. The wealthiest have inspired and annoyed in equal measure throughout history. Today, Britain has highly sophisticated anti-poverty policies yet a more or less laissez-faire attitude towards the very rich. The incomes of those who fall below a strict floor are boosted because, as a society, Britain accepts that there is a minimum living standard below which it would be socially unacceptable for people to have to live. On the other hand, there is no ceiling at the top. Nor is there a norm about what is an acceptable limit.

It was not always so. Indeed, it is a very recent view. For half a century from the great crash of 1929, not only did governments intervene to protect the poor but a social climate emerged that acted as a kind of natural limit to the size of personal fortunes that could be accumulated. This was not imposed. A cultural, political and social consensus developed and was largely observed. The reasons were clear and, at least for a while, widely accepted – that a socially integrated society would be more economically effective and just than one with extremes of poverty and wealth.

Today the dominant view is that the wealth gap no longer matters, that the surge in personal wealth is good for Britain. Higher fortunes are increasingly seen as good for the economy and for encouraging an aspirational culture. Such views began to take hold first in the United States. Before she was disgraced and gaoled for lying about an illicit share deal, the high-profile

American businesswoman and television celebrity Martha Stewart was fond of arguing that inequality not only doesn't matter, it's a good thing.[2] Her consolation on leaving gaol was that she was still estimated to be worth $1 billion. Martin Feldstein, former chairman of the Advisory Committee on Economics under President Bush Sr, described those who are against increases in incomes at the top even if nobody at the bottom end is worse off as 'spiteful egalitarians'.[3]

Similar views hold in Britain. 'Egalitarianism has been the most corrosive, illiberal and murderous of modern beliefs,' as one has put it.[4] Perhaps unsurprisingly, the editor of *Tatler* has applauded what he calls the 'rise of the flashocracy': 'It is about time that we celebrate those who want to spend it. Stealth wealth is so yesterday. And flash cash no longer be sneered at. These spenders, Thatcher's children, are bringing profits and spreading wealth.'[5] One recent polemic celebrating wealth, the rich and modern capitalism was titled *Rich Is Beautiful*.[6] When the *Daily Telegraph* launched its new separate business section, the City editor declared that from now on the paper would 'celebrate what is in this room: power, wealth and influence'. The rich themselves have a common currency that is widely used in their defence – that their activities 'create or save jobs', 'create value', that their rewards are 'in line with the risks they take'. Such views are shared at the highest levels in Britain. Many close to those at the top of politics today have made no secret of their desire to be able to join the ranks of the rich.

There are equally strong reservations as well. Those perturbed by the rise in the wealth gap in fact include a number of New Labour insiders. Geoff Mulgan, head of the Downing Street Strategy Unit under Blair, argued shortly after leaving government that one of its weaknesses was its failure to 'take on the most powerful interests', including 'the super-rich, big business and the City'.[7] In 2005, Lord Giddens, leading New Labour guru and chief architect of the Blairite 'third way', and Patrick Diamond, a former Downing Street adviser, published a book, *The New Egalitarianism*, calling for a set of controversial tax and social measures designed to clip growing inequality and create a more just and socially mobile society. The potential risk has certainly not gone unnoticed even amongst the ranks of the super-rich themselves. Leo Hindery, the multi-millionaire chairman of HL Capital, warned in 2004, 'You're setting up a class system the likes of which we've never seen in the world. The most obvious precedent is the French revolution, where the gap between the extremely wealthy and the middle class grew to be so acute that social unrest ensued.'[8]

There are also plenty of similar siren noises across the Atlantic. It was some of America's richest citizens that led the campaign against President Bush's plans to cut inheritance, capital and other taxes on the rich. Felix Rohatyn, the American investment banker and civic leader, has said that 'a democracy, to survive, must at the very least appear to be fair. This is no longer the case in America.'[9] Michel Camdessus, the former head of the International Monetary Fund, has warned that 'the widening gap between rich and poor within nations [is] morally outrageous, economically wasteful and potentially socially explosive'.[10]

The arguments about whether the growing wealth gap is good or bad for Britain will continue to rage. Those who defend the gap usually make four broad points. First, that the problem of poverty can be tackled without worrying about the rich. Secondly, that economic dynamism requires inequality. Thirdly, that the rich today are mostly deserving of their wealth. And fourthly, that contemporary wealth is mostly gained without harming anyone else. So do these arguments stand up?

Opting out

The dominant political view in Britain today is that all that is important is to act to alleviate serious poverty. Yet it is difficult to reconcile an active policy towards the poor with one that ignores the rich. The rich do not live on a separate planet. As powerful individuals, the decisions they take have a much wider impact on society as a whole. Sometimes their actions are beneficial, sometimes neutral, sometimes harmful. They certainly cannot be dismissed as irrelevant. One of the distinguishing characteristics of being rich is that it buys you the power to opt out. But the process of opting out impacts on others and often on those towards the bottom end of the wealth league. As Giddens has put it, 'the strategies used by the affluent in gaining concentrated access to the best housing, health and education plainly have their effect upon the life chances of poorer groups'.[11]

Take housing as an example. Escalating City and corporate salaries have impacted on many ordinary people by greatly distorting the housing market, especially in the south-east. Although they are not the sole explanation, ever more generous bonuses and rising pay differentials have contributed to the recent sharp increase in the ratio of house prices to earnings, pricing a growing proportion of key workers and young professionals out of the property market. This is not the kind of trickle-down effect that the pro-rich advocates had in mind. In the London borough of Kensington and Chelsea, an area that combines the extremes of wealth and poverty, and which has become an increasingly popular magnet for business tycoons – international and home-grown – as well as pop stars and Hollywood actors, the average cost of a house in 2005 was £1.4 million. No fewer than 7,200 of the borough's 90,000 dwellings are registered as second homes, a situation described by the council's deputy leader as a 'hollowing out' of the local community.[12]

The evidence is also that highly unequal societies exhibit higher levels of ill health, crime and racial discrimination than more equal ones. Greeks are healthier than Americans, even though American incomes are on average twice as high.[13] America is the richest country in the world, yet male life expectancy is lower in the United States than it is in Costa Rica while its infant mortality rate is higher than Malaysia's.

Successive studies have shown that high levels of inequality are associated with higher rates of illness and death amongst the poorest. This is because more egalitarian societies display higher levels of general well-being while unequal ones suffer from higher levels of stress and depression at the bottom of the social ladder. This is the result of the growing psychological importance attached to relative as opposed to absolute positions in modern societies. Above subsistence levels, what seems to undermine our personal sense of well-being most is not our absolute living standard, but 'psychosocial' factors that are related to the size of the gaps between us and those above us. In modern highly visible societies driven mainly by money, poor children and the low paid are only too aware of their lowly status.[14] The evidence is clear: Britain is paying dearly – in higher crime rates, diverging mortality rates and widening levels of educational achievement – for the soaring inequalities that began in the early 1980s.

When the rich choose, as they mostly do, to buy the best education for their children, either directly or by moving house, there is a serious knock-on effect on the rest of the population. Greater social mobility is one of the rallying cries of modern politicians across the political spectrum. Yet educational opportunities are still heavily dependent on social background, with smart poor kids having a slower rate of educational development than dumb rich ones. According to the Prime Minister's own Strategy Unit, 'less able richer children overtake more able poorer children by the age of five'.[15] Moreover, the latest provisional evidence suggests that, far from declining with spreading affluence, the fortunes of birth are becoming harder to overcome as the growing wealth divide makes them even more entrenched. As the wealth and income gap widens so does the opportunity gap.[16]

We have been slowly building a more aspirational culture but without the means of realising it. Ordinary people increasingly aspire to a wealthy lifestyle in a way their parents could not, but that aspiration remains little more than a pipe-dream for the great majority. Comparisons between countries show that the chance of moving through the class hierarchy is greatest in those countries with the smallest wealth gap. This finding – that 'higher rates of social mobility are associated with lower inequalities' – raises big doubts about the merits of an anti-poverty strategy that ignores the improving fortunes of the rich.[17] As one leading expert has suggested, 'inequality of outcome today is a cause of inequality of opportunity in the next generation'.[18]

There is another important way in which the escalation of personal wealth at the top can have damaging social side-effects. To achieve a socially integrated, fully democratic society, all its citizens need to have some sense of social responsibility and belonging. As one observer has put it, 'a society rich in social capital is likely to be a healthy society. A society rich in material capital, but short of social capital, is likely to be unhealthy.'[19] Robin Cook wrote shortly before his death that a core value of a fair society should be 'solidarity – the principle that the strength of a society is measured by the extent that its rich members support their vulnerable fellow citizens.'[20] Yet many, if not most, of the rich are choosing to opt out of those obligations.

'Social exclusion' is usually a term used to describe the effect of poverty. But social disengagement is also a characteristic of many of those at the top of the rich lists. Partly this reflects the way in which the rich are treated as a 'no-go area' by government. Some, though not all, of them are already ring-fencing themselves from wider society. Increasing numbers have chosen to live as tax exiles, even though their wealth derives from Britain. Many choose to exclude themselves from many if not most of the services and activities that the great majority of the populace participate in. These include not merely public services such as state education, the National Health Service and public transport, but also civic involvement. Some have turned their homes into fortresses. The reclusive Barclay brothers run their businesses by moving between their mock-Georgian castle on Brecqhou and their home in Monte Carlo. Property developer Harry Hyams lives a reclusive lifestyle in Ramsbury Manor in Wiltshire's Kennet valley, one of the most beautiful country houses in Britain. The large iron gates carry a notice that says 'Strictly No Admittance'. Hyams reputedly has little to do with his local community except to complain.[21] In a high-profile attempt to exploit a loophole in the legislation, Nicholas van Hoogstraten blocked public rights of way across his land. These are exceptions but the number choosing to live in expensive and exclusive gated communities is rising sharply. As the Royal Institute of Chartered Surveyors has described the growing geographical separation of the poor and the rich, 'there are indications that the upper and lower ends of our society are diverging further than ever before.'[22]

Having chauffeur-driven cars, and, increasingly, access to a private jet, even if they have to share one, the mega-rich rarely use public transport or travel with the wider public. In 2003, Mary Steel, the headmistress of a top girls' private school, complained about the 'values vacuum' being created in a society dominated by money, self-interest and personal ambition. She described how one father used to drop his daughters to school by helicopter and how his relationship with the school was essentially transactional.[23] Today's wealthy super-elite typically choose to live segregated lives, unaware of the reality of ordinary life, increasingly divorced from common experience and independent of the society that enabled them to build the wealth that gives them the choices denied to most of the population. Yet the risk is that, if the rich don't play their part, others will give up too.

Chapter 8 showed that the rich in Britain, and especially the new rich, tend to have a lower than average sense of collective social conscience. The wealth boom has not been accompanied by a philanthropy boom. When the rich do choose to give something back, it tends to be to high-profile, high-status projects in the arts rather than projects that contribute to a more fully integrated society. The rich also appear to be increasingly choosing to opt out of their obligations as taxpayers. Tax is a key part of the social contract, a recognition that social responsibilities and obligations go with rights and the necessary means to building a civilised society. The great majority of citizens pay their dues. In contrast, as shown in Chapter 9, tax avoidance is extensive amongst the rich, and probably growing, despite the greatly lowered tax rates introduced in the 1980s. The poor are constantly reminded of their responsibilities, while no such pressure applies to the wealthiest.

The rich also seem increasingly unwilling to share the ups and downs of business life. It is staff, shareholders and customers who are expected to bear the brunt of the pain when things go wrong, while executives protect themselves even if they are responsible for business failure. This is well illustrated by the finance industry, where dire results for pensioners, savers and investors have rarely been matched by comparable sacrifices by those whose decisions have failed their clients. How many of the directors of successive regimes at the Prudential, Standard Life and Allied Dunbar have fared as badly as many of their clients? As one *Telegraph* headline once put it, 'the fat cats get fatter while the savers suffer'.[24]

It may well be that we are already on course for creating a detached and insular super-class, a parallel at the top to the 'underclass' at the bottom. That is certainly a strong and possibly irreversible trend in the United States, a society where the very rich exercise considerable political power for their own benefit. They have poured money into powerful think-tanks and pressure groups that endorse laissez-faire economic policies, low taxes and cutbacks in welfare programmes. The American election system has become increasingly dependent on high levels of financial support from the very rich, most of it backing the Republicans. As two leading academics have warned, 'if the rich can buy more political influence than other Americans, and if the political process then yields policies that allow the rich to further increase their share of total income, it is hard to reconcile this result with traditional norms about how a democracy should operate'.[25]

In his influential book *Bowling Alone*, Robert Putnam argued that rising social inequality in the United States in the last few decades has coincided with a decline in social cohesion: 'Sometime around 1965–70, America reversed course and started to become both less just economically and less well connected socially and politically.'[26] Similarly, the American social historian Christopher Lasch argued in *The Revolt of the Elites* that 'the general course of recent history no longer favours the levelling of social distinctions but runs more and more in the direction of a two-class society, in which the favoured few monopolise the advantages of money, education and power'. According to him, managerial and business elites are increasingly choosing to isolate themselves from their own national networks and enclaves, abandoning the middle classes and choosing to live in an exclusive world of their own. In doing so they are turning their backs on a sense of commitment and social responsibility and dividing the nation.[27]

Lasch was mainly talking about America, and this is not yet a true picture of Britain. Nevertheless it is slowly heading that way. While the rich tend to be in denial of how wealthy they really are, they are also pulling further away, developing their own separate ethos and choosing to exercise a growing political clout to shape economic policies in their favour.

The goose that lays the golden egg

Shortly after he announced that he was giving a third of his money away, Bill Gates was asked by the *New York Times* if he was a closet liberal. His answer: 'The Republicans often do a good job of figuring out to how to encourage wealth creation while Democrats often do a good job of figuring out how to spread wealth around – and those are both things I think are very important.' He went on, with a smile, 'When people attack the wealth-creation mechanisms, it seems to push me in one direction, and when they don't take spreading the wealth seriously, well, that pushes me in the other direction.'[28]

Gates had captured the very essence of the often fierce battle that has raged, for more than a century, between those backing unconstrained personal wealth creation and those wanting state intervention to create a more equal society. For the former, too much redistribution inhibits the incentives that create the wealth that brings jobs and prosperity. For the latter, excessive inequality breeds divided and unstable societies. Over time, the fortunes of the very wealthy have fluctuated according to which of these two conflicting views has attained political dominance.

The second argument used by those who welcome today's escalating fortunes is that making the rich richer is good news for all of us. They believe that rising inequality is a necessary condition for fostering an enterprise culture, that governments who set out to redistribute wealth simply run out of wealth to redistribute. 'Don't kill the goose that lays the golden egg' is the mantra. Its American advocates like to quote John F. Kennedy: 'a rising tide lifts all boats'. Tony Blair and Gordon Brown have largely accepted the new-right critique that greater equality would inhibit enterprise, that wealth creation would be inhibited by wealth redistribution. When the government is accused of 'redistribution by stealth', most of it has been from the middle rather than the top to the bottom. They have in essence accepted the trickle-down economic theories first promoted by conservative thinkers in the United States.

As Ronald Reagan was fond of arguing, the best way to help the poor is by encouraging the rich through tax cuts and other incentives. This viewpoint might be called the Reagan–Thatcher–Bush–Bush–Blair doctrine, the economic thinking that has driven successive tax cuts on the rich in recent times, especially in America, but also in Britain. In the UK, those who believe that rising inequality is not only necessary but desirable to build a more successful economy certainly remain in the political ascendancy. Blair's governments have been sufficiently in awe of the rich to turn at least a partially blind eye to tax avoidance, for example.

Those who question the growing gap don't dispute that wealth-creators are essential to economic vitality. As seen in Chapter 3, visionary individuals willing to take financial risks have helped to drive the economic progress of the last 150 years. The foundations of the IT revolution of the last decade were laid by bold entrepreneurs whose foresight and enterprise have benefited us all.

But the incentive argument can be taken too far. Were entrepreneurs, bankers and business leaders so demotivated in the post-war era when rewards were much lower? Would more balanced rewards today really lead to an end to enterprise? Would senior Goldman Sachs staff give up work if their bonuses were a little lower? Power, influence and achievement along with generous, indeed exceptionally generous, rewards have usually been sufficient motives to sustain what is undoubtedly a powerful work ethic amongst today's rich elite. As argued in earlier chapters, escalating rewards have been driven much more by greed and opportunity than the need to raise incentives.

Comparisons of the relationship between inequality and economic growth demonstrate that high levels of inequality are not necessary to produce a wealth-creating culture. The era since the Second World War can be divided into two broad periods. The decades immediately following the war brought unprecedented growth, though aided by post-war reconstruction, and wealth equalisation. Historically this period was one in which the rate of creation of new fortunes was low, but this did not appear to act as a brake on growth. During the last twenty years, in contrast, the wealth gap has risen while economic growth has been comparatively lower. Studies of the relationship between growth and inequality, making comparisons within and between countries, have failed to support the trickle-down theorists. There is certainly no evidence that a larger wealth gap brings faster economic progress.[29] The fact that there is no clear link means that the level of rewards at the top should be determined more by ethical and social considerations than economic ones. Societies can choose to have a lower wealth gap without damaging their economic performance and many, including most continental European ones, have indeed chosen to do so.[30]

The evidence on both sides of the Atlantic is that the aggressive tax and cultural stimulants to personal wealth accumulation of the last two decades have helped to enrich a few but not the many. There is no evidence of a rise in the long-term growth or productivity rate as a result of the recent surge in personal wealth making. British productivity (output per worker) remains well below the average of the Group of Seven leading industrial countries. The freeing up of markets has led to a further pulling away of the already rich rather than a general rise in prosperity. It has been a process better described as one of 'trickle-up' than trickle-down. This is true of Britain but especially so of the United States, where most of the gains from growth in recent times have gone to a tiny group of the very rich. Indeed, from 1973 to 1993, while the rich were storming ahead, the incomes of the poorest actually fell in real terms.[31] The same happened in the nineteenth-century wealth explosion, a period that benefited the very rich but nobody else.

The deserving and undeserving rich

A third argument, and one especially popular amongst the rich themselves, is that they are more worthy of their wealth than they once were. The rich see themselves as both more meritocratic and more deserving. The modern wealth revolution is seen as evidence that Britain has become a land of greater opportunity, a sign that people can rise to great heights of wealth and achievement by merit, effort and self-improvement. According to this view, higher levels of inequality are fair because opportunity has replaced privilege as the determinant of one's wealth ranking.

As shown in Chapter 6, this argument doesn't stand up. We are far from the highly socially mobile society that is often claimed and aspired to. The ranks of the mega- and super-rich may contain a slightly higher proportion of those from modest backgrounds than in the nineteenth century, but the restructuring of social opportunities has only been partial. There has been some passing of former social privilege, but it is being replaced by a newly privileged group.

The families of the wealthy elites of the past – the aristocrats and old industrial barons – continue to have a strong, if lesser, hold on the wealth leagues, while the new rich still come from a relatively small and closed circle. Even if Britain had become a meritocracy, which it clearly has not, that would not necessarily justify significantly higher rewards to those at the top, and by implication lower status and rewards at the bottom. It can be argued that legitimate success and aspiration should be tempered by some moderation at the very top. Indeed, as Michael Young warned in *The Rise of the Meritocracy,* a meritocracy carries the danger of legitimising stark inequalities.

Victorian and Edwardian social reformers distinguished between the deserving and undeserving poor in framing the foundations of anti-poverty measures, and such a distinction continues to this day. Yet such logic is just as applicable to the rich. Is it right that we in effect penalise those whom society views as the undeserving poor, but ignore or on occasions even lionise the somewhat less deserving rich? David Lloyd George was one of the first to recognise the concept of the 'undeserving rich' when he sought to justify the doubling of death duties on inherited wealth. What the new Liberal reforms in the opening decade of the twentieth century achieved in essence was a redistribution from the undeserving rich – those who were wealthy by virtue of their father's or grandfather's graft – to the deserving poor – especially pensioners.

Today, even some supporters of the growing wealth gap acknowledge the distinction. David Goodhart, the editor of *Prospect* magazine, who has argued that 'the gap no longer matters', accepts that 'public policy might still want to distinguish between the "good" rich (meritocratic) and the "bad" rich (inherited from ancestors in the slave trade)'.[32] Gordon Brown embraced the distinction when he implemented one of Labour's most popular policies – the windfall tax on the privatised utilities. Few would dispute that some of those at the top of the wealth league deserve their hard-earned places, those who, through a mix of exceptional skill, effort and risk-taking, have contributed to increasing the size of the cake by creating new wealth in ways that benefit others as well as themselves. Most opinion would regard them as 'deserving' of exceptional rewards.

Who could begrudge J. K. Rowling – who toiled away in an Edinburgh café to write her first Harry Potter novel and has given generously to child charities – her runaway success? Entrepreneurs who create new businesses, such as James Dyson and Stelios Haji-Ioannou, would top most popular lists of the deserving rich. They have created wealth and jobs through the invention of a popular new product or service. Sir Tom Hunter and Sir Alan Sugar both left school at sixteen and were small traders before creating successful businesses from scratch. John Caudwell is utterly self-made with a determination to succeed that stems from his modest roots. Entrepreneurship is recognised as the most difficult route to wealth. The single-minded, determined and innovative qualities that are required to build big fortunes are often the same qualities that provide work, bring national prestige and advance economic progress. Without some of the great business creators from Richard Arkwright to Henry Ford, we would undoubtedly be poorer, culturally as well as economically. Many of the pioneering business leaders of the last century and a half have not merely made themselves wealthy but also contributed to improved material living standards for all by reducing costs and expanding markets. This is as true of the car manufacturers and mass retailers of the twentieth century as it is of the ironmasters and cotton manufacturers of the nineteenth.

Not everyone in today's rich lists would be voted into the deserving camp, however. Those who simply live off or fritter away an inheritance, who become super-rich by what Lord Giddens has called 'brute-luck' or who rig the system to enrich themselves by unfairly grabbing a larger slice of the cake at the expense of someone else would be seen as 'undeserving'.[33]

Entrepreneurs themselves are far from a homogeneous group. Those who have founded companies, brands and products, built firms from scratch or added value by improving efficiency or introducing new processes win and deserve higher public esteem than financial raiders who take fewer risks and are much less productive. Even founding entrepreneurs can prove controversial figures. Sir Richard Branson's decision to register most of his business activities offshore and to exploit tax loopholes to the limit has raised question marks about his business methods. Many of those in the rich lists, from Mohamed al-Fayed to Hans Rausing, have greatly enhanced their personal fortunes through the clever use of tax avoidance.

Not all entrepreneurs have made their money cleanly. Many rich business-men have openly or covertly abused their power. John D. Rockefeller and other nineteenth-century moguls may have cut oil prices and improved steel quality, but many were certainly unpopular, often depicted by cartoonists as 'top-hatted, pig-snouted . . . manipulators of politicians and the public'.[34] The directors of Enron, WorldCom and Parmalat have all been exposed for dishonest business dealings. Lord Black treated Hollinger International more like a private fiefdom than a public company, using it to finance a lavish international lifestyle until the company directors pulled the plug.

The wealthy Russian oligarchs such as Roman Abramovich are modern examples of the robber barons of the past. They are in the world's rich lists not because of traditional entrepreneurship and enterprise but because of the way they took advantage of the rush to privatisation of Russia's 'crown jewels' initiated by President Boris Yeltsin. Yeltsin's declared intention was that the benefits of privatisation would be shared through the issuing of vouchers to all fifty-seven million Russian workers and managers, which they could exchange for shares. Instead, the wealth created by earlier generations was inherited by a small, favoured and influential group of insiders, a group that, for the most part, does not appear even to accept that there are obligations associated with such a gain. Most of the wealth plundered in this way, wealth that might have been used to create new Russian businesses and jobs, has ended up financing the international tycoon lifestyles of the country's thirty-odd billionaires. Much of it has ended up in London.

Those who have acquired fortunes that are unrelated to risk, effort or talent would mostly rank lowly in the deserving stakes. The offspring of the rich, from James Murdoch and Mark Slater to Lucas White and the Duke of Westminster, would not justify the same level of recognition as, say, founding entrepreneurs from more humble origins. On the other hand, at least some of these have attempted to build on their good fortune. Others have chosen to simply fritter it away, failing to build on inherited wealth and businesses.

Much of the escalating personal wealth of the last two decades has largely landed in the lap of the lucky recipients. Many have had to do little or nothing, just sit tight and watch their fortunes grow, the beneficiaries of rising property and land values, soaring share prices and benign tax changes. As Michael Lewis describes it, 'making an honest living does not seem like a particularly sensible thing to do anymore when you can simply hold onto stock that simply rises to the stratosphere'.[35] In the early 1990s, fifty-five executives with 'golden handcuffs' at London Weekend Television each made millions, first when they re-won the ITV franchise and then, two years later, when they failed to prevent a hostile takeover by Granada. Most of them were simply in the right place at the right time. They had taken a small risk by buying into the company, but, apart perhaps from a handful of executives at the top, few of them could be said to have earned their newly acquired fortunes. Those at the top who devised the strategy, including Greg Dyke and Christopher Bland, had become wealthy as a result of a mix of ruthless business practice – the downsizing of the company – and a big gamble. Those who bought homes in property hot spots such as Chelsea and Kensington in the 1980s and early 1990s will have enjoyed massive windfall gains. Shareholders and executives in multinational oil companies such as BP and Shell can enjoy huge financial bonanzas as a result of the soaring profits from hikes in oil prices that sometimes follow external events.

Then there are most of the former senior executives of the privatised utilities, who took few risks and displayed minimal skill and little innovation for their remarkable entry into the multi-millionaire class. The privatisation of British Rail proved a particular bonanza for a handful of the industry's managers, and none made more money than the rolling stock company executives. Sandy Anderson, who led the management buy-out team for the purchase of Porterbrook, one of the rolling stock companies, pocketed a personal fortune of almost £40 million for an outlay of £120,000 when the company was sold on only six months later to Stagecoach. Others ended up with sums of between £15 million and £16 million.[36]

Corporate bosses whose salaries seem increasingly beyond control and who can earn lavish rewards and bonuses irrespective of performance have also proved especially unpopular, not least amongst company share-holders. In a 2003 poll of listeners to Radio 4's *Today* programme, company managers were only the sixty-fifth most respected profession, out of a total of ninety-two. Such a low score may in part be down to the traditional anti-business ethos of Britons, but it is also a reflection of the inflated salaries that corporate leaders like to award themselves. Indeed, a more scientific poll found that 65 per cent thought company directors could not be trusted to tell the truth and 75 per cent thought they were paid too much.[37]

The last decade has been one long bonanza for top businessmen, with even failed executives walking off with huge pay-offs known as 'golden parachutes'. The management expert Charles Handy has noted that such payouts have made ineptitude by senior executives the shortest route to millionaire status. They have been dubbed 'golden condoms' because they 'protect the executive and screw the shareholder'.[38] The going rate for the job for top executives seems to bear little relationship to merit, leading the business magazine *Management Today* to condemn the growing gulf in pay between the top and the bottom as defying 'any sense of fairness and undermin[ing] social cohesion'.[39] Other countries, for example Sweden, France and especially Japan, operate successfully with much lower corporate rewards.[40]

City salaries more often reflect greed than contribution. Despite creating little or nothing, many top City executives are on payouts that used to be confined to a handful of the most successful entrepreneurs. Philip Augar, a former top executive at Schroders, has said, 'The money paid to brokers is a social and moral disgrace.' He went on:

With the most basic skills, a broker can earn four times as much as a teacher, twice as much as a GP, and about the same as the finance director of a medium-sized quoted plc. Even if the broker lacks flair but is pushy and determined enough, he or she can earn the same as a leading heart surgeon and more than some chief executives of FTSE-100 companies. All this seems outrageous given that the talent required to earn such sums is not particularly rare and the industry is not very profitable in the City.[41]

Highly paid entertainers and athletes mostly command widespread popular support. Paul Gascoigne used to be greeted onto the pitch with the chant 'he's fat, he's round, he's worth a million pounds'. It is no coincidence that Tony Blair singled out David Beckham as an example of someone worth his salary. Great athletes and sportsmen are usually viewed as part of the 'deserving rich' because success is often linked to exceptional talent and tenacity, and the fact that that they are more likely to break the class barrier, most coming from more modest backgrounds than other members of rich lists.

Few dispute that Beckham is indeed a highly gifted, inspirational and remarkably committed footballer. Whether the scale of reward he and other celebrities enjoy is justified is much more controversial. There are others in sport who have an equal mix of talent, commitment and hard work who earn much less. If Beckham had been born even twenty years earlier, he would not be mega-rich. Equally talented and committed footballers such as Billy Wright, Bobby Charlton and Bobby Moore enjoyed modest rewards and lifestyles. Until 1969 professional footballers were paid a maximum wage of £20 a week in winter and £17 a week in summer. Today top players can virtually name their price. Roger Bannister earned nothing for the first four-minute mile. In 1961, his best year, Stirling Moss competed in fifty-five races, winning £32,700.[42] The dramatic escalation in sports wages might have been justified by a similar dramatic rise in the quality of performance but this has not happened.

Today's top athletes are the beneficiaries not only of rare skills but of the emergence of a global market for sport, a growing competition for television rights and the birth of world product marketing. Beckham is very rich because he was born in an era of intense international competition for talent and because he has been signed up by a host of sponsors. Through his £40 million deal to become the face of Gillette, he became the highest-paid advertising star in Britain. Half the proceeds went to his club, Real Madrid, who bought him only partly because of his football prowess. The club estimated correctly that he could bring them a big rise in revenue from joint sponsorship. Although he has rare skills, which he exploits to the full, it is the commercialisation of sport that has thrust him into today's rich lists.

The soaring wealth of today's top celebrities is down to what has been described as 'winner-take-all markets', in which those who are the best in their field, from sport and films to rock music and fashion, can command a dramatic earnings premium.[43] Top players may have the equivalent of monopoly skills, but, while we regulate monopoly power amongst companies, we have been reluctant to do so amongst individuals. This has led to spiralling fees for those deemed the best and poorer rates for those just below the top. A marginal superiority in talent can mean a massive upping in earning power. Top film stars such as Tom Cruise, Cameron Diaz and Arnold Schwarzenegger can command up to $30 million for one film. Steven Spielberg earned £120 million in 2002. In 2004, Nicole Kidman was paid $2 million for four days' work on an advertisement for Chanel No 5 as part of a $5 million contract to be the face of Chanel. Sven-Goran Eriksson's basic salary of more than £3 million a year is way above the pay of the coaches of the more successful French and Italian national teams.[44] If Eriksson, and some of his team, were paid on results, the international salary bill would shrink.

Public support for the kinds of reward on offer certainly has its limits, and many question the increasingly skewed nature of relative rewards, and their supposed link to skill and responsibility. Is a pop singer with an indifferent voice or a chat show host with questionable talent really worth so much more than surgeons or headteachers with much greater responsibilities? Should accountants who dream up clever ways of avoiding tax be paid the equivalent of scores of nurses? Should a speculating hedge fund operator, who does little more than sit in front of a trading screen, end up wealthier than a risk-taking and wealth-creating entrepreneur? Why do fund managers as a group continue to be so highly paid even though the great majority of them fail to beat the market?

A zero sum game?

A final argument used to defend the wealth gap is that personal wealth accumulation is said not to hurt anybody else. One strong critic of egalitarianism has argued,

There is not a shred of evidence that wealth in itself harms those without it . . . Nor does it harm me that Sir Elton John and the Duke of Westminster are hugely better off than me, even if the work of one is embarrassingly vulgar, and the wealth of the other due to birth. To resent their good fortune would be to succumb to the nasty, small-minded vice of envy.[45]

This is the essence of the argument used by Tony Blair to defend inequality in his interview on BBC's *Newsnight* in the run up to the 2001 general election. It is common nowadays to argue that wealth is not the zero sum game that it was in, say, the nineteenth century, when land-owning and big industrial fortunes were created through exploitation of farm labourers and industrial workers.

This may be true of some wealth but not all. While some personal fortunes are the result of real wealth creation that harms nobody, others are largely the product of carefully manipulated transfers from one group in society to another. Sometimes such transfers are the legitimate reward for competitive business behaviour resulting from outstripping the opposition. Tesco has overtaken Sainsbury's as Britain's top supermarket chain, transferring wealth between the two companies and their respective shareholders as a result, through superior business methods. But this is not always the case.

When Dennis Kozlowski used millions of dollars of company money to finance his lavish personal lifestyle before he was convicted of fraud, a lot of British as well as American pension fund holders were effectively subsidising it. Such transfers do not only stem from fraudulent business behaviour. They are often the product of the flexing of muscles by powerful groups who simply take full advantage of their bargaining strength. Higher profits to the stores and lower prices to the consumer will often come at a price to others. We rarely stop to think how it is that discount retailers like Wal-Mart and Primark are able to offer such cut-price clothes. The big supermarkets have become increasingly powerful agents who can make or break smaller suppliers around the world. The truth is that, in recent years, the increasingly monopolistic buying power of the retail giants has forced scores of small farmers in developing and developed countries out of business because of the increasingly brutal deals demanded by the chains.

Philip Green is a brilliant businessman whose personal wealth is to a large extent the product of his cost-cutting skills. Green's ability to improve efficiency was recognised in the 2005 'wealth creation league tables' published by the Department of Trade and Industry. Nevertheless, although

Arcadia emerged at the top of the table, not all of this gain could be described as pure 'value added' – that is, free of external costs on others. Some of it has been the product of the much tougher deals he has secured from suppliers and the way in which he, along with other high street retailers, has switched from more expensive British and western European suppliers to cheaper factories in eastern Europe, China and elsewhere. Some of his 'gain' will thus have been bought at the expense of 'losses' incurred by suppliers who have either forfeited business or ended up with a lower payment.

A similar logic applies to Green's record dividend payment of £1.2 billion from Arcadia in October 2005, a dividend that was paid for by taking out a loan for that amount. In essence the company mortgaged itself to the banks. There is nothing untoward about such a strategy, which is a common form of financial engineering used in private equity companies. Nevertheless, as Anthony Hilton of the *Evening Standard* pointed out, the wealth in this case is not 'created, it is diverted. For there to be a winner, there has to be a loser and in this case the loser is the taxman, and therefore all taxpayers.'[46] This is because the additional interest charges on the loan will reduce profits and lower Arcadia's corporation tax. In effect, the taxpayer is subsidising a sizeable chunk of Green's, or rather his wife's, dividend.

There are numerous other examples. Bill Gates may be one of the most popular men in America in recognition of his undoubted business genius. Nevertheless, his wealth is in large part the result of his aggressive tactics in creating a monopoly through the ruthless destruction of rival software, from the WordPerfect word-processing system to the Netscape Navigator internet browser. At least part of his fortune is the product of his ability to charge premium prices by creating a near-monopoly product. His star rating certainly took a heavy knock during the succession of monopoly hearings from 1999, and his popularity may now be linked as much to his philanthropy as to his business skills. In 2004, Microsoft was fined a record £333 million by the European Union for illegal use of its near monopoly, this time to try and crush competitors in media players and server software.

Property developers create wealth when they make improvements or build new housing or offices, but not when the value of their assets rises because of property inflation resulting from excess demand or new public investment. The rise in property prices in the areas serviced by the development of the new Jubilee line in London gave a huge windfall gain to local landowners at the expense of new buyers, tenants and taxpayers. The announcement of the London Olympic Games, to be held in 2012, will create huge fortunes for some of the richest men in the UK, with the biggest windfall going to the Reuben brothers, who have been developing land on the edge of the site. A good deal of the cost of the games – paid for heavily by national and local taxpayers – will end up in the pockets of the already rich. The rising wealth of the old landowners in recent times has come mainly from soaring land prices and rents, and thus paid for by small tenant farmers and leaseholders.

The dramatic rise in the salaries of premiership footballers has been bleeding clubs dry and has been paid at least in part by the inflation in ticket prices of recent times. It is not just the players themselves who make a killing out of modern football. So do their agents. In 2004, Manchester United paid out £5.5 million to players' agents, equivalent to more than 20 per cent of its pre-tax profits. The payments included £1.13 million to the agents of Cristiano Ronaldo for his £10.6 million transfer from Sporting Lisbon and £1.2 million to Ruud van Nistelrooy's agent for a renegotiation of his contract. The scale of the payments heightened concerns that football was being drained of cash. In 2005, the president of FIFA, Sepp Blatter, launched a stinging attack on the game he governs. He described some footballers' salaries as 'pornographic' and claimed that greed was ruling the game. He accused modern football of indulging the appetites of the rich at the expense of nourishing the game's roots. It is no wonder that premiership football has become an increasingly middle-class spectator sport.

The soaring fees demanded by BBC celebrity television presenters are paid for by a mix of a higher licence fee and smaller budgets on other programmes. Tax avoidance – costing Britain at least £25 billion in lost revenue – is paid for by taxpayers who pay up. The financial industry is mostly engaged in non-productive activity, activities that involve the transfer of existing wealth rather than its creation. Investment bankers are able to earn such large rewards because the market in which they operate has been effectively rigged in their favour against the interest of shareholders. No other industry would be allowed to operate the commission structures and the hidden cartels that characterise the profession. Such is their power. The proceeds of most of the personal finance scandals of the 1980s and 1990s involving the deliberate selling of inappropriate products from endowment mortgages to precipice bonds lined the pockets of the companies and advisers promoting the schemes at the expense of those unwittingly buying them.

The business methods used by some executives to enrich themselves has often been at the expense of employees. This is true of large-scale redundancy programmes designed to increase shareholder value. Another classic example is the decision taken by many boardrooms in the 1990s to take advantage of the rising stock market to take pension contribution holidays. By stopping paying into their employee pension schemes they boosted short-term profits and pushed up the share price, thus increasing the value of their share option packages. This, in turn, contributed to the subsequent serious crisis in many final-salary schemes. It is impossible to prove in most cases, but few doubt that City insiders have taken advantage of their unique access to deal in shares in advance of forthcoming takeover bid announcements.

When Wall Street analysts were cynically promoting shares they knew to be dud in the 1990s, they were in effect picking their investors' pockets. In the last two decades, corporate decisions justified by maximising shareholder value were often dreamed up to make fast bucks for the company executives and their Wall Street and City advisers rather than ensure the long-term health of the company. Roy Disney, Walt's nephew, seemed to sum it up. When he was forced from the board of the Walt Disney Company following a simmering row with chief executive Michael Eisner, Disney's resignation letter accused Eisner of turning the company into an operation that is 'rapacious, soulless and always looking for a quick buck'. Shareholders and staff have often paid for the hike in wealth of corporate executives. Little of the financial engineering and restructuring activity of the 1980s and 1990s created new products or new jobs. The rise in leveraged buy-outs and takeovers during the 1980s ended for many companies in bankruptcy. During the 1980s, *Fortune* 500 companies eliminated 3.2 million jobs in the name of shareholder value in order to pay for the $1 trillion of debt incurred for takeover, merger and restructuring activity.[47] One detailed analysis has described the diversion of wealth from shareholders to executives through unmerited compensation schemes throughout the 1990s 'an atrocity'.[48]

The pursuit of personal fortunes in the 1990s has also resulted in some very wasteful investment decisions that have had to be paid for by others. A classic example is the desperate American telecom race to achieve early dominance and the monopoly power that was assumed to come with it. In the late 1990s, telecom companies laid tens of millions of miles of cable across the United States and under the ocean, paid for by America's leading financial institutions and biggest banking conglomerates. The result was and still is a 'mountainous glut', with a utilisation rate of less than 3 per cent. This did not stop some of those involved enriching themselves before the consequences were clear and some of the companies, including Global Crossing, Qwest and WorldCom, got into serious financial difficulties after the crash of 2000. As one writer has described the enrichment, 'it should not be thought that the entrepreneurs behind the great telecoms bust were so clumsy as to get caught up in the financial carnage they left in their wake. Between 1997 and 2001, insiders cashed in some $18 billion in shares.'[49] Those who paid the price included the 500,000 workers who were laid off, small investors who failed to see the carnage coming and the smaller supply companies who saw their profits plunge.

One of the dangers of today's modern, wealth-driven culture is its increasingly unquestioning reverence for the rich. The rich and their backers like to argue that their rising share of the cake in recent times reflects their growing importance to society, that they have been contributing that much more than those who have ended up with a shrinking share. But is this really the case? Are their rewards really proportionate to their contributions? Has their contribution to wider economic and social well-being really been outstripping the rest of society's to that degree?

Of course there are many individual examples of outstanding entrepreneurship and business endeavour that few would be mean enough not to recognise. But most of the wealth explosion of recent times is down to skilful financial manipulation and/or brute luck. The list of the undeserving probably stands higher, possibly much higher, than that of the deserving. Moreover, however much we might argue about which boxes the rich should be placed in, the signs are that the wealth revolution of the past two decades is far from a temporary phenomenon. If anything, the steady rise in the extreme income and wealth divide may not yet have reached its peak.

The next and final chapter will look at the future prospects for the rich and at what measures could be taken to ensure a fairer cutting of the cake.

11

A permanent revolution

> We can have a democratic society or we can have great concentrated wealth
> in the hands of the few. We cannot have both.
> (Louis Brandeis, Supreme Court Justice)[1]

In 2001, six bond traders from Barclays Capital met for a meal at Gordon
Ramsay's Michelin-starred restaurant Pétrus in London's Mayfair, a venue
renowned for its fine wines and top menus but also its prices. Indeed, the
table managed to run up a bill of £44,007, most of it going on vintage wine.
It was not merely a record for the most expensive meal, it proved an
expensive outing for the traders, one that cost five of them their jobs as the
bank expressed its displeasure at such a public show of ostentation in the
middle of a deep financial recession. For a while after what became the
notorious Barclays meal, such open displays of extravagance had to take a
back seat. But not for long. In April 2004, the Swiss financier Dieter
Behring, who had made a fortune running hedge funds, treated another six
bankers to dinner at Pétrus, at a cost of £42,000 including a four-figure tip.
This time there was no such fuss.

Many of the world's super-rich may have woken with a severe headache in
the aftermath of the world stock market crash that began in the spring of
2000, but they did not have to nurse their hangovers for as long as those who
had lost out in earlier crashes. This time the rich bounced back quickly. All
the signs are that, with economic conditions and the political culture
working in their favour, the wealthy super-class is not just back, but is set to
continue to prosper.

Not only has the somewhat short-lived belt-tightening of the immediate
post-millennial years gone, wealth levels have been rocketing. This has been

driven by a continuing upward trend in executive compensation, record dividend payments in private companies, a continuing property boom and the return of generous City bonuses after the slump that followed the millennial crash. By 2005, six- and seven-figure sums were becoming commonplace once again, especially amongst City bankers. Although secrecy continues to surround the issue, bonus payments in 2005 were estimated to be twice those of 2004. At Goldman Sachs, a handful of top executives were set to receive bonuses for the year of between £5 million and £10 million. Similar sums were being talked about at Morgan Stanley, Merrill Lynch and J. P. Morgan. Hedge fund managers were said to be in line for even bigger rewards.[2]

Big spending is also back. In 2004, Peter Toner, who runs ToffsWorld.com, a website catering for the seriously wealthy, was able to declare, 'There's so much money swimming around Europe at the moment . . . We are talking absolutely bucket loads.'[3] In the same year, Porsche salesmen and upmarket estate agents started to lick their lips again. The rich are firmly back on the upward path they enjoyed throughout the feast years of the 1990s. City wealth consultants are predicting a continuing rise in the number of very rich Britons. The parties thrown for and by the super-rich have got bigger and better.

The political consensus persists that the growing wealth gap does not matter. The limit of the moderate left's ambition today is to improve the lot of the poorest. New Labour has embarked on an ambitious programme to tackle poverty. Despite some success in this, in 2004, Britain still had a level of relative poverty that was higher than in the late 1970s and higher than in most developed countries – only Ireland, Greece, Italy and the United States had higher rates.[4] What progress has been achieved is the result of redistribution from middle rather than rich Britain. While those on lower incomes have got richer, so have the rich themselves and at a faster rate than the poor. Hence the rising wealth and income gap between the very top and the bottom.

All this is good news for the rich, of course. But is there a limit to the rate at which the very rich can continue to enrich themselves in modern societies? And if there is no built-in limit, should one be imposed?

Some experts have argued that there is a natural economic limit to the degree of inequality that is sustainable and that levels above this will self-correct. Certainly, highly unequal societies have had a habit of imploding. The American economist Raveendra Batra has warned that 'extreme inequality has generated some of the worst economic disasters in history'. In his book *The Great Depression of 1990*, published in 1987, he argued that, above a certain level, inequality causes economic instability.[5]

His thesis is that there is a link between the economic and wealth cycles, in which extremes of wealth concentration can trigger deep recessions. This, he argues, is because such concentration encourages speculative excess and risky investments by the rich while simultaneously raising the demand for loans by the large non-wealthy portion of the population who do not have the assets to sustain them. He showed how recessions – such as those of the late nineteenth century and after 1929 – coincided with rising concentrations of wealth that peaked in the late nineteenth century and then in the 1920s.

Of course, economic factors are only one possible source of a limit to inequality. Democracy is another. Some of the key turning points in the history of the fortunes of the rich – the introduction of the redistributive tax and welfare policies at the beginning of the twentieth century, the egalitarian thrust of the post-war era – have been triggered at least in part by a hostile public mood. It is possible that there is still a socially driven self-correcting mechanism, one triggered by what some have called the 'outrage constraint'.[6]

There is certainly no shortage of outrage about some of the rich, especially about the increasingly lavish rewards even failed corporate bosses are able to claim, and not merely from angry shareholders. The self-made billionaire mobile phone entrepreneur John Caudwell is scathing about fat-cat rewards for failed executives: 'It's a disgrace . . . It sends a bad signal to people earning modest salaries when they see lousy bosses pick up big pay-offs just to go away. It really galls me.'[7] Another billionaire, Philip Green, seems to share his distaste. In his usual direct way, he once dismissed such executives as 'tossers'.[8] Ferdinand Mount, former head of 10 Downing Street's Policy Unit, has called such payments 'obscene'.[9]

Aware of the risk of hostility, corporate compensation packages have been designed specifically to camouflage the true level of compensation, to 'let CEOs reward themselves lavishly while minimizing the associated outrage'.[10] In the event, such 'camouflage' has been exposed on both sides of the Atlantic. Yet the outburst of public and professional indignation at such blatant and indefensible attempts at personal enrichment have failed to bring moderation to company boardrooms. The public's patience may have been severely tested by the revelations of corporate excess and widespread self-serving but, unlike in earlier periods, that has not yet been translated into a change in direction.

Today the public have a mixed attitude towards the rich, ranging from support for self-made entrepreneurs and celebrities and athletes with exceptional talent to outright hostility to business executives who seem to be primarily serving their own interests. Surveys have shown that citizens are prepared to accept substantial inequality where it is based on talent, effort or even luck, but they also believe that differentials should be limited. One survey has shown that eight out of ten people think that company chairmen are overpaid. It is a view that seems to be shared by company shareholders, who expressed their opposition to rising executive pay by turning up in unprecedented numbers throughout 2003 and 2004 to vote against the remuneration packages being offered to top executives.

In a survey in 2002, 82 per cent said they thought the income gap between the top and bottom was too large; just over 60 per cent thought that ordinary people were not getting a 'fair share of the nation's wealth'. These figures had changed little over the previous twenty years.[11] Most people think that we have gone beyond what is an acceptable limit. Indeed, surveys have put the acceptable gap between the poorest and the richest at around twenty-five to one. More than 100 years ago, the business financier and guru J. P. Morgan – then one of a handful of the most powerful men in America – argued that executives should earn no more than twenty times the pay of the lowest paid company workers. Yet today, individual company ratios are commonly way beyond this level – sometimes several hundred or in some cases a thousand.

Hierarchies are necessary and desirable. Elites have existed and always will exist. The rich are here to stay. Some degree of inequality is needed to maintain incentives and to allow a properly opportunistic culture. But all societies ultimately only function effectively if the distribution of rewards is seen to be fair, if they are believed to be in line with people's individual contributions to society. The rich who build personal wealth that contributes to economic or social progress deserve to be well rewarded. Indeed, entrepreneurs who continue to own the companies they create from scratch or turn around are only worth what society judges those companies to be worth. Those who create little, give little back and who are rich by virtue of their ability to rig the system to suit their own interests need to be reined back. Societies would also judge wealth more generously if it has been acquired through merit rather than privilege, and where everybody of ability has a chance to make it to the top.

Even committed egalitarians would accept that equality is not a practical or a desirable goal. What is needed is a system of rewards that is fair and commands popular consent. The present distribution of rewards – in which the top 1 per cent enjoy 23 per cent of all wealth (and over 60 per cent of liquid assets) while the poorest half manage only 6 per cent – is neither. The popular political view that a rising wealth and income gap does not matter is simply wrong. Tackling poverty is not enough. The rising inequality of recent times is not necessary to bring extra prosperity. It has also clashed sharply with the widely accepted goal of improving social mobility. Indeed, while the modern consensus may have switched its emphasis from the goal of equality of outcomes to one of equality of opportunities, the hard truth is that we are receding from both objectives.

It is popular today to argue that governments have no power in increasingly market-driven and global economies to prevent rising inequalities, that they can do little to stall the upward march of the rich, even if they wanted to. But this is simply not the case. It was fashionable too not so long ago to argue that governments could do nothing about unemployment. To build the foundations of the welfare state, the reforming Liberal government of 1906 had to overcome similar scepticism about the value of government action and the idea that you could do nothing about the super-rich. There is nothing inevitable about rising inequality. With the exception of the United States, no other developed economy has experienced such a scale of escalating fortunes at the top.

The key explanation for the rising Anglo-Saxon gap is the move from a post-war culture that held back runaway greed to the new ethos of 'anything goes' that evolved from the 1980s. The rising concentration of wealth at the top has been driven by government policy, from tax cuts to deregulation. There is no reason why that predominant ethos should not be challenged and reversed. Whether it happens is ultimately a matter of political choice.

In Britain, there have been calls for policies that would cap the progress of the rich, especially those deemed undeserving. Some favour a higher tax rate of 50 per cent on those earning over £100,000, pointing out that Margaret Thatcher retained a top rate of 60 per cent for six years before she cut it to 40 per cent. Some have argued that the proceeds could be used to pay for policies that would improve the life chances of children born into poor families and whose chance of social improvement has been falling.[12] Such a targeted use for the tax might make it much more politically palatable.

Some want the introduction of greater restraint by employers through the use of voluntary pay ratios. These would limit the gap between top and bottom pay levels as advocated by Morgan. Even in the more pro-rich United States, there has always been some concern about excessive ratios. In 1942, Franklin D. Roosevelt proposed a 100 per cent tax rate on all individual income over $25,000 – about $300,000 in today's terms.[13] In 1943, America's very richest paid 78 per cent of their total incomes in federal taxes, even after exploiting every tax loophole they could find. J. K. Galbraith has long argued for a limit between the maximum and minimum wage within the firm. 'The most forthright and effective way of enhancing equality within the firm would be to specify the maximum range between average and maximum compensation.'[14]

In 2003, William McDonough, president of the New York Federal Reserve, and earning a 'modest' $297,500, asked whether there should not 'be both economic and moral limitations on the gaps created by the market-driven reward system'. He went on to argue that today's vast increases in executive compensation were 'terribly bad social policy and perhaps even bad morals'.[15] At the beginning of 2004, one American fund manager, Catholic Funds, proposed limiting pay at seven companies they held investments in to 100 times the pay of the average worker, unless shareholders explicitly approved more because of the attainment of some clear performance goal that was attributable to the chief executive.[16] In 2005, Congressman Martin Sabo from Minnesota had a bill in Congress, the Income Equity Act, that would prevent any corporate tax deductions on executive pay that totalled more than twenty-five times the pay of a company's lowest-paid worker. Others have argued that government contracts could be made conditional on companies behaving more responsibly when it comes to executive pay as a way of limiting the gap in the same way that they have to conform with racial and gender equality policies.

Some Japanese and European firms voluntarily impose ratios limiting the pay gap.[17] Income differentials within large Japanese corporations are much lower than in their Anglo-Saxon equivalents, mainly because group cohesion is more highly valued than individual reward. The Royal Navy has a de facto differential of eight. One proposal is to pool a 'total remuneration package for senior executives, with limits on any one individual's pay. This is the model used effectively by US basketball teams. In one Brazilian company, managers propose their own salary and colleagues either endorse or reject it.'[18]

Others have called for the imposition of a maximum wage akin to the minimum wage. A variation on this is for 'no limit on nominal earnings but

100 per cent cut-off beyond a certain point, say £1 million, with the funds going into a personal trust or company foundation for charitable purposes'.[19] This would be a kind of enforced philanthropy. Advocates of a maximum wage have pointed out that it would be a logical development from the introduction of the national minimum wage, which is already a constraint on employers and market forces. It would be a way of introducing a moral boundary on the market. If the poor are expected to make sacrifices in order to claim the rewards of the new opportunity-based economic policy, it is argued, why shouldn't some equivalent responsibility be placed on the rich?

Such proposals have mostly fallen on deaf government and corporate ears. Some of them may well be policies that would be impractical in a market-driven economy. But there is no shortage of effective and acceptable ways of ensuring greater fairness in the way rewards are distributed. There are also some signs that the tide of influential opinion may be moving. In his call for a 'new egalitarianism', Lord Giddens has argued that, in relation to the rich, 'we can and should take action if their earnings, and how they are achieved, set them apart from the rest of society. We should tackle social exclusion at the top as well as at the bottom.'[20]

There are a number of steps that could be taken to build a fairer structure of rewards, one with built-in limits that would correct some of the more unacceptable trends of recent times, that would help to create a much more level playing field than the one we have at the moment. First, measures are needed to reverse the recent move towards a more regressive tax system under which the poor pay more tax proportionately than the rich. One study has suggested that as much as 40 per cent of the rise in inequality of the past twenty years may be explained by tax changes that have benefited the richest groups.[21] Partly because of Labour's nervousness about the politics of taxation, about not wanting to be seen as the party of tax and spend, the government has set its back against a higher tax rate on higher earners, but there are other ways of making the tax system more progressive. National insurance contributions could be made fairer by withdrawing the £32,000 ceiling. Council taxation – which is highly regressive – could be reformed rather than ducked as the government did when they dropped the proposed review of property values. Capital taxes including inheritance taxes could also be made more effective. Giddens and Patrick Diamond have called for higher taxes on the transfer of wealth from parents to children, including lifetime gifts as well as inheritances.[22] Although taxes on inheritance and wealth transfer, which essentially tax luck and windfall gains, are amongst the fairest of taxes, the idea was not exactly greeted with open arms by the Treasury.

Second, a much tougher attack on tax evasion and avoidance is also needed. Tax avoidance, a form of 'legalised theft', is costing society – and other taxpayers – upwards of £25 billion a year. Although the Treasury and HM Revenue and Customs have started to talk tougher language, too many of the measures introduced have proved toothless. Recovery of some of this sum could fund lower tax rates on the broad span of taxpayers. The rich have been proving time and again that, despite the declining tax rates they have enjoyed in recent times, they are poor citizens by their apparently increasing refusal to meet their social obligations on tax as the bulk of the population do. They are almost encouraged to do so by government tax policy that seems to treat the rich as a special case, as the only group that should be allowed to opt out of their obligations if they choose. The public are only too aware of the rich's special status on tax, a key factor in the growing antipathy to some taxes such as inheritance tax. Perhaps the principle, adopted by some local councils, of naming and shaming citizens guilty of serious anti-social behaviour or of environmental crime such as fly tipping, could be adopted by national governments against persistent tax avoiders. It was not so long ago that leading politicians were open about denouncing over-greedy and unscrupulous businessmen, declaring, in Edward Heath's phrase, that capitalism had its 'unacceptable face'. Maybe it is now time for our political leaders to give similar leadership and call the bluff of the undeserving super-rich. Reining in the increasing use of tax havens, for example, is not a utopian goal, though it may require international action. Chapter 9 showed that in the fight against terrorism, President Bush has been happy to use US political muscle to force some offshore havens into providing information on bank accounts of suspected terrorists.

Third, despite the voluntary measures introduced by industry in recent years to prevent the abuse of executive power, the system of corporate remuneration remains largely out of control. Self-regulation has failed to work, institutional shareholders have proved toothless. Industry bosses have continued to award themselves rises in remuneration that are not justified by business performance. The boardroom culture seems to be one of 'grab as much as you can while you can'. Greater, if necessarily statutory, measures are needed to ensure that non-executive directors act in a less spineless way and to empower shareholders to help them check the scandal of boardroom excess. That this is possible is shown by the resolve of one City investment firm, F&C Asset Management, which has led a campaign against unreasonable payoffs. They have hired a law firm to devise a directors' contract that would allow companies to claw back salary and bonus payments after poorly performing executives have left troubled companies. There is no reason why such an arrangement should not become a widespread requirement.

Fourth, measures are needed to tackle the issue of land and planning. Up and down the country, big urban public transport and rural housing developments, and more recently the successful Olympics bid, are bringing huge and totally untaxed windfall gains to a tiny group of Britain's mainly aristocratic and in some cases entrepreneurial landowners. One estimate suggests that planning permission to build on a greenfield site can boost the value of a hectare (2.5 acres) of land more than a hundredfold. A land value tax – such as the 'planning gain supplement' being considered by the government – would be one way of ensuring that at least some of the gains generated by social decisions were shared more widely for public benefit and not preserved for a group benefiting not by merit but by a quirk of birth.[23] The restructuring of planning laws would also do a lot to spread the benefits of planning gain more widely.

Fifth, Britain's political and business leaders seem to have accepted the superiority of the American business model with its aggressive pursuit of shareholder value as its primary goal. The adoption of that model, one driven by short-term gains, has been fuelling the personal wealth revolution without any obvious benefits to society as a whole. Yet there are no overwhelming reasons to believe that the prioritisation of the short-term profit rate is best for industry or society. Of course, shareholders need to be protected but, as the Work Foundation has shown, there are other attributes of success including creativity and innovation, an understanding of what customers want, an awareness of other stakeholders including the wider community and treating workers well. A study of 1,000 companies by the foundation found that those in the top half on these criteria were 42 per cent more productive than the bottom half.[24] A shift in business culture that brought a new emphasis on these wider and longer-term goals might limit profitability in the short term but is much more likely to win long-term success.

Sixth, a much tougher set of policies is needed to tackle the continuing barriers to social mobility. As shown in Chapter 6, far from moving towards a more opportunistic society, social mobility from the bottom to the top has if anything receded in recent times. Britain only really pays lip service to the creation of a genuinely aspirational culture, one that enables those with the right blend of effort and skill to rise to the top whatever their background. Despite decades of rhetoric, our current system of education and recruitment is still rigged heavily in favour of those from privileged backgrounds. It is the rich who, unsurprisingly, ensure that their own children are first in the queue to the best schools, universities and jobs.

Our educational system has failed to tackle the barriers that have long beset bright children from poor backgrounds. Britain's most elite universities have failed to increase the share of students coming from state schools and low-income families.[25] Indeed, despite government pressure, Britain's top universities took in a lower proportion of students from state schools in 2005 than they did the year before. One recent study has concluded that 'the expansion of higher education . . . appears to have disproportionately benefited children from richer families rather than the most able'.[26] Since the mid-1980s, the proportion of children from the richest fifth of households collecting degrees has more than doubled from 20 to 47 per cent. In contrast, amongst the poorest fifth, just 9 per cent graduate – up from 6 per cent.[27] In no better evidence of how money buys results, the top 100 schools ranked by A-level results in 2004 are all private. Even within the state sector, covert and back-door selection policies result in an increasing number of ghettoised schools where the chances of improvement are slim. At every level of the education system, clever working-class children are being beaten by their less able middle-class counterparts.

Britain is in danger of falling into the trap that has ensnared the United States, a country that has little social mobility but pretends that it has. Britain likes to think of itself as a much more opportunistic and open country than it once was. But, just as in the United States, this is largely a myth, and one perpetuated by those who have a strong vested interest in the status quo. We should aim to build a society where wealth can genuinely be worn as a badge of success rather than be so heavily dependent on privilege. One possible way of showing a declaration of intent might be to introduce an 'opportunity tax', a tax that would effectively draw on existing and new taxes on all sources of unmerited increases in wealth, including inheritance, capital transfers, windfall gains from property and land revaluation and unfair wealth transfers. All the proceeds could then be earmarked for improving the opportunities for those with more limited life chances, just as Gordon Brown's tax on the utility companies' excess profits was used to fund employment programmes.

Seventh, it needs to be recognised that promoting social mobility is not enough on its own to bring about fairness. Equality of opportunity alone is a recipe for unsustainable inequality. The distribution of rewards should be a central issue of public policy. It is a matter of public interest that criminal QCs, clever as they undoubtedly are, are often paid close to twenty times the salary of a headteacher, that chat show hosts get twice a fireman's annual salary for a single appearance, that a partner at Goldman Sachs receives the equivalent of around a thousand times the salary of a care assistant in an old people's home. The market has its place, and it is right to reward rare talent, but too many jobs are disproportionately rewarded for the skill and contribution involved.

Such a strategy – built around these seven key measures – would be popular and practical. It would chime with ordinary people's innate sense of fairness and is within the power of government – national and international. The measures may invite accusations of being motivated by envy, of reinventing the class war. But they would enhance, not undermine, incentives, they would not prevent the achievement of great wealth where it is deserved, they would lead to a distribution of rewards which is easier to defend and justify.

Rich Britain has argued that the rising inequality of recent times has above all been driven by a cultural shift, a new political acceptance of the pursuit of personal enrichment. Such a package of measures would send out a new political signal that rewards based on merit are to be welcomed while those built at the expense of others are unacceptable. It would mean building a new 'social norm' that signalled support for a society in which fairness and social justice are as important as prosperity, one that accepts socially agreed limits to the degree of inequality, one built on fair economic and tax policies that reward people for success and contribution.

New Labour has largely deferred to wealth and power. Yet the strategy of indulging the rich while trying to tackle poverty does not square. Only minimal attempts have been made, in the words of the pro-market *Economist*, 'to punish corporate wrong-doers and to fill the power vacuum that is leading executives to line their bank accounts; to separate business and government in order to preserve government's role as an arbitrator and counterweight, rather than as a corporate poodle'.[28]

Britain has a clear choice. On the one hand, it could call a halt to present trends, introduce measures that bring a closer alignment of merit and reward, that encourage the deserving rich who create wealth and limit the opportunities open to the undeserving to redistribute wealth away from the economically weak. Of course, public opinion may yet force a limit to the degree of inequality that they are prepared to tolerate. A number of factors could trigger a sufficient backlash to force the government's hand – economic downturn triggered by excess, a growing perception by the middle majority that they were not getting a fair share of growing prosperity, that they were carrying an excessive burden of taxation, that they were bearing too much of the risk associated with unequal societies, from rising crime to soaring debt. Frustration could build against blatant greed or corruption or unreasonable attempts by the rich to exploit their good fortune. There is almost certainly a point at which the 'outrage constraint' may begin to bite, a limit to the patience with which the public will accept unwarranted personal enrichment and excessive limitations on social mobility.

On the other hand, it is possible that the economic and social self-correcting mechanisms that acted as barriers to excessive wealth concentrations in the past may now be much weaker, or will only be triggered at even higher levels of concentration. Despite the public's willingness to tick the anti-inequality box in opinion surveys, for example, there is no sign as yet of the sort of mood swing sufficient to force political action and it is possible that the public are now prepared to accept higher degrees of wealth concentration than proved sustainable in the past.

If so, Britain is likely to continue down the road of ever-rising inequality, towards a society closer to the American model, one characterised by even more extreme levels of wealth at the top, one that leads to much deeper levels of social polarisation and one that perpetuates the myth of wider opportunity. If that does prove to be the case, then the age of equality will have proved to be a temporary phase, a mere blip in the long history of the hegemony of the super-rich.

Appendix

The data sources

This appendix summarises the evidence on trends in income and wealth inequality in Britain and the United States referred to in the book. There are a great many sources for comparing wealth and income distributions at a single moment in time but few that measure trends from as far back as the opening decades of the twentieth century to the present day.

Trends in the distribution of income in the UK

Table A1 shows trends in the distribution of after-tax income covering the period 1937 to 1999. This shows that the share of income (after tax) received by the top 0.5 per cent and top 1 per cent fell sharply and continuously from 1937 to the mid-1970s. The late 1970s, however, was to prove the nadir for those at the top. Since then, top income recipients have started to pull away again, and inequality has risen. In the period from 1978 to 1999, for example, the share of income enjoyed by the very richest 0.5 per cent and top 1 per cent has more than doubled, returning to levels close to those prevailing in 1937 (evidence before 1937 is patchier and mainly based on gross incomes).

Economic historians are split about the scale and trend of inequality during and after the Industrial Revolution. What is clear is that income inequality was much higher in the late nineteenth century than it is now, despite the increased inequality of the last two decades. The best evidence is that the impact of the Liberal government reforms and the First World War was to raise incomes at the bottom end and bring about a steady equalisation over the period from the middle of the opening decade of the twentieth century, a process that accelerated after 1929.[1]

Table A1: Percentage shares of total after-tax incomes, United Kingdom, 1937–1999

	Top 1%	Top 0.5%
1937	12.6	9.0
1949	6.8	4.2
1954	5.7	3.4
1959	5.5	3.3
1964	5.7	3.5
1971	5.0	2.9
1975	4.2	2.5
1978	4.2	2.4
1985	5.8	3.5
1990	8.0	5.4
1995	8.7	5.9
1999	10.2	7.2

Source: A. B. Atkinson and W. Salverda, 'Top Incomes in the Netherlands and the UK over the Twentieth Century', *Journal of the European Economic Association* (2005), vol. 3, no. 4, 883–913.

During the last quarter-century, income inequality rose sharply during the 1980s, stabilised in the early 1990s, fell slightly during John Major's Conservative governments, rose again during Blair's first two governments and then fell back to 1997 levels in 2004. Under Labour, inequality has therefore remained roughly static at relatively high historical levels.[2]

Trends in the distribution of wealth in the UK

The extent of wealth inequality depends on the definition used. The distribution of 'liquid assets' (that is, cash and privately owned assets easily convertible into cash, including savings, bonds and shares) is very unequal. According to the specialist wealth consultants Tulip Financial Research, in 2005, the wealthiest 1 per cent enjoyed no less than 62 per cent of all liquid assets while the poorest half owned less than 1 per cent. The top 135,000 individuals – a mere 0.3 per cent of the population – enjoyed as much as a half of all wealth, with average liquid assets of more than £6 million. The top 1,000 had liquid assets averaging £70 million. The distribution of wealth at the top is just as inequitable as amongst the overall population, with the richest enjoying the largest concentrations.

Extending the definition, for example by including the value of homes owned, results in lessened inequality. Table A2 shows the trends in top wealth shares where wealth is defined as liquid assets plus all houses.

Table A2: Trends in the distribution of marketable wealth

Percentage of total personal wealth owned by:

	Top 1%	Top 5%	Top 2%–5%	Bottom 50%
1923	61	82	21	0
1938	55	77	22	0
1950	47	74	27	0
1960	34	59	25	0
1970	30	54	24	0
1976	21	38	17	8
1986	18	36	18	10
1991	17	35	18	8
1996	20	40	20	7
1999	23	43	20	6
2000	23	44	21	5
2001	22	42	20	6
2002	23	43	20	6

Source: For figures from 1923–1970, A. Atkinson, *The Economics of Inequality*, 2nd edn, (Oxford: Clarendon Press, 1983, p. 168); figures for 1976 onwards come from HM Revenue and Customs statistics. Figures for 1923 and 1938 relate to England and Wales, those for 1950–1970 are for Great Britain and figures from 1976 onwards are for the United Kingdom. Because the figures relate to different regions and because of changes in the method of calculation, they are not strictly comparable over time. The raw data, based on estate returns, will almost certainly understate the actual share of wealth enjoyed by the top 1 per cent and 5 per cent because it is based on declared levels of wealth, and most of the rich have ways of disguising the true level of their worth. The definition includes property (but not accrued pension rights) as well as liquid assets such as cash, savings, and shares and bonds.

Wealth tends to be much more concentrated than incomes. This is mainly because of the effect of life cycle savings and because it can be passed on through the generations. People build up their assets during the course of their working life, draw on them in retirement and then pass on what's left at death. Nevertheless, the degree of inequality is greater than can be explained by this. As shown in Table A2, the level of wealth concentration has followed a similar pattern to that of incomes. The share accruing to the top 1 per cent, for example, fell from around 60 per cent in the 1920s to a low of some 17 per cent in 1991. This trend towards greater equality came to a halt at the beginning of the 1990s and then went into reverse, with the wealthiest groups increasing their share. In 2003, the wealthiest 1 per cent had increased their share to 23 per cent. In contrast, the poorest half of the population shared only 6 per cent of wealth between them, down from 10 per cent in 1986.

The primary explanation for the shift to greater wealth equality up to the 1980s was the spread of home ownership, which boosted the holdings of the top half of the wealth distribution below the very top. If property is excluded, the level of inequality rises sharply. (When homes are excluded, the share of wealth owned by the top 1 per cent rises, in 2001, from 22 to 32 per cent and by the top 5 per cent from 42 to 57 per cent.)[3]

A second, less important, reason has been the gradual change in the pattern of wealth distribution within families. In the 1920s, a family's wealth was concentrated in the hands of the oldest male and the practice of primogeniture – the passing of wealth down the male line – remained widespread. Gradually, the tradition has weakened, partly to avoid the impact of estate duty. As a result wealth today is spread more evenly between family members. The primary effect of this latter change has been a redistribution of wealth amongst the rich themselves, specifically from the top 1 per cent to the next 4 per cent. As Table A2 shows, the decline in the wealth share of the top 1 per cent is much greater than that of the top 5 per cent. Indeed, the share of wealth enjoyed by the top 2–5 per cent has barely changed over the period from 1923 to 2000, starting at 21 per cent and finishing at 20 per cent.

While the shift in the share of the top 1 per cent from a low of 17 per cent in 1991 to 23 per cent in 2002 is a significant jump, the growth in wealth inequality in the last decade is less pronounced than in the case of incomes. It may seem surprising that the surge in income inequality has not been fully reflected in the wealth figures. Partly this will reflect the nature of the data collected by HM Revenue and Customs (HMRC), which almost certainly fails to pick up the large fortunes at the very top that have occurred in recent years. HMRC, for example, does not publish information on the distribution of wealth amongst the top 0.5 per cent. Partly it is because wealth represents 'congealed income' and so wealth inequality will lag behind income inequality.[4] It takes time to accumulate fortunes large enough to get you into the top 1 per cent. Nevertheless, the shift towards greater inequality is all the more remarkable given that some of the equalising factors – the extension of wealth to those with few assets through the growth of home ownership and the spreading of family fortunes – has continued over the last twenty years.

The income and wealth distribution in the United States

The US has experienced a similar pattern of change to the UK. Income inequality was at its greatest in the period up to the early 1930s. It then fell sharply and continuously from the 1929 stock market crash, through the great recession of the 1930s and then especially sharply through the Second World War years. For the thirty years from 1945 until the mid-1970s, the income gap between the top and the bottom remained remarkably static. Since then top earners, as in Britain, have been pulling sharply away from the rest. In consequence the gap in incomes between the very top and the bottom in 2000 is back at levels last seen before the crash of 1929.[5] Indeed, between 1979 and 2000, the after-tax incomes of the top 1 per cent of families rose by 201 per cent in real terms. In contrast, the after-tax incomes of those in the middle fifth of the distribution rose by 15 per cent and of the bottom fifth by 9 per cent. Significantly, the gains are higher the nearer you get to the very top. The big winners have been the very rich. 'The top five per cent have done better than the next 15 per cent, the top one per cent better than the next four, and so on up to Bill Gates.'[6]

In 1970, the top 0.01 per cent of taxpayers had 0.7 per cent of total income – that is, they earned seventy times the average. By 1998, their share had risen to 3 per cent of all income – they had incomes 300 times the average. The 13,000 richest families in America had almost as much income as the 20 million poorest households.[7] Today, the United States tops the international league table on income inequality.[8]

What about the pattern of wealth inequalities? Until the last few decades, rich Americans had a generally smaller slice of the cake than their European counterparts. Despite their stronger entrepreneurial culture and belief in the reward for effort, the level of wealth inequality in the United States was more equal than in Britain in the pre-war era. While the top 1 per cent in Britain controlled some 60 per cent of wealth in the 1920s, the comparable share in the United States varied from a low of 32 per cent in 1922 to a peak of 36 per cent in 1929 (some experts put the peak at 40 per cent).[9] This may seem surprising in view of the fact that, as shown in Chapter 2, top American fortunes were much greater than in Britain at the time, and always have been. Britain experienced greater inequality because it had relatively more people at the bottom of the distribution with little or no wealth. Over time this disparity has evened out, with the level of inequality in the United States falling more slowly in the post-war era than in Britain. By the late 1980s, wealth inequality in the United States had become more concentrated than in Britain. As one author put it, by the 1990s, the US was replacing Europe as 'the pinnacle of Western privilege and inequality'.[10]

It is likely that the United States at its founding had about the same level of wealth concentration as in the mid-1970s. Wealth concentration probably increased slightly up to the end of the Civil War in 1865 and then became markedly more unequal up to 1900 with the process of industrialisation. After 1900 it began a slow decline, though one interrupted during the boom of the 1920s. The share of the top 1 per cent in the United States reached its peak of 36 per cent in 1929 and then proceeded to fall through the 1930s, during the Second World War and into the late 1940s. It then remained roughly static through the 1950s and 1960s, fell in the early 1970s and rose again from the early 1980s. The main explanation for the decline through the 1930s and 1940s was the effect of the great depression, the war and the introduction in the 1930s of steep rates of estate taxation on the very rich. These were only relaxed in the 1980s. These factors had the effect of fracturing very large wealth-holdings and reducing the rate of wealth accumulation for the very rich. In addition the level of share and property ownership became more even in the post-war era.

There is limited official information on more recent trends in the distribution of wealth in the United States, and it has been left to independent analysts to gather the evidence. Some studies show it rising sharply during the 1990s, with the share of wealth enjoyed by the top 1 per cent around a third.[11] The explanation for the rising concentration in recent years has been explored throughout this book.[12]

A comparison between the trends in the income and the wealth distributions shows that, in the last decade, as in the UK, there has been a much greater surge in income than in wealth inequality in the United States. Again, one reason for this apparent disparity is that it takes time to accumulate a large fortune out of earnings:

> The top 0.1 per cent (about 20,000 individuals) average income in the late 1990s is around $10 million while the top 0.1 per cent wealth holding is around $60 million. Thus even with substantial savings rates, it would take at least a decade for the average top 0.1 per cent income holder to become an average 0.1 per cent wealth holder.[13]

As shown in Chapter 5, America experienced an even greater explosion of executive compensation in the late 1990s than in Britain, but few of the richest Americans listed on the annual *Forbes* survey are salaried executives. Most of them are still successful entrepreneurs or family heirs.

Nevertheless, although wealth inequality appears not to have risen as fast as income inequality, experts claim that this may be partly the result of the limitations of the data, which seems to have failed to pick up the escalating wealth enjoyed by a small group of the super-rich in the last decade. This is clear from a study of the *Forbes* top 400 (a group corresponding to 0.0002 per cent of wealth holders), which shows that the share of total wealth by this small group of the mega-rich rose sharply from just above 1 per cent in the early 1980s to just below 3 per cent in 2002.[14]

After adjusting for inflation (to 2001 money levels), the average level of wealth enjoyed by the top 400 rose from $921 million in 1989 to $2.1 billion in 2002. The strongest gains in wealth occurred amongst the very richest.[15] Official figures therefore missed the surge in wealth of the very richest Americans and thus failed to show the sharp increase in wealth inequality at the top end in the years to 2002.

The annual rich lists published by the *Sunday Times*

These began in 1989, but the first survey included only 200 people, and contained a number of errors. The second survey in 1990 had a larger sample of 400 people and was more reliable. The sample size was increased to 500 in 1995 and then to 1,000 in 1998. The annual estimates attempt to identify 'identifiable wealth' – including land, property, racehorses, art and significant shares in publicly quoted companies. The definition excludes bank accounts and private share portfolios, which are not accessible, but attempts to allow for liabilities. Other assets such as pensions are difficult to identify and value. Valuations arising from the sale of successful businesses include an estimate for the tax paid on sale proceeds at a lower rate than the notional 40 per cent level. Since the rich generally have a clear interest in hiding their true wealth, and often pay professionals large fees for doing so, the figures are inevitably estimates and not necessarily accurate. The valuations are deliberately cautious and the lists are, in general, likely to understate the total value of wealth holdings by individuals and groups. Nevertheless they are a useful additional source outside HMRC and provide a good guide to trends.

Notes

Introduction

1. HM Revenue and Customs.
2. 'Liquid assets' includes money held in cash, bank and building society deposits, shares, bonds and unit trusts and so readily available. Figures are from successive years of the *Global Wealth Reports* by Datamonitor. See too figures provided by wealth consultants Tulip Financial Research.
3. Rich Lists, *Sunday Times*, 4 March 1990 and 3 April 2005.
4. *Daily Express*, 25 January 2005.
5. *Sunday Times*, 3 April 2005.
6. M. Brewer, A. Goodman, J. Shaw and A. Shephard, *Living Standards, Inequality and Poverty* (London: Institute for Fiscal Studies, 2005); C. Jencks and G. Burtless, 'American Inequality and its Consequences', in H. Aaron, J. Lindsey and P. Nivola (eds), *Agenda for the Nation* (Washington: Brookings Institution, 2003); A. Atkinson, 'Distribution of Income and Wealth', in A. Halsey and J. Webb (eds), *Twentieth Century Social Trends*, 3rd edn (Basingstoke: Palgrave Macmillan, 2000), p. 367.
7. K. Phillips, *Wealth and Democracy* (New York: Broadway Books, 2002), p. 109.

Chapter 1

1. S. Lansley and A. Forrester, *Top Man: How Philip Green Built His High Street Empire*, (London: Aurum Press, 2005).
2. C. Rojek, 'Leisure and the Rich Today: Veblen's Thesis after a Century', *Leisure Studies* (2000), vol. 19, no. 1.
3. *Observer*, 9 June 2002.
4. J. Mack and S. Lansley, *Poor Britain* (London: Allen and Unwin, 1985).
5. *New York Times*, 15 October 2000.
6. Datamonitor, *Global Wealth Reports*, 2004.
7. *Times*, 18 October 2005.
8. There are no official published estimates of the number of people in Britain with wealth levels

of over £50 million, £5 million or even £1 million. Private organisations that set out to measure the numbers of very wealthy at the top include the *Sunday Times*, Tulip Financial Research and Datamonitor. They all use slightly different definitions, which sometimes include just liquid assets, sometimes investment property and sometimes all property. This explains the wide variation in estimates presented in this paragraph. The higher figures for the numbers worth more than £1 million and more than £5 million are based on Tulip data, which includes investment property, but excludes homes and second homes. For the definition of wealth used by the *Sunday Times*, see Appendix.

9.   *Sunday Times*, 3 April 2004.
10.   *Wall Street Journal*, Europe, 6 May 2005.
11.   *Observer*, 6 June 2004.
12.   F. Mount, *Mind the Gap* (London: Short Books, 2004), p. 107.
13.   P. Johnson, 'When are you seriously rich?', *Forbes*, 10 November 2004.
14.   Ibid.
15.   Ibid.
16.   *Sunday Times*, 30 April 2000.
17.   F. Partnoy, *F.I.A.S.C.O.: Blood in the Water on Wall Street* (London: Profile, 1997), p. 40.
18.   Ibid., p. 25.
19.   *Sunday Times*, 3 April 2005.
20.   M. Bishop, 'Survey: the new rich', *Economist*, 16 June 2001.
21.   K. Phillips, *Wealth and Democracy* (New York: Broadway, 2002), p. 56.
22.   *Forbes*, 30 March 2002.
23.   *Daily Telegraph*, 28 February 2003.
24.   K. Cahill, *Guardian*, 29 January 2001.
25.   Ibid.
26.   *Sunday Times*, 7 April 2002.
27.   Datamonitor, *Global Wealth Reports*.
28.   That is, after adjusting for inflation.
29.   The inflation-adjusted entry price for 1990 would be £75 million.
30.   *Guardian*, 6 August 2005.
31.   The figures have not been adjusted for inflation.
32.   *Forbes*, 22 September 2004.
33.   S. Pizzigati, 'Toward a maximum wage', *Too Much*, 3 June 2005.
34.   For comparisions of income inequality across nations, see J. Hills, *Inequality and the State* (Oxford: Oxford University Press, 2004), p. 29 and G. Burtless and C. Jencks, 'American Inequality and Its Consequences', in H. Aaron, J. Lindsay and P. Nivola (eds), *Agenda for the Nation* (Washington: Brookings Institution, 2003), fig. 4.
35.   *Sunday Times*, 3 April 2005.
36.   *World Wealth Reports* 2004 and 2005 (New York: Merrill Lynch Gemini). Assets exclude housing and pension entitlements.

Chapter 2

1.   See for example D. Goodhart, *Guardian*, 29 July 1999 and D. Aaronovitch, *Observer*, 25 May 2003.
2.   *Independent*, 6 August 2004.

3.   J. Rentoul, *The Rich Get Richer* (London: Unwin Hyman, 1987).

4.   M. Dean, *Guardian*, 11 August 2004.

5.   W. Paxton and M. Dixon, *The State of the Nation: An Audit of Social Injustice* (London: Institute of Public Policy Research, 2004), p. 24; A. Atkinson and W. Salverda, 'Top Incomes in the Netherlands and the UK over the Twentieth Century', *Journal of the European Economic Association* (2005), vol. 3, no. 4, 883–913.

6.   As measured by the proportion falling below an income equal to 60 per cent of median income.

7.   M. Brewer, A. Goodman, J. Shaw and A. Shephard, *Living Standards, Inequality and Poverty* (London: Institute for Fiscal Studies, 2005).

8.   J. Hills, *Inequality and the State* (Oxford: Oxford University Press, 2004), p. 29; A. Atkinson, 'The Distribution of Income in Industrialized Countries', in *Income Inequality Issues and Policy Options: A Symposium Sponsored by the Federal Reserve Bank of Kansas City*, Jackson Hole, Wyoming, August 27–29, 1998; Brewer et al., *Living Standards, Inequality and Poverty*, pp. 11–12.

9.   The official figures on wealth (which are published for only the top 1 per cent) probably underplay the extent of concentration at the top. If property is excluded, the top 1 per cent enjoy an even higher share of the nation's wealth, while the distribution of liquid assets is even more unequal. According to Tulip Financial Research, the specialist wealth consultants, the top 45,000 people (0.1 per cent of the population) today enjoy a third of all liquid assets (marketable wealth that includes cash, savings and shares), averaging more than £8 million each. See Tulip, *Britain's Millionaires: The Powerhouse of Private Investment* (London: Tulip Financial Research, 2002).

10. Office of National Statistics, *Share of the Wealth*, December 2004.

11. W. Rubinstein, *Men of Property: The Very Wealthy in Britain since the Industrial Revolution* (London: Croom Helm, 1981), p. 45.

12. A. Smith, *An Inquiry into the Nature and Causes of the Wealth of Nations* (Oxford: Clarendon Press, [1784] 1976).

13. D. Cannadine, *The Decline and Fall of the British Aristocracy* (London: Picador, 1992), p. 49.

14. Ibid., p. 48.

15. A. Carnegie, 'Wealth', *North American Review* (1889), vol. 148, no. 391, 653–665.

16. S. Lansley, *After the Gold Rush: The Trouble with Affluence – 'Consumer Capitalism' and the Way Forward* (London: Century, 1994).

17. A. Sampson, *The Midas Touch: Money, People and Power from West to East* (London: Hodder and Stoughton, 1989), p. 24.

18. A. Sampson, *The New Anatomy of Britain* (London: Hodder and Stoughton, 1971), p. 206.

19. Rubinstein, *Men of Property*, p. 232.

20. See Appendix for more details.

21. Royal Commission on the Distribution of Income and Wealth, *Report No. 1: Initial Report on the Standing Reference*, Cmnd 6171, July 1975.

22. P. Golding and S. Middleton, *Images of Welfare* (Oxford: Martin Robertson, 1982).

23. *Money*, March 1984.

24. V. Packard, *The Ultra Rich* (Boston: Little Brown, 1980), p. 11.

25. Sampson, *Midas Touch*, p. 24.

26. A. Sampson, *Who Runs This Place? The Anatomy of Britain in the 21st Century* (London: John Murray, 2004), p. 354.

27. C. Gardner and J. Sheppard, *Consuming Passion: The Rise of Retail Culture* (London: Unwin Hyman, 1989), p. 63.

28.   *Guardian,* 27 October 2005.
29.   *Mail on Sunday,* 12 June 2005.
30.   *Daily Mail,* 11 June 2005.
31.   W. Rubinstein (ed.), *Wealth and the Wealthy in the Modern World* (London: Croom Helm, 1980), p. 21.
32.   F. Jaher, 'The Gilded Elite', in Rubinstein, *Wealth and the Wealthy in the Modern World,* p. 193.
33.   M. Josephson, *The Robber Barons* (New York: Harcourt Brace, 1934).
34.   T. Veblen, *The Theory of the Leisure Class: An Economic Study in the Evolution of Institutions* (New York: Macmillan, 1899).
35.   Quoted in *Washington Post,* 3 March 2002.
36.   K. Phillips, *Wealth and Democracy: A Political History of the American Rich* (New York: Broadway, 2002), p. 240.
37.   Ibid., p. 312.
38.   Ibid., p. 356.
39.   A study showed just how concentrated it was, with some 40 per cent of the 200 largest corporations controlled by single families exercising either absolute or effective control. These families included the Rockefellers of Standard Oil, the Vanderbilts of New York Central Railroads, the Fords and the duPonts. See F. Lundberg, *America's 60 Families* (New York: Vanguard, 1937).
40.   Phillips, *Wealth and Democracy,* p. 61.
41.   In 1978, the two richest American families, the duPonts and the Mellons, were estimated to be worth some $2 billion–$5 billion each, but both would have comprised some several dozen family members. The next richest, the Gettys and self-made shipping magnate Daniel K. Ludwig, were estimated to be worth $2 billion–$3 billion and the Rockefellers some $1 billion–$2 billion. No other families or individuals were worth more than $1 billion, which was the equivalent of less than $200 million in 1910 dollars. In 1914, Rockefeller was worth $1 billion. Rubinstein, *Wealth and the Wealthy in the Modern World,* p. 39.
42.   Phillips, *Wealth and Democracy,* p. 76.
43.   D. Reisman, *Thornstein Veblen,* (New York: Scribner's Sons, 1953).
44.   Jaher, 'Gilded Elite', p. 203.
45.   Phillips, *Wealth and Democracy,* p. 110.
46.   P. Johnson, 'When are you seriously rich?', *Forbes,* 11 October 2004.
47.   B. Burrough and J. Helyar, *Barbarians at the Gate: The Fall of RJR Nabisco* (New York: Random House, 1990).
48.   M. Lewis, *Liar's Poker: Two Cities, True Greed* (London: Coronet, 1990), p. 11.
49.   Ibid., pp. 15–18.
50.   *Economist,* 3 January 1998.

Chapter 3

1.   *Economist,* 28 June 2003.
2.   A. Atkinson, *The Economics of Inequality,* 2nd edn (Oxford: Clarendon Press, 1983), p. 179.
3.   D. Hobson, *The National Wealth: Who Gets What in Britain* (London: Harper Collins, 1999), p. 531.
4.   J. Wedgwood, *The Economics of Inheritance* (London: George Routledge and Sons, 1929).

5. M. Hay, P. Reynolds et al., *Global Entrepreneurship Monitor: 2000 Executive Report* (London: London Business School, 2000).
6. L. Abramovsky, 'Is the UK Innovative Enough?', *IFS Update*, Summer 2004.
7. W. Rubinstein, *Men of Property: The Very Wealthy in Britain since the Industrial Revolution* (London: Croom Helm, 1981), Tables 3.3–3.7.
8. Ibid., pp. 44–5.
9. A. Sampson, *The Midas Touch* (London: Hodder and Stoughton, 1989), p. 13.
10. Ibid., p. 22.
11. *Guardian*, 27 April 2005.
12. T. Bower, *Branson* (London: 4th Estate, 2000), p. 1.
13. *Observer*, 17 November 2002.
14. Bower, *Branson*, p. 10.
15. J. Stewart, *Den of Thieves* (New York: Simon and Schuster, 1991), p. 22.
16. J. Baskin and P. Miranti, *A History of Corporate Finance* (Cambridge: Cambridge University Press, 1997), p. 295.
17. *Management Today*, October 2000.
18. Ibid.
19. *Sunday Times*, 3 April 2005.
20. *Sunday Times*, 11 July 2004.
21. Sampson, *Midas Touch*, p. 13.
22. *Sunday Telegraph*, 20 November 2005.
23. J. Micklethwait and A. Wooldridge, *The Company* (London: Weidenfeld and Nicolson, 2003), ch. 3.
24. Ibid., p. 85.
25. Sampson, *Midas Touch*, p. 56.
26. Ibid., p. 55
27. *The Mayfair Set*, BBC2, July 1999.
28. Ibid.
29. Sampson, *Midas Touch*, p. 54.
30. B. Burrough and J. Helyar, *Barbarians at the Gate; The Fall of RJR Nabisco* (New York: Random House, 1990).
31. Ibid., p. 620
32. Ibid., pp. 615–6.
33. J. Helyar, 'From ashes to ashes', *Fortune*, 13 October 2003.
34. B. Burroughs, 'The 00's finale of the 80's tycoons', *New York Times*, 5 June 2000.
35. Sampson, *Midas Touch*, p. 59.
36. W. Hutton, *The State We're In* (London: Jonathan Cape, 1995), p. 163.
37. *Economist*, 27 November 2004.
38. Ibid.
39. *Herald*, 8 May 2005.
40. *Sunday Times*, 8 May 2005.
41. *Scotsman*, 5 December 2002.
42. *Forbes*, 17 March 2003.
43. *Guardian*, 8 May 2001.
44. R. Shiller, *Irrational Exuberance* (Princeton: Princeton University Press, 2000).
45. C. Kindleberger, *Manias, Panics and Crashes; A History of Financial Crises*, 4th edn (New York; John Wiley and Sons, 2000).
46. *Guardian*, 8 May 2001.

Chapter 4

1. *Observer*, 24 July 2005.
2. *Times*, 26 April 2005.
3. *Guardian*, 4 August 2005, 27 August 2004, 11 July 2003.
4. *Observer*, 14 May 1995.
5. D. Hobson, *The National Wealth: Who Gets What in Britain* (London: HarperCollins, 1999), p. 562.
6. *Guardian*, 4 August 2005.
7. *Guardian*, 31 July 2003, 4 August 2005.
8. Under the new rules, shareholders can only register their opposition to the packages being offered; the votes are retrospective and carry no direct power to reverse pay deals. Not that it is always easy to simply ignore the protests.
9. D. Osler, *Labour Party PLC: Party of Business* (Edinburgh: Mainstream, 2002), p. 188.
10. P. Krugman, *New York Times*, 20 October 2002.
11. D. Henwood, 'A New Economy', speech to the Friday Forum, University YMCA, University of Illinois at Urbana-Champaign, October 1999.
12. J. Cassidy, 'The Greed Cycle', *New Yorker*, 23 September 2002.
13. J. Stiglitz, *The Roaring Nineties: A New History of the World's Most Prosperous Decade* (New York: W. W. Norton, 2003), p. 122.
14. Cassidy, 'Greed Cycle'.
15. Ibid.
16. Hobson, *National Wealth*, p. 1234.
17. *Financial Times*, 31 July 2002.
18. R. Brenner, 'Towards the Precipice', *London Review of Books*, 6 February 2003.
19. *Daily Telegraph*, 19 November 2005.
20. *Fortune*, 28 April 2003.
21. Cassidy, 'Greed Cycle', p. 313.
22. *Economist*, 16 November 2002; F. Partnoy, *Infectious Greed: How Deceit and Risk Corrupted the Financial Markets* (London: Profile, 2004), p. 288.
23. *New York Times*, 29 April 2003; *Guardian*, 6 February 2004.
24. E. Chancellor, 'The croupier takes too much', *Prospect*, February 2003.
25. *Evening Standard*, 5 October 2005.
26. P. Augar, *The Greed Merchants: How the Investment Banks Played the Free Market Game* (London: Allen Lane, 2005).
27. J. Stewart, *Den of Thieves* (New York: Simon and Schuster, 1991).
28. Cassidy, 'Greed Cycle'.
29. Augar, *Greed Merchants*, pp. 170–71.
30. N. Barry, 'Why capitalism needs a new Gordon Gekko', *Business*, 1 September 2002.
31. Hobson, *National Wealth*, p. 1096.
32. Letter to *Financial Times*, 18 June 1997.
33. *Guardian*, 6 March 2004.
34. *Guardian*, 13 September 2005.
35. *Observer*, 23 October 2005.
36. *Guardian*, 31 July 2003.
37. *Evening Standard*, 19 June 2003.
38. Ibid.
39. *Financial Times*, 12 July 2004.

40.   J. Bevan, *Trolley Wars: The Battle of the Supermarkets* (London: Profile, 2005), p. 219.

41.   *Financial Times*, 7 May 2005; paper by Martin Conyon and Graham Sadler to the annual conference of the Royal Economic Society, 2005.

42.   See the biannual international surveys carried out by *Management Today*, July 2003 and September 2005. They show that although Germany was way behind the UK in 2003, it caught up and overtook Britain over the next two years.

43.   Hobson, *National Wealth*, p. 576.

44.   Quoted in J. Useem, 'Have they no shame?', *Fortune*, 28 April 2003.

45.   P. Krugman, 'For richer', *New York Times*, 20 October 2002.

46.   Useem, 'Have they no shame?'.

47.   *Financial Times*, 24 July 2003.

48.   *Guardian*, 1 August 2003, 14 June 2004.

49.   P. Gregg, S. Machin and S. Szymanski, 'The Disappearing Relationship between Directors' Pay and Corporate Performance', *British Journal of Industrial Relations* (1993), vol. 31, no. 1; M. Conyon, 'Boardroom Compensation in the UK', unpublished paper, December 1994.

50.   *Observer*, 29 February 2004.

51.   J. Collins, *Good to Great: Why Some Companies Make the Leap – and Others Don't* (New York: HarperBusiness, 2001).

52.   *Guardian*, 23 July 2002.

53.   *Times*, 8 March 1995.

54.   K. Phillips, *Wealth and Democracy: A Political History of the American Rich* (New York: Broadway, 2002), p. 154.

55.   *Sunday Telegraph*, 4 May 2003.

56.   *Financial Times*, 7 July 2005.

57.   *Sharing in the Boardroom 2000: Incentive Arrangements in Large UK Companies*, May 2000.

58.   *Evening Standard*, 13 October 2005.

59.   *Investors Chronicle*, 22 December 2004

60.   'One billion dollars', *Financial Times Magazine*, 13 November 2004.

61.   Krugman, 'For richer'; a similar emphasis on changing social norms to explain the rising income share of the top has been made by T. Piketty and E. Saez, *Income Inequality in the United States 1913-1998*, NBER Working Paper 8467 (Cambridge, MA: National Bureau of Economic Research, 2001).

62.   Krugman, 'For richer'.

Chapter 5

1.   Quoted in D. Hobson, *The National Wealth: Who Gets What in Britain* (London: Harper Collins, 1999), p. 49.

2.   Ibid., p. 49.

3.   D. Cannadine, *The Decline and Fall of the British Aristocracy* (London: Papermac, 1996), p. 640.

4.   *Sunday Times*, 7 April 2002.

5.   Hobson, *National Wealth*, p 49.

6.   M. Benn, 'The legacy lottery', *New Internationalist*, June 1991.

7.   Cannadine, *Decline and Fall of the British Aristocracy*, p. 9.

8.   Ibid., p. 17.

9.   Ibid., p. 69.
10. J. Camplin, *The Rise of the Plutocrats: Wealth and Power in Edwardian England* (London: Constable, 1978), p. 16.
11. W. Rubinstein, *Men of Property: The Very Wealthy in Britain since the Industrial Revolution* (London: Croom Helm, 1981), p. 74.
12. Cannadine, *Decline and Fall of the British Aristocracy*, p. 342.
13. Ibid., p. 111.
14. W. Guttsman, *The British Political Elite* (London: MacGibbon and Kee, 1963), p. 132.
15. J. Paxman, *Friends in High Places: Who Runs Britain?* (London: Penguin, 1991), pp. 24 and 26.
16. P. Mandler, *The Fall and Rise of the Stately Home* (New Haven: Yale University Press, 1997), p. 317.
17. Guttsman, *British Political Elite*, pp. 41 and 94. The aristocrats were a mix of baronets, Irish peers and sons of peers and baronets.
18. The ten leading landowners in 1880 were the Duke of Westminster, the Duke of Buccleuch, the Duke of Bedford, the Duke of Devonshire, the Duke of Northumberland, the Earl of Derby, the Marquess of Bute, the Duke of Sutherland, the Duke of Hamilton and the Earl of Fitzwilliam. See Rubinstein, *Men of Property*, p. 194.
19. Paxman, *Friends in High Places*, p. 22.
20. K. Cahill, *Who Owns Britain* (Edinburgh: Canongate, 2001), p. 5.
21. Ibid., p. 56.
22. A. Sampson, *The New Anatomy of Britain* (London: Hodder and Stoughton, 1971), p. 208.
23. Cannadine, *Decline and Fall of the British Aristocracy*, p. 651.
24. *Observer*, 20 May 2001.
25. *Guardian*, 23 March 2005.
26. Hobson, *National Wealth*, p. 49.
27. Ibid., p. 47.
28. Ibid., p. 41.
29. *Sunday Times*, 2 September 1990.
30. Cannadine, *Decline and Fall of the British Aristocracy*, p. 658.
31. D. Riley, *Taken for a Ride: Taxpayers, Trains and HM Treasury* (Teddington: Centre for Land Policy Studies, 2001).
32. Cahill, *Who Owns Britain*, p. 54.
33. S. Jenkins, *England's Thousand Best Houses* (London: Penguin, 2003).
34. Benn, 'Legacy lottery'.

Chapter 6

1.   T. Nicholas, 'The Myth of Meritocracy: An Inquiry into the Social Origins of Britain's Business Leaders since 1850', mimeo, London School of Economics, 1999, p. 26.
2.   J. Rentoul, *The Rich Get Richer* (London: Unwin Hyman, 1987), p. 138.
3.   D. Hobson, *The National Wealth: Who Gets What in Britain*, (London: HarperCollins, 1999), p. 532.
4.   S. Lansley and A. Forrester, *Top Man, How Philip Green Built His High Street Empire* (London: Aurum Press, 2005).
5.   W. Rubinstein, *Men of Property: The Very Wealthy in Britain since the Industrial Revolution* (London: Croom Helm, 1981), pp. 125–6.

6.   Ibid., p. 120.
7.   W. Rubinstein, 'Men of Property: Occupation, Inheritance and Power', in P. Stanworth and A. Giddens (eds), *Elites and Power in British Society* (London: Cambridge University Press, 1974), p. 146.
8.   Rubinstein, *Men of Property*, p. 82.
9.   Ibid., p. 146.
10. Ibid., p. 135.
11. Ibid., p. 138.
12. W. Rubinstein (ed.), *Wealth and the Wealthy in the Modern World* (London: Croom Helm, 1980), p. 28.
13. The 1990 list is more reliable than the first *Sunday Times* list published in 1989. It had doubled in size to 400 names and some of the teething troubles had been ironed out.
14. C. Lasch, *The Revolt of the Elites and the Betrayal of Democracy* (New York: W. W. Norton, 1995), p. 51.
15. R. Smith, *The Wealth Creators: The Rise of Today's New Rich and Super-rich* (New York: St Martin's Press, 2001), p. 284.
16. C. Wright Mills, 'The American Business Elite: A Collective Portrait', *Journal of Economic History* (1945), vol. 5, supplement, 20–44.
17. Rubinstein, *Men of Property*, p. 132.
18. E. Pessen, 'The Egalitarian Myth and American Social Reality: Wealth, Mobility and Equality in the "Era of the Common Man"', *American Historical Review* (1971), vol. 76, no. 4, 1012.
19. A. Kerckhoff, 'The Current State of Social Mobility Research', *Sociological Quarterly* (1984), vol. 25, no. 2.
20. Rubinstein, *Men of Property*, p. 133.
21. Lasch, op cit, p 77.
22. A. Krueger, *New York Times*, 14 November 2002; for the British data see L. Dearden, S. Machin and H. Reed, 'Intergenerational Mobility in Britain', *Economic Journal* (1997), vol. 107, no. 440, 47–66.
23. Ibid.
24. K. Phillips, *Wealth and Democracy: A Political History of the American Rich* (New York: Broadway, 2002), p. 114.
25. Smith, *Wealth Creators*, p. 310.
26. *Forbes*, 13 September 2002.
27. *Forbes*, 17 March 2003.
28. *Economist*, 17 May 2003.
29. F. Jaher, 'The Gilded Elite', in Rubinstein, *Wealth and the Wealthy in the Modern World*.
30. Phillips, *Wealth and Democracy*, p. 118.
31. Ibid., p. 116.
32. *Forbes*, 12 October 1998, p. 47.
33. Phillips, *Wealth and Democracy*, p. 119.
34. Ibid., p. 118.
35. P. Saunders, *Unequal but Fair?: A Study of Class Barriers in Britain* (London: Institute of Economic Affairs, 1996), p. 7.
36. R. Breen and J. Goldthorpe, 'Class, Mobility and Merit: The Experience of Two British Birth Cohorts', *European Sociological Review* (2001), vol. 17, no. 2.
37. J. Blanden, A. Goodman, P. Gregg and S. Machin, *Changes in Intergenerational Mobility in Britain* (London: Centre for Economic Performance, London School of Economics, 2002); J. Blanden, P. Gregg and S. Machin, *Intergenerational Mobility in Europe and North America*

(London: Centre for Economic Performance, London School of Economics, 2005).

38. S. Aldridge, 'Social Mobility', paper to Performance and Innovation Unit, Cabinet Office, March 2001; S. Aldridge, *Life Chances and Social Mobility*, paper to Prime Minister's Strategy Unit, March 2004.

39. Breen and Goldthorpe, 'Class, Mobility and Merit'. The data on which this finding is based relates to two large groups of children born in Great Britain in one week in 1958 and in 1970. Their subsequent class positions are compared for the years 1981 and 1996.

40. C. Harbury and D. Hitchens, *Inheritance and Wealth Inequality in Britain* (London: George Allen and Unwin, 1979), p. 131.

41. Study by Bill Rubinstein for the television series *Fortune*, London Weekend Television, 1985.

42. T. Nicholas, *The Myth of Meritocracy; An Inquiry into the Social Origins of Britain's Business Leaders since 1850* (London: London School of Economics, 1999), p. 26.

43. J. Goldthorpe and P. Bevan, *The Study of Social Stratification in Great Britain 1946–1976* (Turin: Fondazione, 1977).

44. The study, by Hemmington Scott, was reported in the *Sunday Times*, 12 October 1997.

45. *Sunday Express*, 13 April 2003.

46. Author's calculations.

Chapter 7

1. A. Adonis and S. Pollard, *A Class Act: The Myth of Britain's Classless Society* (London: Penguin, 1998), p. 67.

2. *Evening Standard*, 8 August 2000.

3. *Guardian*, 3 February 2004.

4. A. Sampson, *Who Runs This Place?: The Anatomy of Britain in the 21st Century* (London: John Murray, 2004).

5. A. Neil, *Full Disclosure* (London: Macmillan, 1996), p. 265.

6. Ibid., p. 351.

7. P. Stanworth and A. Giddens, *Elites and Power in British Society* (London: Cambridge University Press, 1974).

8. See, for example, J. Paxman, *Friends in High Places: Who Runs Britain?* (London: Penguin, 1991).

9. Adonis and Pollard, *Class Act*, p. 67.

10. Sampson, *Who Runs This Place?*, p. 355.

11. *Evening Standard*, 22 September 1997.

12. F. Jaher, 'The Gilded Elite', in W. Rubinstein (ed.), *Wealth and the Wealthy in the Modern World* (London: Croom Helm, 1980), p. 215.

13. A. Burr, *The Portrait of a Banker: James Stillman 1850–1918* (New York: Duffield, 1927), p. 278.

14. Jaher, 'Gilded Elite', p. 215.

15. H. Hughes, *My Life and Opinions*, ed. R. Eaton (Chicago: Best Books Press, 1972), p. 202.

16. A. Giddens, *The Third Way and Its Critics* (Cambridge: Polity Press, 2000), p. 96.

17. R. Conniff, *The Natural History of the Rich: A Field Guide* (London: William Heinemann, 2003), p. 75.

18. A. Sampson, *The Midas Touch: Money, People and Power from West to East* (London: Hodder and Stoughton, 1989), p. 49.

19.   *The Mayfair Set*, BBC2, July 1999.
20.   *Times*, 15 October 2003.
21.   Ibid.
22.   *Times*, 2 November 2004.
23.   A. Sampson, *Who Runs This Place?*, p. 251.
24.   D. Hobson, *The National Wealth: Who Gets What in Britain* (London: HarperCollins, 1999), p. 591.
25.   Healey, *The Time of My Life* (London: Michael Joseph, 1989), p 427.
26.   Hobson, *National Wealth*, p. 981.
27.   Ibid., p. 768.
28.   Ibid., p. 985.
29.   S. Lansley and A. Forrester, *Top Man: How Philip Green Built His High Street Empire* (London: Aurum Press, 2005).
30.   *Guardian*, 24 September 2005.
31.   *Guardian*, 10 March 2004.
32.   J. Maskow, 'Poor Representation Creates Voter Apathy', *Battalion*, 2 November 1998.
33.   Ibid.
34.   K. Phillips, *Wealth and Democracy: A Political History of the American Rich* (New York: Broadway, 2002), p. xvi.
35.   R. Morris, *Encyclopedia of American History*, p.417.
36.   Phillips, *Wealth and Democracy*, pp. 322–3.
37.   *New Statesman*, 12 January 2004.
38.   P. Krugman, *The Great Unravelling: From Boom to Bust in Three Scandalous Years* (London: Allen Lane, 2003), p. 3.
39.   R. Goodwin, 'The selling of government', *Los Angeles Times*, 30 January 1997.
40.   K. Phillips, 'Too much wealth, too little democracy', *Challenge*, September 2002.
41.   *Guardian*, 19 November 2003.
42.   *Guardian,* 27 October 2004.
43.   J. Stiglitz, *The Roaring Nineties: A New History of the World's Most Prosperous Decade* (New York: W. W. Norton, 2003).
44.   G. Hodgson, *More Equal than Others: America from Nixon to the New Century* (Princeton: Princeton University Press, 2004).
45.   *New Yorker*, 2 September 2002.
46.   P. Krugman, *New York Times*, 31 October 2001.
47.   D. Osler, *Labour Party Plc: Party of Business* (Edinburgh: Mainstream, 2002), p. 11.
48.   *Observer*, 29 August 2004.
49.   Neil, *Full Disclosure*, p. xxv.
50.   N. Chenoweth, *Virtual Murdoch: Reality Wars on the Information Highway* (London: Secker and Warburg, 2001).
51.   *Guardian*, 14 June 2005.
52.   M. Wolff, *Autumn of the Moguls: My Misadventures with the Titans, Poseurs, and Money Guys Who Mastered and Messed Up Big Media* (London: Flamingo, 2003).
53.   *Guardian*, 27 October 2004.
54.   R. Cook, *The Point of Departure* (London: Simon and Schuster, 2003), pp. 72–3.
55.   *Guardian*, 1 November 2004.
56.   *Spectator*, 12 November 2005.
57.   Osler, *Labour Party Plc*, p. 147.
58.   *Sunday Times*, 1 February 2004.

Chapter 8

1. J. Paxman, *Friends in High Places: Who Runs Britain?* (London: Penguin, 1991), p. 246.
2. *Herald,* 6 July 2000.
3. L. Edwards, *A Bit Rich?: What the Wealthy Think about Giving* (London: Institute for Public Policy Research, 2002).
4. *Sunday Times,* 3 April 2005.
5. Giving List, *Guardian,* 17 November 2003.
6. J. Banks and S. Tanner, *The State of Donation: Household Gifts to Charity 1974–96* (London: Institute of Fiscal Studies, 1997); B. Egan, *The Widow's Might: How Charities Depend on the Poor* (London: Social Market Foundation, 2001); Edwards, *A Bit Rich?,* p. 12.
7. *Observer,* 9 June 2002.
8. *Daily Telegraph,* 21 October 2003.
9. *Business,* 15 June 2003.
10. R. Conniff, *The Natural History of the Rich: A Field Guide* (London: William Heinemann, 2003), p. 112.
11. Ibid., p. 113.
12. *New York Times,* 19 September 1997.
13. *New York Times,* 16 April 2000.
14. *Times,* 14 November 2003.
15. Quoted in the *New York Times,* 24 November 2002.
16. F. Jaher, 'The Gilded Elite', in W. Rubinstein (ed.), *Wealth and the Wealthy in the Modern World* (London: Croom Helm, 1980), p. 207.
17. A. Carnegie, 'Wealth', *North American Review* (1889), vol. 148, no. 391, 653–665.
18. K. Phillips, *Wealth and Democracy: A Political History of the American Rich* (New York: Broadway, 2002), p. 238.
19. *New York Times,* 9 December 1997.
20. Jaher, 'Gilded Elite', p. 205.
21. D. Hobson, *The National Wealth: Who Gets What in Britain* (London: HarperCollins, 1999), p. 548.
22. Jaher, 'Gilded Elite', p. 205.
23. *Financial Times,* 17 January 2004.
24. Ibid.
25. R. Smith, *The Wealth Creators: The Rise of Today's Rich and Super-Rich* (New York: St Martin's Press, 2002), p. 323.
26. *New York Times,* 16 April 2000.
27. *New York Times,* 25 August 1996.
28. Interview on Larry King show, quoted by CNN Interactive, 19 September 1997.
29. H. Ford and S. Crowther, *Moving Forward* (Garden City, NY: Doubleday, Doran, 1930), pp. 6–7, 107–8.
30. Jaher, 'Gilded Elite', p. 211.
31. Hobson, *National Wealth,* p. 548.
32. Conniff, *Natural History of the Rich,* p. 105.
33. A. Huffington, 'Doing Ted Turner One Better', *Philanthropy,* March–April 2000.
34. *Economist,* 30 May 1998.
35. M. Dowie, *American Foundations: An Investigative History* (Cambridge, MA: MIT Press, 2001).
36. *Western Daily Press,* 18 April 2003.

37.   *Financial Times*, 10 July 2004.
38.   *Sunday Tribune*, 3 August 2003.
39.   L. Edwards, *A Bit Rich? What the Wealthy Think about Giving* (London: Institute for Public Policy Research, 2002).
40.   Ibid., p. 21.
41.   Ibid., p. 25.
42.   *Times*, 19 September 2003.
43.   *Times*, 13 October 2005.

Chapter 9

1.   *Mail on Sunday*, 18 July 1999.
2.   *Sunday Times*, 18 July 2004; *Observer*, 6 June 2004.
3.   *Financial Times*, 26 May 1998.
4.   *Guardian*, 11 April 2002.
5.   A. Mitchell, P. Sikka, J. Christensen, P. Morris and S. Filling, *No Accounting for Tax Havens* (Basildon: Association of Accountancy and Business Affairs, 2002), p. 11.
6.   J. Christensen, *Tax Distortions, Fiscal Dumping and Tax Fraud* (London: Tax Justice Network, 2003).
7.   Tax Justice Network, 27 March 2005.
8.   Mitchell et al., *No Accounting for Tax Havens*, p. 61; S. Milne, *The Enemy Within: The Secret War against the Miners*, rev. edn (London: Verso, 2004); T. Bower, *Gordon Brown* (London: HarperCollins, 2004), pp. 253–9.
9.   *Guardian*, 12 April 2002.
10.   *Economist*, 31 January 2004, p. 68.
11.   *Times*, 10 July 2000.
12.   *Mail on Sunday*, 20 January 2002.
13.   *Guardian*, 15 April 2003.
14.   *Independent*, 4 February 1998.
15.   *Economist*, 20 March 1999.
16.   *Times*, 3 September 2000.
17.   *Observer*, 24 December 2000.
18.   *Guardian*, 17 November 2003.
19.   *Guardian*, 12 April 2002.
20.   Christensen, *Tax Distortions, Fiscal Dumping and Tax Fraud*.
21.   *International Herald Tribune*, 14 January 2004; *Observer*, 25 January 2004.
22.   *Daily Telegraph*, 13 March 2004.
23.   K. Phillips, *Wealth and Democracy: A Political History of the American Rich* (New York: Broadway, 2002), p. 355.
24.   A. Atkinson, *Unequal Shares: Wealth in Britain*, rev. edn (Harmondsworth: Pelican, 1974), p. 115.
25.   D. Cannadine, *The Decline and Fall of the British Aristocracy*, rev. edn (London: Papermac, 1996), p. 132.
26.   Phillips, *Wealth and Democracy*, p. 355.
27.   F. Lundberg, *America's 60 Families* (New York: Vanguard Press, 1937).
28.   *Economist*, 20 January 1990, p. 8.

29.   P. Krugman, *New York Times*, 14 September 2003.
30.   Ibid.
31.   *New York Times*, 30 June 2002.
32.   *New York Times*, 14 February 2001.
33.   *Washington Post*, 13 April 2003.
34.   HMRC annual reports – only some of the amount would have been recovered from rich and corporate taxpayers.
35.   *Guardian*, 13 April 2002.
36.   *Guardian*, 25 October 2005.
37.   T. Bower, *Gordon Brown* (London: HarperCollins, 2004), p. 269.
38.   Mitchell et al., *No Accounting for Tax Havens*, p. 60.
39.   Ibid., p. 60.
40.   *Guardian*, 24 January 2004.
41.   *Guardian*, 15 April 2003.
42.   *Economist*, 31 January 2004.

Chapter 10

1.   *New Statesman*, 27 September 2004.
2.   P. Krugman, *New York Times*, 20 October 2002.
3.   M. Feldstein, 'Is Income Inequality Really a Problem?', in *Income Inequality Issues and Policy Options: A Symposium Sponsored by the Federal Reserve Bank of Kansas City*, Jackson Hole, Wyoming, August 27–29, 1998.
4.   A. O'Hear, 'Equality', *New Statesman*, 23 April 2001.
5.   G. Greig, 'Welcome to the flashocracy', *Observer*, 6 June 2004.
6.   R. North, *Rich Is Beautiful: A Very Personal Defence of Mass Affluence* (London: Social Affairs Unit, 2005).
7.   G. Mulgan, *Prospect*, May 2005.
8.   *Guardian*, 23 November 2005.
9.   V. Packard, *The Ultra Rich: How Much Is Too Much?* (Boston: Little, Brown, 1989), p. 16.
10. *Guardian*, 6 August 2003.
11. P. Diamond and A. Giddens, *New Statesman*, 27 June 2005.
12. *Guardian*, 15 November 2005.
13. Only about a quarter of the difference is explained by dietary and lifestyle differences, including smoking.
14. R. Wilkinson, 'The Impact of Inequality: How to Make Sick Societies Healthier', in *Unhealthy Societies: The Afflictions of Inequality* (London: Routledge, 1996); R. Wilkinson, 'Health, Redistribution and Growth', in A. Glyn and D. Miliband (eds), *Paying for Inequality: The Economic Cost of Social Injustice* (London: Rivers Oram Press, 1994).
15. *Independent*, 24 November 2003.
16. S. Aldridge, 'Social Mobility', paper to Performance and Innovation Unit, Cabinet Office, 20 March 2001; S Aldridge, *Life Chances and Social Mobility*, Cabinet Office, March 2004.
17. Aldridge, *Life Chances and Social Mobility*.
18. A. Atkinson, 'Preface', in A. Atkinson and J. Hills (eds), *Exclusion, Employment and Opportunity*, CASE Paper 4B (London: London School of Economics, 1998), p. vi.
19. M. Kohn, *Prospect*, 20 September 2001.

20. R. Cook, *Guardian*, 4 February 2005.
21. *Daily Mail*, 26 June 2001.
22. *Sunday Telegraph*, 2 March 2003.
23. *Observer*, 16 November 2003.
24. *Daily Telegraph*, 30 October 2004.
25. G. Burtless and C. Jencks, *American Inequality and Its Consequences* (Washington: Brookings Institution, 2003).
26. R. Putnam, *Bowling Alone: The Collapse and Revival of American Community* (New York: Simon and Schuster, 2000), pp. 358–9.
27. C. Lasch, *The Revolt of the Elites and the Betrayal of Democracy* (New York: W. W. Norton, 1996), p. 29.
28. *New York Times*, 16 April 2000.
29. A. Glyn and D. Miliband (eds), *Paying for Inequality: The Economic Cost of Social Injustice* (London: Rivers Oram Press, 1994); A. Alesina and D. Rodrik, 'Distribution, Political Conflict and Economic Growth: A Simple Theory and Some Empirical Evidence', in A. Cukierman, Z. Hercowitz and L. Leiderman (eds), *Political Economy, Growth and Business Cycles* (Cambridge, MA: MIT Press, 1992); C. Garrison and F. Lee, 'Taxation, Aggregate Activity and Growth: Further Cross-country Evidence on Some Supply-side Hypotheses', *Economic Inquiry* (1992), vol. 30, no. 1, 172–6 (for a summary, see R. Frank, *Luxury Fever: Why Money Fails to Satisfy in an Era of Excess* (New York: Free Press, 1999), ch. 15); Burtless and Jenks, *American Inequality and Its Consequences*.
30. A. Atkinson, 'Is Rising Inequality Inevitable?: A Critique of the Transatlantic Consensus', WIDER annual lecture, United Nations University, Oslo, 1 November 1999.
31. J. Stiglitz, *The Roaring Nineties: A New History of the World's Most Prosperous Decade* (New York: W. W. Norton, 2003), p. 286.
32. D. Goodhart, *Guardian*, 29 July 1999.
33. A. Giddens and P. Diamond, *The New Egalitarianism* (Cambridge: Polity Press, 2005), p. 117.
34. *Newsweek*, 16 November 1998.
35. *Sydney Morning Herald*, 13 February 2000.
36. C. Wolmar, *Broken Rails: How Privatisation Wrecked Britain's Railways* (London: Aurum Press, 2001), pp. 76–7, 110.
37. *Management Today*, 13 January 2003.
38. G. Haigh, *Bad Company: The Strange Cult of the CEO* (London: Aurum Press, 2004), p. 86.
39. *Management Today*, 13 January 2003.
40. Burtless and Jencks, *American Inequality and Its Consequences*.
41. P Augar, *The Death of Gentlemanly Capitalism: The Rise and Fall of London's Investment Banks* (London: Penguin, 2001), p 331.
42. D. Hobson, *The National Wealth: Who Gets What in Britain* (London: HarperCollins, 1999), p. 873.
43. R. Frank and P. Cook, *The Winner-Take-All Society: How More and More Americans Compete for Ever Fewer and Bigger Prizes, Encouraging Economic Waste, Income Inequality, and an Impoverished Cultural Life* (New York: Free Press, 1995).
44. *Sunday Times*, 4 April 2004.
45. A. O'Hear, 'Equality', *New Statesman*, 23 April 2001.
46. *Evening Standard*, 24 October 2005.
47. Haigh, *Bad Company*.
48. R. Monks and A. Sykes, *Capitalism without Owners Will Fail: A Policymaker's Guide to Reform* (London: Centre for Studies of Financial Innovation, 2002).

49.   R. Brenner, 'Towards the precipice,' *London Review of Books*, 6 February 2003; see also Stiglitz, *Roaring Nineties*, p. 17.

Chapter 11

1.   Louis Brandeis, Supreme Court Justice, speaking about America at the beginning of the twentieth century; K. Phillips, *Wealth and Democracy: A Political History of the American Rich* (New York: Broadway Books, 2002), p. 418.
2.   *Observer*, 2 October 2005; *Evening Standard*, 4 February 2004; *Times*, 11 December 2003.
3.   *Daily Telegraph*, 30 October 2004.
4.   S. Ashridge, *Life Chances and Social Mobility*, paper to Prime Minister's Strategy Unit, March 2004.
5.   R. Batra, 'An ominous trend to greater inequality', *New York Times*, 3 May 1987; R. Batra, *The Great Depression of 1990*, rev. edn (New York: Simon and Schuster, 1987).
6.   L. Bebchuk, J. Fried, and D. Walker, 'Managerial Power and Rent Extraction in the design of Executive Compensation', *University of Chicago Law Review* (2002), vol. 69, no. 3.
7.   'One billion dollars', *Financial Times Magazine*, 13 November 2004.
8.   *Observer*, 9 March 2003.
9.   F. Mount, *Mind the Gap: The New Class Divide in Britain* (London: Short Books, 2004), p. 260.
10.   P. Krugman, *The Great Unravelling: From Boom to Bust in Three Scandalous Years* (London: Allen Lane, 2003), p. 125.
11.   A. Park, J. Curtice, K. Thomson, L. Jarvis and C. Bromley (eds), *British Social Attitudes: Continuity and Change over Two Decades* (London: Sage, 2004), ch. 4.
12.   See, for example, P. Toynbee, *Guardian*, 2 April 2004.
13.   *New York Times*, 28 April 1942.
14.   J. Galbraith, *Economics and the Public Purpose* (Boston: Houghton Mifflin, 1973), p. 260.
15.   *Financial Times*, 25 February 2003.
16.   *International Herald Tribune*, 27 January 2004.
17.   *Guardian*, 6 August 2003.
18.   A. MacGillivray and I. Christie, 'Social Exclusion and the Rich', *Renewal* (2001), vol. 9, no. 4, p. 55.
19.   Ibid., p. 56.
20.   *New Statesman*, 27 September 2004.
21.   T. Clark and A. Leicester, 'Inequality and Two Decades of British Tax and Benefit Reforms', *Fiscal Studies*, 2004, vol. 25, no. 2.
22.   A. Giddens and P. Diamond (eds), *The New Egalitarianism* (Cambridge: Polity Press, 2005), p. 117.
23.   See, for example, C. Huhne, *New Statesman*, 27 September 2004; S. Brittan, 'Redistribution yes, equality no', *Financial Times*, 13 August 2004.
24.   *The Missing Link: From Productivity to Performance* (London: Work Foundation, 2003).
25.   Higher Education Statistics Agency.
26.   S. Machin and A. Vignoles, 'Educational Inequality: The Widening Socio-economic Gap', *Fiscal Studies* (2004), vol. 25, no. 2, 107–128.
27.   Office of National Statistics, *Focus on Social Inequalities*, 2005.
28.   *Economist*, 28 June 2003.

Appendix

1. A. Atkinson, 'Distribution of Income and Wealth', in A. Halsey and J. Webb (eds), *Twentieth Century Social Trends* (Basingstoke: Macmillan, 1999), pp. 365–6.
2. M. Brewer, A. Goodman, J. Shaw and A. Shephard, *Living Standards, Inequality and Poverty* (London: Institute for Fiscal Studies, 2005).
3. HMRC, Table 5.26.
4. J. Hills, *Inequality and the State* (Oxford: Oxford University Press, 2004), p. 31.
5. T. Piketty and E. Saez, *Income Inequality in the US 1913–1998*, NBER Working Paper 8467 (Cambridge, MA: National Bureau of Economic Research, 2001); the data refers to gross incomes not net of tax.
6. P. Krugman, 'For richer', *New York Times*, 20 October 2002; see also R. Greenstein and I. Shapiro, *The New, Definitive CBO Data on Income and Tax Trends* (Washington, DC: Center on Budget and Policy Priorities, 2003).
7. Piketty and Saez, *Income Inequality in the US*.
8. Hills, *Inequality and the State*, p. 29; A. Atkinson, 'The Distribution of Income in Industrialized Countries', in *Income Inequality Issues and Policy Options: A Symposium Sponsored by the Federal Reserve Bank of Kansas City*, Jackson Hole, Wyoming, August 27–29, 1998.
9. A. Atkinson, *The Economics of Inequality*, 2nd edn (Oxford: Clarendon Press, 1983), pp. 173–4; W. Kopczek and E. Saez, *Top Wealth Shares in the US 1916–2000: Evidence from Estate Tax Returns*, NBER Working Paper 10399 (Cambridge, MA: National Bureau of Economic Research, 2003).
10. Atkinson, *Economics of Inequality*, pp. 173–4; G. Harding, *We, the People* (1995), http://members.aol.com/trajcom/private/therich.htm; K. Phillips, *Wealth and Democracy: A Political History of the American Rich* (New York: Broadway, 2002), p. xii.
11. See, for example, E. Wolff, *Recent Trends in Wealth Ownership 1983–1998*, Working Paper 300 (Annandale-on-Hudson, NY: Levy Economics Institute of Bard College, 2000).
12. See also Kopczek and Saez, *Top Wealth Shares in the US*.
13. Ibid.
14. Ibid.
15. A. Kennickell, *A Rolling Tide: Changes in the Distribution of Wealth in the US 1989–2001* (Washington, DC: Federal Reserve Board, 2003).

Index